Salaam.Peace

AN ANTHOLOGY OF
MIDDLE EASTERN–AMERICAN DRAMA

Salaam.Peace

AN ANTHOLOGY OF
MIDDLE EASTERN–AMERICAN DRAMA

Edited by

Holly Hill and Dina Amin

THEATRE COMMUNICATIONS GROUP
NEW YORK
2009

Salaam.Peace: An Anthology of Middle Eastern–American Drama is copyright © 2009 by Theatre Communications Group

"What's in a Hyphen?" is copyright © 2009 by Dina Amin
"New Threads" is copyright © 2009 by Holly Hill

Salaam.Peace: An Anthology of Middle Eastern–American Drama is published by Theatre Communications Group, Inc., 520 Eighth Avenue, 24th Floor, New York, NY 10018-4156

All rights reserved. Except for brief passages quoted in newspaper, magazine, radio or television reviews, no part of this book may be reproduced in any form or by any means, electronic or mechanical, including photocopying or recording, or by an information storage and retrieval system, without permission in writing from the publisher.

Professionals and amateurs are hereby warned that this material, being fully protected under the Copyright Laws of the United States of America and all other countries of the Berne and Universal Copyright Conventions, is subject to a royalty. All rights including, but not limited to, professional, amateur, recording, motion picture, recitation, lecturing, public reading, radio and television broadcasting, and the rights of translation into foreign languages are expressly reserved. Particular emphasis is placed on the question of readings and all uses of this book by educational institutions, permission for which must be secured from the authors' agents.

Due to space constraints, copyright, author contact information and photo credits for the individual plays are found at the back of the book.

This publication is made possible in part with public funds from the New York State Council on the Arts, a State Agency.

TCG books are exclusively distributed to the book trade by Consortium Book Sales and Distribution.

CIP data information is on file at the Library of Congress, Washington, D.C.

Cover art "Ana wa Inta" copyright © El-Iqaa (www.olivetones.com)
Cover, book design and composition by Lisa Govan

First Edition, December 2009

For Vanya, of course

· ✦ ·

Vanya Exerjian was a splendid actress and producer. Of Armenian-Egyptian heritage, she was a founding member of Hassan El Geretly's El Warsha company and played the leading role in the group's creation of the al-Hilaliyya epic, based on traditional Egyptian heroic poetry, and performed it internationally, including a run at The Kennedy Center.

Dina Amin, Vanya's best friend since university days, directed her solo performance in Alfred Farag's drama of marital abuse, *al-Mishwar al-Akhir* (*The Last Walk*), performed in Arabic at Cairo's historical site, wikalet al-Ghuri, in 1998, and in English at Marvin Carlson's Conference on Egyptian Theatre at The Graduate School of The City University of New York in 1999. For the conference, Vanya and Dina stayed with Holly.

Vanya Exerjian died in 2003, heroically, but vainly, trying to save her father during a brutal knife attack by a neighbor who had been released from a mental asylum only one day before. She was mourned nationally.

Contents

What's in a Hyphen?

By Dina Amin

> Sometimes it's so hard. I had no idea, none, when I left my country, what a life-changing thing it would be. It's much harder than I'd ever thought could be possible. I wasn't prepared for how much I would miss them—and for how much worse simply knowing I can't return makes me feel. And of course there's no way I could have known any of this before I'd left, when I was so young and excited and thought I was ready for anything at all.
>
> —Diana Abu-Jaber, *Crescent*

Today the Middle East is virtually always at the forefront of the news, yet many still do not know for sure which countries constitute that part of the world. While some may ask: "The Middle East is in the middle of what?" It seems that that question had a reasonably straightforward answer in the nineteenth century. Historically, the Middle East was labeled "middle" because of its proximity from the reigning empire of the nineteenth century, namely the British, as it is halfway between England and the Far East. And, naturally the Far East was considered "far" by virtue of its location from England as well. It is obvious then, that as a powerful empire, Britain was construed as the center of the universe, and all other regions of the world were defined by their geographical distance from that powerful hub.

From this point of view, the countries that fall between that center and the Far East are the twenty-two Arab countries extending from the Persian Gulf to the Atlantic Ocean (many of them were British protectorates in the nineteenth century), as well as Iran, Turkey and the state of Israel, which was established in 1948.

While the four areas that constitute the Middle East today share a predominant religion, Islam, and a great deal of history, they don't all speak the same language or share common cultural grounds. Moreover, contrary to common knowledge, there are large Christian and Jewish populations living there. However, after 9/11, the overall perception of the Middle East has become one of reprehension. Today, more often than not, these four areas are treated as a monolithic entity irrespective of the national character, historical background or political affiliations of each. This wholesale negative perception has resulted in stereotyping the denizens of this region as fanatical and religiously intolerant among many others. While this attitude is not conducive to a global dialogue and understanding, it is particularly taxing on immigrants whose image in their new homelands has been tarnished by association.

This anthology aims to represent a few artistic visions of those who are labeled or self-identify as "Middle Eastern–Americans," artists who do not necessarily have a unified vision or constitute a movement within American theatre so far, but have become visible, for both positive and negative reasons, only after 9/11, because of their ethnic background. While attention suddenly focused on them as "the other," many of those artists struggle with that categorization and refuse to be studied/viewed only from that thin prism, which, according to them, is an oversimplification of their situation, after all they *are* U.S. citizens, albeit a second generation of Middle Eastern–Americans who grew up American and are trying to reconfigure their place in the U.S. and the world at large since 9/11. This collection of plays, by hyphenated American dramatists with ancestral ties to the Middle East and whose ethnicity adds to their uniqueness, tries to encompass the dramatic talent of some exceptional authors, who must, we hope, be appreciated for their excellence, not their ancestral difference.

Pure breeds usually do not need identity definitions, they are already defined. It is the work of hyphenated/hybrid authors that usually require an overture for their ethnic origins; these explanations usually digress from the authors' talent, focusing instead on their familial, racial or religious backgrounds. Such prefaces may typically explore definitions of hybridity and raise such questions as: "Can a person belong to two worlds equally? It is hard enough to understand an immediate cultural heritage, so how does one begin to understand/ belong to a distant past or even an imaginary homeland?" But then, this is the plight of most second-generation writers who have strong ties to more than one regional identity and homeland.

Reading my co-editor Holly Hill's excellent introductory essay on the history of Middle Eastern–American theatre in the States, one cannot help but notice the (much needed) strong emphasis that she puts on the biography of the playwrights and producers as though their lives *were* the stories. The reason for this is quite clear: Readers want to know about the lives of hyphenated/hybrid artists, asking: "Why do they write what they write? What stories have they to share with their audience?" Invariably, there is an interest in the identity, background and life stories of hyphenated creators of art, and discovering those works can turn into an activity of exoticism. While aware of that heightened interest in their origins, hybrid artists create for a variety of reasons; defensiveness is certainly an element, but there is also the wish to challenge stereotypes, sometimes even to shock the pigeon-holing reader/spectator. In all cases, writing on the one hand, and viewing/reading on the other, the works of hyphenated authors is always a process of negotiating identities—it is almost a diplomatic mission more than a literary/artistic one. But is this really how hyphenated, particularly Middle Eastern–American artists, wish their works to be construed?

While many describe the work of hyphenated artists as a search for (or introduction to) an identity and home, many of those artists seem to think that their artistic productions are themselves representations of "their identity" and home, thus to know their work is to know them, if anyone is interested. In their minds their art "is the thing," and if it reflects notions of self and homeland, it is in a universal sense, in the same way that Kahlil Gibran spoke of spiritual matters or Henry James reflected on the character of the "American." From this point of view one asks: "Are self-identifications and contexts necessary or can a work stand alone? Do works by nationally hybrid authors differ in nature and objective than those by single-identity writers?"

Best forms of writing are explorations of the self. Writing is a means by which to reconcile contradictions and make sense of our world especially if that world seems to be limiting or exclusive to some over others. Writing at best is harmonizing and at worst disturbingly divisive. Writing is a contribution to human culture and, from this point of view, the more inclusive it is the more comprehensive our understanding of our humanity will be. Yet everywhere in the world there are canons that place restrictions on literature and art; canons that include and exclude expression, that place narratives into centers and margins. Those canons at times ignore hyphenated expression wholesale. Reasons for such dismissals vary from willful suppression of certain realities to genuine bafflement. In either case, there is a certain simplification to categorizing culture that eliminates/dismisses, at times, what we do not understand. Such eliminations can only be a loss to humanistic arts as it stands the chance of missing out on great human experiences and deep reflections on the human soul.

From this point of view comes the importance of our anthology, *Salaam*. It is a contribution to American theatre, its students and practitioners. The works included here were considered, not because they contribute to the exoticism of art and artists, but because they are excellent works that need to be read, studied and given stage performances. Essentially they tell stories about the American way of life, America that is loved and sought after because of its international and historical popularity for being "a melting pot." A quick look at the works presented, we notice that they are about living in America today with links to other cultures; those connections are not portrayed as the "other" rather as just the way things are. They are stories about love, family, relationships, enemies becoming friends—if we look closely at the meanings behind the writings, is this so different from Shakespeare, Molière, Chekhov, Brecht or Wasserstein?

Finally, since arts and humanities are still bent on categorizing, one final question remains: "Where does the work of these playwrights fall in their country of residence (which, in most cases, is their only home) as well as in their ancestral homelands?" Are they considered genuine Arab, Iranian, Israeli or Turkish literary productions? One obvious obstacle in the inclusion in the literary and performance canons of their respective ancestral homelands is language. Therefore, in order for their works to be produced there, they will have to be translated into their ancestral language. Once translation is in the balance, the works will invariably be one step removed from being considered a national art form. Therefore, the natural place for these works is within the boundaries of the Anglo-American literary and performance canon, and this anthology hopes to firmly instate them in that heritage.

New Threads

By Holly Hill

On September 12, 2001, author Laura Shamas received two packages of red pistachio nuts from Syria. "They were ripped apart and the address was obscured," she recalls, "but they were delivered to me. There was a handwritten note: 'You know what to do with these, George' . . . a very strange thing to happen on September 12, it started a trajectory of odd events, including someone suggesting that the package was perhaps a terrorist sleeper-cell activation signal, and that I had received them because I'm part Lebanese." Though she called the FBI and Customs, Shamas never learned anything about the mysterious packages from Syria. But she did write a play.

The tragedies of 9/11 might have silenced Middle Eastern–American theatre artists, but voices rose through the clouds of outrage, condemnation and suspicion that threatened them individually and communally. Betty Shamieh began her drama *The Black Eyed* (included here) the day after the terrorist attacks. A newly formed Middle Eastern–American theatre collective in New York started doing interviews for a play based on the question: "What comes to mind when you hear the word 'Arab'?" Two Middle Eastern–American businessmen from Chicago wanted to do something to counter anti-Arab and anti-Muslim feelings and, in classic American tradition, they decided to put on a show.

The plays in this anthology did not exist ten years ago. They came to public life in workshops, readings and festivals. They have been nurtured by two pioneering theatres and one cooperative created by Middle Eastern–Americans for their artists and communities. Finding stages Off-Broadway and in regional theatres, Middle Eastern–American plays are beginning to add unique designs to a quilt crafted over the last fifty years by such illustrious predecessors as The Negro Ensemble Company, Pan Asian Repertory Theatre and El Teatro Campesino. Through *Salaam.Peace: An Anthology of Middle Eastern–American Drama*, we share in the weaving of these vibrant new threads into the national patchwork.

Prior to 9/11, the only Middle Eastern–American play I had seen was Palestinian-American Betty Shamieh's *Chocolate in Heat: Growing Up Arab in America*, five interlocking stories (with Shamieh playing the female roles), which I saw at the New York International Fringe Festival in summer 2001. Shamieh allowed me to make copies of her manuscript for use in a Women in Theatre class, and it became my students' favorite play. I thought Israeli-American Rebekah Maggor's *Two Days at Home, Three Days in Prison* was promising, when I saw it in its MFA-candidate performance at American Repertory Theater. But it wasn't until fall 2004, when Iraqi-American Heather Raffo brought *9 Parts of Desire* to New York, that my knowledge of the growing body of work by Middle Eastern–American artists shouted: "These should be published!" Dina Amin, an Egyptian-American scholar and director, who is co-editor of this anthology, was already championing Middle Eastern–American talent through her work.

Salaam.Peace: An Anthology of Middle Eastern–American Drama actually began its journey in 1993, when I first visited Egypt and, like so many before me, fell in love with the country and its people. Visiting the Abydos temple of Seti I, where the Osiris Passion Play had been performed for nearly two thousand years, I wondered what had become of Egyptian drama. A colleague, Mohamed Baha'a Wasfy, Associate Professor of English Drama at Zagazig University, generously took it upon himself to search out English translations of Arabic dramas and send them to me. I became fascinated, even to the point of beginning to study Arabic at the age of fifty-six.

Hélas, I failed at that, but succeeded in interesting George White, founding director of the Eugene O'Neill Theater Center in Connecticut, in bringing Arab theatre artists to the 1997 Conference at the O'Neill. Dina Amin, then a Ph.D. candidate at Penn, was interpreter when we hosted Lotfy El Sayeed, Artistic Director of the Cairo Puppet Theatre, to the O'Neill Puppetry Conference; playwright Sameh Mahran

and director Nasser Abdel Moneim to the Plawrights Conference (where
Artistic Director Lloyd Richards had the Egyptian artists and Dina present a panel on Arab theatre for the entire Conference) and composer/
director Ashraf El Noamany to the Music Theater Conference. George,
Lloyd, et. al, treated their Egyptian visitors like princes and the Arabic
Theater Project (with me as Director and Dina as Associate Director)
was founded.

We began with Egyptians because Cairo is the capital of the
Arabic-language theatre world, but the idea for the project was that
we would foster exchanges among a broad selection of Middle Eastern
and American theatre artists, critics and scholars. George and Lloyd
had, after all, never heard of Arab theatre before; it wasn't even mentioned in the current edition of Oscar G. Brockett's *History of the
Theatre* (the theatre student's "bible").

The Arabic Theater Project had some successes, but I proved to be
a lousy fundraiser and the wheels slowed. After 9/11, Dina and I sadly
reflected that though support for our work might come because fun-
ders would finally understand the importance of cultural bridges
between America and Middle Eastern countries, we'd never be able to
get visas for the artists to enter the U.S. The growing body of work by
Middle Eastern–American artists inspired us, and this anthology
became a thrilling new direction for us to serve our cultural, scholarly
and theatre communities.

We put out a call for plays through numerous Arab, Iranian,
Turkish and Israeli communities, asking for plays from writers who
self-identified as Middle Eastern–Americans. We did not ask anyone to
designate her/his specific heritage. Although we had no response
from Turkish writers (except one emailed reproof for including Turkey
in the Middle East), and only a few submissions from playwrights
identifying themselves as Israeli-American, the overall response and,
in our judgment, the quality of the writing was excellent.

We had not stipulated in our call for plays that a work be about
the author's heritage, but every play we received was. And the dream
of peace is woven through each—not just peace in political terms—
the peace yearned for may be within families, between lovers and
friends and colleagues, within the self. But the yearning is palpable—
to be at peace.

Another great yearning, felt throughout the plays, is to be heard,
to tell one's story and have that story be acknowledged as human and
valuable, to have one's story heard without prejudgment.

Before the 2001 terrorist attacks made the American public acutely
aware of Middle Eastern people and subjects, few were interested. In

September 2001, I was on sabbatical leave in Dallas, Texas, fulfilling a dream of working in a bookstore through a part-time job at Borders. Suddenly there was a huge demand for books about the Middle East, about Islam, about the three Abrahamic faiths. Churches invited imams to speak about Islam; the mosque in nearby Richardson held open houses for non-Muslims; and universities, sociopolitical organizations and museums began to offer lectures, panels and exhibits.

National events similarly created chinks in a wall of negative attitudes toward Middle Eastern people, particularly Arabs and Muslims, by news coverage and, from their inception, by American films and television (as documented by Jack G. Shaheen in *Reel Bad Arabs: How Hollywood Vilifies a People* [Olive Branch Press, 2001, 2009] and *Guilty: Hollywood's Verdict on Arabs After 9/11* [Olive Branch Press, 2008]). Though theatre is usually ahead of mass media, exploring controversial subjects before the rest of society is willing to deal with them, this hadn't been the case with Middle Eastern subjects—there is a wide gap between plays written about people and issues of the Middle East before and since 9/11.

Native Language Theatre

Though mainstream theatres weren't producing much Middle Eastern work before 9/11, there was an exception with immigrant communities, who were supporting performances done in Arabic or Farsi (the language of Iran, also called Persian). Since 1989, AJYAL has produced comedies about the challenges facing Arab immigrants in the Arab-American cultural capital of Dearborn, Michigan. Additionally, the sizable Iranian population in the Bay Area of California supports a Farsi-speaking theatre group. Darvag, founded there in 1985, produces classical and contemporary Iranian dramas, Farsi translations of Western plays and new work. With help from a Rockefeller grant in 1994, Darvag began to mount bilingual productions, hoping to introduce Iranian drama to American audiences.

While these and other Arabic and Farsi theatres have not directly generated today's generation of Middle Eastern–American artists, their portrayal of émigrés' personal and cultural concerns has built bridges for the new writers, actors, directors and producers who choose to create Middle Eastern work in English. Torange Yeghiazarian, author of this anthology's *Call Me Mehdi* and founder of Golden Thread Productions in San Francisco, told me: "The fact that Darvag had already created a strong theatre audience in Berkeley through fifteen years of work in Persian made the Bay Area a fertile ground for

Golden Thread's work. Having an audience that was ready to listen, watch and respond and, more importantly, provide financial support, made all the difference for us."

Golden Thread Productions

Torange Yeghiazarian is the Margo Jones–founding-mother-figure of Middle Eastern–American theatre. This Iranian-Armenian producer/ director/ actress/author initiated her company in 1997 with a production of her MA thesis adaptation of Aristophanes' *Lysistrata*. She describes the debut: "*Operation No Penetration* was about Israelis and Palestinians getting together and going on a sex strike to end the conflict. It was a shoestring production—the technical values I would be ashamed to describe—but it was spirited, with great music and nice dance sequences, and we gave it everything we had. We had full houses for the six performances we gave at The Next Stage Theater in San Francisco, which was surprising and encouraging."

From 1997–2000, Golden Thread Productions did one play per year, including three world premieres. Its 1999 program of staged readings of one-acts evolved into the annual ReOrient Festival in 2000. They performed in rented spaces where, with the financial and hands-on help of colleagues, family and friends, Yeghiazarian piloted the ship while working full-time in her medical research career. In 2001, Yeghiazarian says, "We were just ready," and she quit her day job, recruited a board of trustees and established Golden Thread as a not-for-profit theatre. Their mission: To present theatre that explores Middle Eastern cultures and identities as represented throughout the globe.

9/11 occurred just two weeks before the opening of the company's second ReOrient Festival of Short Plays. Issuing a statement condemning the "inhumane and atrocious acts," expressing sympathy and condolences to all who had lost loved ones in the tragedy, Golden Thread affirmed: "Now more than ever it is crucial to go forward with a cultural event that we hope will foster a deeper understanding of our shared humanity." And go forward they did.

Their 2001 mainstage play explored the issue of female circumcision in a drama about an American father and his Egyptian-American daughter. Among the ReOrient offerings was *Stoning*, a work about the practice of stoning women who committed adultery, and Yeghiazarian's *Abaga*, a play about forbidden love between an Armenian man and a Turkish woman in 1915 Istanbul, and their daughter's love of a Jewish man in 1940s Jerusalem. Works in succeeding seasons have dealt with such post-9/11 problems for Middle Eastern–Americans as suspicion, hostile stereotyping, surveillance, suspension of civil rights and rendition. There have also been comedies—from classical Egyptian author Tawfiq al-Hakim's *The Donkey Market* to a reality-based tale about a Middle Eastern–American singer who is told she will have to *Learn to Be Latina* in order to have a successful commercial career.

Golden Thread has also highlighted facets of Islam. *Island of Animals*, based on a tenth-century Ismaili Islamic fable, was a major production in 2006. The 2009 season includes a commissioned project adapted from a Sufi fable, and in development is a multimedia performance piece exploring Ta'ziyeh, the Iranian Passion Play about the martyrdom of the prophet Muhammad's grandson Hussain (which led to the Shia-Shiite division among Muslims).

Golden Thread's Youth Program began in 2002 with a short summer camp for children from the local Iranian community, and it expanded the following year to a camp in an Armenian school. The program now includes The Fairytale Players, an ensemble that creates and performs plays based on children's stories from the Middle East. In addition, each Golden Thread season features special events: a playwriting workshop with MacArthur "genius" awardee Naomi Wallace (whose one-acts about the Middle East have been produced in ReOrient festivals), two nights of work by emerging Iranian playwrights, and an annual theatre and dance event celebrating International Women's Day.

Yeghiazarian estimates that "at least half of our audiences are white and younger. We get a lot of students. We do outreach to campuses, we provide students with big discounts, we hire them as interns. Our Middle Eastern audiences vary from production to production. When we did *Nine Armenians* [by Leslie Ayvasian], I'd say ninety percent of the houses were Armenians, and then none of them showed up for other productions. If we do an Iranian play, we get Iranians. We haven't marketed to the mosques or to the conservative community, except when we did *Island of Animals*. The Islamic community was very supportive of that production; then some of them came to ReOrient and it was too much for them. You can understand that—*Island of Animals* was about everyone learning to get along, and who can take issue with that? ReOrient is all about questioning and confronting."

People outside Middle Eastern–American communities often think of insiders monolithically, as "Arabs" and "Muslims." Inside those communities (as the bios of our authors demonstrate), identities are much more complex. In 2006, Yeghiazarian wrote about herself for Iranian.com: "First name: Persian. Last name: Armenian. In Iran, people always asked: 'Are you Iranian or Armenian?' In the U.S. they ask:

'Are you Muslim or Christian?' I always give the same answer: 'Both.' For years I worked in hospitals and laboratories. Then decided to change careers and focus on theatre, adding one more dichotomy to my identity, that of the scientist versus the artist. When people ask: 'Which are you?' I answer: 'Both.'"

Silk Road Theatre Project

Complex genealogies and experiences also characterize Jamil Khoury and Malik Gillani, two Chicago businessmen who founded their Silk Road Theatre Project as a response to 9/11.

Born in Chicago, Khoury is the son of a Polish-American mother and a Syrian-born Orthodox Christian father. In September 2001, he was a cross-cultural trainer for an international relocations consulting firm, preparing clients for overseas work assignments. He loved theatre and was working on a play, but had no expectation of theatre as his life work.

Neither had Gillani, who was born in Pakistan to Shia-Ismaili Muslim parents of Syrian heritage. Shortly after 9/11, Gillani found that strangers were crossing the street when they saw him coming; one of his employees at his family business quit because he didn't want to work for a Muslim; photographs of Osama bin Laden with darts through his head were placed in an office he frequently visited. Khoury and Gillani wanted to do something to counter anti-Arab and anti-Muslim feelings. The show they produced to achieve that goal (*Precious Stones*, the play that Khoury had been working on) blossomed by summer 2002 into Silk Road Theatre Project.

Silk Road takes its name from the trade route from Japan to Italy traversed for more than eighteen hundred years. There are more than 1.5 million people of Silk Road heritage in metropolitan Chicago, but Khoury and Gillani recognized a void of representation in the city's thriving theatre community. "We feel it's a very strong and compelling mission," Khoury states. "We do plays by people of Middle Eastern, Asian and Mediterranean backgrounds. In the work we select, the playwrights have been very directly affected by their upbringing, cultural milieu, family, heritage—all that has become a part of their voice."

Once founded, the theatre's first production was Khoury's *Precious Stones*, which opened in January 2003. Set in Chicago in 1989 (at the time of the first intifada: the 1987–1993 Palestinian uprising against Israeli rule), the drama is about a Jewish and Palestinian woman who together organize a Jewish/Arab dialogue group and find themselves falling in love. Influenced by issues Khoury faced growing up as an Arab-American and self-described "queer feminist," his working and studying in the Middle East for five years, and his experience of living with his life partner, Malik, *Precious Stones* explores the Israeli/Palestinian conflict and issues of sexuality and class. After a successful seven-week run, the play went on college tour. In 2003, Silk Road also launched an annual staged-reading series: Al Kasida ("the ode" in Arabic).

The business and marketing skills of Khoury and Gillani, who became, respectively, Artistic Director and Executive Director, brought Silk Road early dividends. Gillani contacted the Reverend Philip Blackwell at Chicago Temple about buying group tickets to *Precious Stones*, and some weeks after the run ended, Silk Road was invited to become the resident theatre at Chicago Temple, a United Methodist church that had a diverse congregation and wanted to house a secular multicultural arts organization. Silk Road moved into a flexible ninety-nine-seat theatre space in a historic building at the center of Chicago's Loop theatre district. From its first major production in 2003, Silk Road's season grew to three full productions in its 2007–2008 season.

Silk Road has become an important participant in Chicago's cultural life. Khoury and Gillani, in conversations with journalist Novid Parsi, helped inspire a cover story in *TimeOut-Chicago* (July 27, 2006) about how the city, with no ethnic or racial majority, failed to reflect this diversity in its theatre scene. The magazine suggested that Chicago's theatre scene did not, in effect, look like Chicago. So Khoury and Gillani created their 2008 initiative: Looks Like Chicago.

For ninety-eight dollars, Looks Like Chicago subscribers can see four shows from four different theatres—Silk Road, Congo Square Theatre (primarily dedicated to work from the African Diaspora), Teatro Vista (Latino culture) and Remy Bumppo (devoted to the Anglo-American tradition). Subscribers can choose the plays and dates that suit them, and they are invited to a Town Hall forum to discuss the season at its end. "I'm not familiar with another program like this in the country," says Lyle Allen, previously Managing Director of the League of Chicago Theatres. "It's very innovative and I can see it as a promotion for years to come."

In February 2008, Silk Road received the League's 2008 Broadway in Chicago Emerging Theater Award, which includes a five-thousand-dollar prize and marketing-support package. Barely five years after its first production, Silk Road's honors also include the 2008 City of Chicago Human Relations Award, a Chicago Community Trust "Hopie" for creativity and inspiration, and a 2007 Columbia College Arts Entrepreneurship Award.

Silk Road and Golden Thread have been of incalculable value to Middle Eastern–American playwrights. In a 2003 online panel sponsored by the Non-Traditional Casting Project, Yussef El Guindi said of his writing career: "My biggest challenge is finding theatres open to doing Arab-American plays . . . the more theatres [like Golden Thread and Silk Road] that spring up, the more inclined I am (and other writers I'm sure) to explore issues around immigration and the Middle East. Before the creation of these theatres, I was somewhat hesitant to tackle subjects that I felt would not get past the first reader at a theatre."

Nibras

Another pioneering Middle Eastern–American theatre collective is the New York–based community of artists: Nibras. One of the founders, Maha Chehlaoui, an actress and director whose father is Syrian and mother Filipino, was inspired by the work of Ma-Yi Theater Company, an Asian-American theatre in New York that did only Filipino work in its early years. "I wondered if Arab-Americans had stories worth telling. I was learning that when you get people of a shared heritage together, stories come out that you might not hear in a diverse group." What began as an online 1998 conversation between Chehlaoui, Rana Kazkaz and Dahlia Sabbour, developed into a small network of Arab-American artists (Chehlaoui, Kazkaz, Najla Said, Leila Buck, Omar Koury and Afaf Shawwa), who got together in June 2001. They chose the name Nibras, meaning "lantern lighting the way," and began planning a documentary-theatre piece.

Most members of the group went off that summer to visit family abroad. They came home to the terrorist attacks of 9/11. "When we left each other we were so excited at finding other Arab-American artists and it was very lighthearted," Chehlaoui remembers. "We returned to this horror, and we wanted to make sure that our voices were heard in the mourning and in the recovery."

Nibras members based their first piece on interviews they conducted that asked: "What comes to mind when you hear the word 'Arab'?" and developed it into *Sajjil*, meaning "record," inspired by a line from Palestinian Mahmoud Darwish's famed 1964 poem *Identity Card*: "Write down! / I am an Arab." Chehlaoui says, "We asked people of different backgrounds and faiths, some Arab, some not. We made a collage of perception of immigrant experience and a very immediate projection of how things were different." Directed by

Chehlaoui, produced and acted by Nibras members, *Sajjil* was performed in 2002's New York International Fringe Festival. It won the Festival's Best Ensemble Award.

"It was very well received," Chehlaoui recalls. "People at that time were hungry for any work by actual Middle Eastern people, who were often being spoken about and spoken for. It was quite interesting after that, because we didn't have to do much, we just had to show up and a lot of attention was being paid. *Sajjil* brought a lot of confidence to people in our company and to individuals who had been doing work alone. Part of it was that there were many talented Middle Eastern–American theatre artists who came out of the woodwork. I think that doing even one show can create a movement whether you intend to or not."

Nibras has never sought not-for-profit status. Instead it operates through donations; its members share financial responsibility for the company's workshops and reading series. Nibras members (including playwrights Nathalie Handal and Sam Younis, whose work is included here) present work within and outside of the collective's banner. Founding member Leila Buck, for example, performed her one-woman show *ISite* at the Martin E. Segal Theatre Center of the City University of New York Graduate Center in 2003. The daughter of a Lebanese mother and American diplomat father, Buck describes *ISite* as "a piece based on my father's experiences moving from Lebanon to Oman to Iraq under Saddam, to Saudi Arabia to Canada to the U.S., struggling to define identity and home somewhere in between."

The event was co-sponsored by Nibras and the Graduate Center's Middle Eastern and Middle Eastern–American Center, established in 2001 as the only U.S. center to incorporate Middle Eastern–American experience into Middle East studies. The Segal Theatre, often in partnership with Nibras, has subsequently welcomed many performances and forums by Middle Eastern–American artists and scholars.

Among the collective's achievements have been inclusion in the Mahrajan Al-Fan—Festival of Arab World Culture, where Nathalie Handal's *The Details of Silence* was performed at New York's Symphony Space; the participation of members' Handal, Leila Buck and Elias El-Hage in the Lark Playwright Development Center's first roundtable on developing Arab voices in theatre; and its co-producing of six one-acts for *Acts for Palestine*, a benefit for a "Made in Palestine" art exhibition. Among the benefit plays was *Palestine*, written and performed by Nibras founder Najla Said (the daughter of scholar Edward Said, whose work on Orientalism challenged and redefined the views of the West about the Near and Middle East) about her first visit with her father to his homeland of Palestine.

A significant turning point for Nibras came in winter 2006, when members Chehlaoui, Buck, Said and Younis each contacted New York Theatre Workshop during the furor over its cancellation of *My Name Is Rachel Corrie*, a play about a young American peace activist killed by an Israeli army bulldozer while she was trying to prevent its destruction of Palestinian homes in Ramallah. The controversy was long and complicated, with NYTW receiving a great many angry emails from activists around the world. Nibras members "reached out individually as artists and Arab-Americans," recalls Leila Buck. "I took the moment to explain why people, not primarily Arab-Americans, but many from the theatre communities, were so angry. Whether NYTW was doing so or not, theatre about and from Palestine was actively censored in America. People might have been misplacing their anger, but their outrage came from years of experience."

NYTW's Artistic Director James Nicola was immediately receptive, and Chehlaoui brought in more Nibras members to talk with him and NYTW Associate Artistic Director Linda Chapman. NYTW and the Lark Playwright Development Center invited Nibras members to participate in panels and other activities regarding Middle Eastern theatre. When New York's Public Theater asked NYTW to present two evenings of play readings in The Public's 2006 Arab-Israeli Festival, NYTW brought Nibras in as a co-producer.

Nathalie Handal's drama *Between Our Lips* (included here), Buck's *In the Crossing* (based on Buck's being with her Jewish husband in Lebanon under the Israeli bombardment during summer 2006) and Said's *Lebanon* and *Palestine* were among the plays presented, Chehlaoui was one of the directors, and both performances were followed by panels moderated by James Nicola. Soon after the evenings at the Public, Buck, Handal and Said were invited to become NYTW Usual Suspects (the term for its extended family of affiliated artists), and Nibras became a company-in-residence at NYTW.

NYTW presented a mainstage production of Betty Shamieh's *The Black Eyed* in 2007. Buck and Said were chosen to develop their work at NYTW's summer retreat and Handal was invited to work on her new play, *The Oklahoma Quartet*, in 2008. The journey from an initial meeting among Middle Eastern–American theatre artists eager to know and help each other and their community, to residence at one of New York's premier institutional theatres was accomplished in five years.

Cornerstone Theater Company

It has been harder for other Middle Eastern and Middle Eastern–American dramatists to find welcome in U.S. regional theatres. "For the longest time, Arab issues or Muslim issues had not been on the radar . . . they were regarded as too complex," Yussef El Guindi told *New York Times* reporter Dinitia Smith in 2006. Then came 9/11 and, he said, "Suddenly there were calls for plays." Smith commented that El Guindi "is one of a small group of Arab-American playwrights who have gained a higher profile since the terrorist attacks."

A unique exploration of Middle Eastern–American concerns has, however, been pursued for nearly two decades by Los Angeles's Cornerstone Theater Company, which maintains an ensemble that operates on consensus and involves professional artists and members of specific communities in creating and performing plays. Their first work was *Ghurba* (roughly translated as "diaspora"), a response to the Gulf War of 1990–1991. As Shishir Kurup, the Bombay-born and Kenya-raised South Asian–American, who wrote and directed *Ghurba* explains: "I had a group of Arab-American professional actors come in and we interviewed each other. Then as a team we went and interviewed members of the Arab community. In the Pan-Arab community there are Druze, Jews, Christians, Muslims—we were looking for their stories." The resulting play ran for three weeks as part of the 1993 Los Angeles Festival and sold out. "It was incredible," Kurup remembers. "They came to the play, they sang with the play, they came back to the play seven or eight times."

Just five weeks after 9/11, Cornerstone opened *The Festival of Faith*, a work they had been developing long before the attacks. *The Festival of Faith* explored feelings about being Muslim, as well as South Asian and Sikh (Sikhs were mistaken for Muslims and attacked after 9/11), and presented twenty-one theatrical offerings at a Buddhist temple, a Baha'i center, a Methodist church, a Jewish temple and an Islamic school.

For its 2002 season, Cornerstone commissioned Yussef El Guindi to write a play. The result, *Ten Acrobats in an Amazing Leap of Faith* (included in this anthology), upset conservative members of the Muslim community at its initial reading and was withdrawn (it would find difficulty in 2005 as well, when Silk Road staged it). The main reason was the portrayal of possible homosexuality. As Kurup recalls: "There was such a hue and cry that it was decided not to go down that road. Within and without the theatre and Muslim community there were people arguing for both sides."

Ironically, because the spirit of El Guindi's comedy has so much in common with *You Can't Take It with You*, a Muslim version of the Kaufman and Hart classic was produced during Cornerstone's 2003 season (the first time in the comedy's seventy-year history that the Kaufman and Hart estate approved a contemporary adaptation), with the madcap Vanderhof/Sycamore family becoming Muslim-American and the straitlaced Kirbys rendered as Pakistani-American. "During the performance," Kurup, who played the Pakistani mogul, remembers, "we got a lot of hijab-wearing women, sitting there and laughing, and that in itself was a coup."

The withdrawal of Yussef El Guindi's commissioned play from Cornerstone demonstrates the fear of negative perceptions of Middle Eastern–American culture, by both its own artists and its audiences. At Golden Thread, the fall 2001 production of *Stoning* was criticized by some Iranian audience members as untimely in the context of the post-9/11 hate wave against Arabs and Muslims. People complained that an Iranian would never behave in the way presented in the play's biting portrayal of the practice of stoning adulterous women. A play for Golden Thread's next season, *Tamam*, by author Betty Shamieh, was assailed "as stereotyping Middle Eastern men as violent," Yeghiazarian relates, "and we were attacked for promoting negative images of Middle Eastern families by presenting issues regarding domestic violence."

Cornerstone accommodated the bruised sensibilities in 2002 and 2003, but tackled the issue head on in 2005 with *A Long Bridge Over Deep Waters* (written by James Still and directed by Bill Rauch), a play that included a Muslim man struggling with his homosexuality. As Kurup relates: "The young male character was struggling with his sexuality and his faith, and saying that when he was a good Muslim he felt like a bad homosexual, and when he was a good homosexual he felt like a bad Muslim. There were amazing meetings with members of the community and Cornerstone's. In that case we chose not to leave gay people out of the play. And there were repercussions. There were a lot less Muslim people in the audience."

Not only that, says Rauch, Co-Founder and Artistic Director of Cornerstone from 1986–2006, and now Artistic Director of the Oregon Shakespeare Festival, but: "We ended up losing several cast members over the issue. Some of them that we lost on religious grounds were part of a panel discussion that we did at the TCG Conference in Seattle that very summer. It was pretty remarkable, because the man (who had played the gay Muslim) and the woman (who had been playing his sister) and her husband, both of whom had quit the play on religious grounds, were part of the panel, as were James Still, Mark Valdez (who had directed our *You Can't Take It with You*) and I. It was unbelievably honest about the pain that was involved in the situation, and yet there we all were, sitting together on the stage to tell the story. It was one of the proudest moments in my life."

Middle Eastern–American playwrights must struggle with whether and how to represent many controversial issues about the communities of their heritage. It is one thing to grapple with volatile subjects within a community; quite another to expose them to outsiders who are already saturated with negative images of Arabs and Muslims. El Guindi comments: "Because there are so few depictions of Arab-American life in our theatre, people have wanted me to give it a very, very affirmative view of who we are . . . But in order to humanize a people, you need to show them warts and all. Our humanity lives in our cracks and wounds. How can you affirm something without talking about everything?"

Israeli–American Theatre

When searching for plays, Dina and I were surprised to find few playwrights who thought of themselves as Israeli-American. In addition to this anthology's Misha Shulman, we located Rebekah Maggor, who most recently has been a playwriting fellow at the Huntington Theatre Company in Boston and the recipient of an MIT commission; Iris Bahr, whose remarkable *Dai (Enough)* has enjoyed acclaim Off-Broadway and at the Edinburgh Festival; Zohar Tirosh, whose *Pieces* was presented in tandem with *My Name Is Rachel Corrie* at Watertown, Massachusetts' New Repertory Theatre and Meron Langster, whose *b'Shalom* received a reading at the New Rep. All but one of these playwrights had volunteered for service in the Israeli army.

Another Israeli Defense Forces veteran Ami Dayan, whose father is Israeli and mother American, settled in the U.S. in 1999, and has had an international career as a playwright, director, performer and producer. He is primarily known in America as an adaptor and director—his Off-Broadway staging of Israeli writer Ilan Hatsor's *Masked*, about three Palestinian brothers in the intifada, was recognized by *New York* magazine as one of the three "Theatrical Events of the Year" in 2007. Asked why finding playwrights who self-identified as Israeli-American was difficult, Dayan commented: "This category may confine a writer to the 'conflict' and/or 'jewish' themes. It is said that 'one is the reflection of one's homeland.' I've always identified with this line and feel very much Israeli."

Though their members may not be or may not identify them-selves as Israeli-American or Middle-Eastern–American, there are established Jewish theatres in the U.S. that have welcomed Middle Eastern/Middle Eastern–American issues and artists. San Francisco's Traveling Jewish Theatre, a collaborative ensemble, researched and created *Blood Relative*, about Israel and Palestine from both perspec-tives, for its twenty-sixth season in 2005. In the past decade, Washing-ton, D.C.'s Theater J (Ari Roth, Artistic Director) has workshopped and produced many works dealing with the conflict in the Middle East. Among the plays for its 2009 Voices from a Changing Middle East Festival, is Iris Bahr's *Dai,* and a commissioned work from the Travel-ing Jewish Theatre's Artistic Director, Aaron Davidman, *A Jerusalem between Us* (previously titled *Chasing Justice/Seeking Truth: Musings on the Parallel but Radically Different Lives and Deaths of Rachel Corrie and Daniel Pearl*).

Casting

Not as much an issue of controversy but of practicality is the chal-lenge of casting productions with Middle Eastern characters. Big cities may have growing pools of professional Middle Eastern–American actors, but this is rare for the majority of U.S. regional theatres. Ultimately, and with the blessings of playwrights, however, casting can be a matter of imagination and determination. Yussef El Guindi states: "The facts simply dictate that you have to seek other ethnicities to play your characters when Arab–Middle Eastern actors are not available. My one criterion is that they be good actors!"

Torange Yeghiazarian says: "There is something unique about what a Middle Eastern actor brings to the process that is invaluable. However, I'm a believer in the cross-cultural exchange and the ability of a good actor to embody the experience of another. Embodying the experience of another is a big part of why I write and produce plays about the Middle East."

Changing Times, Post 9/11

Artists in the first generation of Middle Eastern–American playwrights are building bodies of work and moving slowly toward productions in "mainstream" regional theatres. Just a few signs of the progress in the 2007–2008 season were Shamieh's *Territories* (Magic Theatre world premiere), Raffo's *9 Parts of Desire* (productions by eight TCG constituent theatres), the selection of Najla Said and Leila Buck for The Public Theater's first Emerging Writers Group, El Guindi's ACT Seattle Award for *Language Rooms* and the American Theatre Critics Association's M. Elizabeth Osborn New Play Award for his *Our Enemies: Lively Scenes of Love and Combat*, which premiered in March 2008 at Silk Road Theatre Project in Chicago.

THE AUTHORS OF SALAAM.PEACE

Yussef El Guindi

Of this anthology's playwrights, Yussef El Guindi is the only first-generation Arab-American, though Dina Amin told *New York Times* reporter Dinitia Smith: "He tries to see the Arab-American predicament from within the second [generation]." El Guindi's parents fled Egypt in 1963, when President Gamal Abdel Nasser began nationalizing Egyptian businesses, and settled in London. After Nasser's death, his father sent him to the American University in Cairo for his undergraduate work in 1978, and in 1983 El Guindi came to America in 1983 to earn an MFA in Playwriting from Carnegie Mellon. He became a U.S. citizen in 1996.

He is prolific, having written short stories, stage adaptations (Chekhov's *The Marriage Proposal* in an Arab-American setting and Egyptian feminist Salwa Bakr's short stories, for example), radio plays, short film scripts, short plays for both the Arab-American Comedy Festival and the ReOrient Festival at San Francisco's Golden Thread, and full-length works, which have been produced in Anchorage, Los Angeles, San Francisco, Seattle, Chicago and New York.

In *American Theatre* magazine, critic Misha Berson described El Guindi's *Back of the Throat* as a "chilling, ambiguous tale of an Arab-American writer who is visited by two menacing government agents, tracking down suspects after an act of urban terrorism, [which] plays like a section of the USA Patriot Act—as dramatized by David Mamet and Franz Kafka."

Of the El Guindi works available when we were reading plays in 2006, *Ten Acrobats in an Amazing Leap of Faith* impressed us as a classic family comedy in the tradition of *You Can't Take It with You* and *The Royal Family*. As Malik Gillani, a producer of the play's debut run, described it: "The play allows a non-Muslim audience an inside peek at a Muslim-American family and provides them a chance to see them as real people facing real challenges." El Guindi told Misha Berson that *Ten Acrobats* is "my sentimental American drama." Ironically, this "sentimental" play has provoked considerable controversy.

Nathalie Handal

Nathalie Handal is originally from Bethlehem, a city with which she closely identifies: "I often go to Bethlehem, and its narrow streets, stone houses, the olives trees, lemon trees, orange trees, the smell of rosewood in the prayer beads, the nativity church, constantly roam inside of me . . . even if it is a fragmented experience."

Handal has lived in France, Latin America, the U.S. and the Middle East.

The Neverfield, Handal's first volume of poetry, was published in 1999, followed by *The Lives of Rain* (2005) and, most recently, *Love and Strange Horses* (forthcoming in 2010). She has also edited the award-winning anthology *The Poetry of Arab Women* (2000) and co-edited *Language for a New Century: Contemporary Poetry from the Middle East, Asia, and Beyond* (2008)

In the summer of 2008, Handal related in the Riyadh publication *Qawafil*: "I cannot but acknowledge my diasporic life. I have navigated borders most of my life. Dislocation has not been an easy place to exist in. It is a place where the dark is suspended around me all the time, but I have also found in this exilic journey, windows of sensual light. Today, I feel deeply connected to the world. Yes, I am Palestinian but I am also French, Latina, American. People think that fragments cannot be whole. I don't view it that way. I cannot separate myself from all that is me. Just like I cannot separate myself from the world—being attentive to the life-beats around us is what is most divine in us."

Involved in professional theatre as a producer since 2002 and as a director since 2003, Handal made her playwriting debut in 2005 with *Between Our Lips*, compelling for its intensity of relationship and situation.

This short play was quickly followed by the full-length *The Details of Silence*, in which a reporter interviewing Arab women about their lives discovers the details of her own personal tragedy. Other plays presented between 2006 and 2008 are *La Cosa Dei Sogni* (about the dilemma a Palestinian soccer player faces in Italy), *The Stonecutters* (about a family's journey on the eve of Deir Yassin), and in development at New York Theatre Workshop, *The Oklahoma Quartet* (a family drama). In March 2009, Handal's play *Hakawatiyeh* was produced by The John F. Kennedy Center for the Performing Arts, Washington, D.C.

Heather Raffo

Heather Raffo's father was born into a Christian family in Mosul, Iraq. After coming to study in America, her father, a civil engineer, married an American art teacher and watercolorist, and Raffo was born and raised in Michigan. She first visited her Iraqi relatives as a four year old and returned in 1993 after the Gulf War.

Raffo began her theatre career as an actress. She earned her BA at the University of Michigan and an MFA from the University of San Diego, where she created the first draft of *9 Parts of Desire* as a thesis project.

Raffo has been performing *9 Parts of Desire* since its acclaimed debut at the Edinburgh Festival in August 2003. In 2004, *9 Parts* opened Off-Broadway. It was greeted by rave reviews, including the *New Yorker*'s John Lahr, who called it "an example of how art can remake the world."

Misha Shulman

Jerusalem was the city of Misha Shulman's birth and childhood. After serving in the Israeli Defense Forces as Commander in Charge of Education in the Communications Unit of Lebanon from 1996 to 1999, Shulman came to America to enroll in the Theatre Department at Hunter College. There, with the support of Professor Michael Rutenberg, he developed his first produced play *The Fist* (2004), about a decorated Israeli soldier who refuses to continue serving in the army and the repercussions of his actions within three generations of his family. Shulman's drama in this anthology, *Desert Sunrise*, was produced a year later.

The writings of his father David Shulman, an Israeli professor of humanities who received the Rothschild Prize for culture and a 1987 MacArthur "genius" fellowship as an historian of religion, have been a great influence on his work. Both father and son are devoted to Ta'ayush (Arabic for "life in common"), a grassroots movement of Arabs and Jews working to construct an equal partnership and peace. Shulman considers both *The Fist* and *Desert Sunrise* to be Ta'ayush (or activist) works.

As a participant in outreach efforts to Palestinian residents of the South Hebron Hills, Misha Shulman has been a teacher in a drama camp for Palestinian children and an Israeli observer in efforts to gain safe passage for Palestinian residents to their ancestral water wells. During these actions in 2004 and 2005, Shulman met cave dwellers in the Hebron Hills and used some of their own words in *Desert Sunrise*. "Everything in the Middle East is fuzzy and you don't know where the truth is," Shulman observed, "but with the cave dwellers, everything is crystal clear." The headline of the *New York Times* review called the play "a West Bank Godot," with critic George Hunka concluding that in this play "the Godot who never comes is peace."

Sam Younis

Sam Younis's parents, both Christians, met at Saint Joseph University in Beirut. Younis's father, a Lebanese born in Senegal, was enrolled in medical school and his mother, half Lebanese and half Syrian, was in the pharmacy program. They moved to Houston a few years before Younis was born. Unlike most of his fellow anthology authors, he did not grow up speaking the native language of his parents. "I grew up as an American kid—my parents spoke Arabic to each other but not to me."

Younis majored in Spanish and sociology at Vanderbilt and minored in theatre before earning an MFA in acting from Columbia University. "I didn't experience my ethnicity as a boundary. I played a lot of Shakespeare and [immediately after graduating Columbia] landed an understudy role on Broadway in *The Tale of the Allergist's Wife*. When the run ended in September 2002, I went out on auditions and found that I was consistently up for Middle Eastern terrorist roles. I felt kind of defensive at this point and turned down some auditions on principle, but I wanted to work. I met a lot of Arab-American friends at these casting calls and it got kind of comic: 'Who's going to get this one?' A small community grew.

"I was contacted by the Arab-American Comedy Festival, which was just getting started and wanted comedy sketches of up to fifteen minutes. I wrote *Browntown*, just two guys talking in an audition waiting room—it was like a journal entry of my life. I played Malek. It was very well received and I was encouraged to develop it as a play for the New York Fringe Festival in 2004."

The full version of *Browntown* won the 2004 FringeNYC Award for Overall Excellence in Playwriting. The manuscript was the first that Dina Amin and I received, and we found it a delightful new twist on a long tradition from Sheridan's *The Critic* to Rattigan's *Harlequinade* to Stoppard's *The Real Inspector Hound*.

Betty Shamieh

Born to Christian parents who emigrated to America from Ramallah in Palestine, Betty Shamieh grew up in San Francisco, where her first play on record, *One Arabian Night*, was a finalist in the Young Playwrights Festival. The drama was given a Harvard student production, about which the *Harvard Crimson* critic wrote, "*One Arabian Night*, by Betty Shamieh '96, is both bold and honorable in trying to address the ways in which Arab-American women must negotiate their sexuality within American and Arab-American society."

While studying playwriting at the Yale School of Drama, from 1997 to 2000, Shamieh worried about being pigeonholed as Arab-American, but nevertheless wrote her first two plays exploring her heritage. *Chocolate in Heat* and *Roar* were both produced in New York shortly after her graduation. "They're not about politics," Shamieh told *New York Times* reporter Liesl Schillinger, "but they're inherently political. Because if you've never heard a perspective, it makes it political."

The setting and the four characters' quest are unique in *The Black Eyed*, Betty Shamieh's poetic drama. The first draft of the play was her immediate response to the Twin Towers' destruction: "It just came out of me," she told *TimeOut–New York* writer Diane Snyder. "I was really interested in sinking my teeth into what it was like being a Palestinian-American living in New York after 9/11. I realized that to write political theatre with any sort of sense of humor, or humanity, you have to put it in cultural historic context. So I started with Delilah."

"I'm always trying to create work that you don't know whether it's comedy or tragedy," Shamieh told San Francisco reporter Jean Schiffman. "Are you going to laugh or have your gut pulled out? It's my sensibility as a person. Life is so great—but people are dying in Somalia . . . I want to write about Arab-Americans hopefully in the way Tennessee Williams wrote about Southerners . . . Southern culture is very different from the rest of the country, but everybody identifies with Blanche DuBois, she's so intensely human."

Torange Yeghiazarian

Born in Iran to a Muslim mother and Christian father of Armenian heritage, Yeghiazarian came to America in 1978, right before the Iranian

Revolution in 1979. Her family settled in Boston, where she acted in plays in multiple languages: in English at her high school, in Persian with an Iranian theatre company, and in Armenian through the arts wing of an Armenian organization of which she was a member.

"I didn't pursue a degree in theatre because I didn't think I'd get work," she reflects. "My dream career as a child was to become a heart surgeon." By the time she earned her BS in 1990 from Northeastern University in Boston, however, she was disillusioned with the practice of American medicine and decided to pursue her MA in theatre. "In a way, theatre for me is like practicing medicine. It's healing and has its roots in magic and ritual." While doing AIDS research and co-authoring scientific articles with titles like "Quantification of Human Immunodeficiency Virus Type 1 RNA Levels in Plasma by Using Small Volume-Format Branched-DNA Assays," she earned an MA in theatre from San Francisco State University.

Not only is Yeghiazarian the author of *Call Me Mehdi*, the gentle comedy of cross-cultural marriage, she is also the founder of the first Middle Eastern–American theatre company, Golden Thread Productions, which evolved from a production of Yeghiazarian's thesis play, a Middle Eastern adaptation of Aristophanes' *Lysistrata* called *Operation No Penetration*. "It was important to me to attach a name to the company and, as I was reading Greek mythology at the time, I was inspired by the tale of Ariadne giving Theseus a ball of golden thread to lead him out of the labyrinth. For me theatre is that golden thread that helps you find your way in life."

Younger authors are following this anthology's dramatists in development and production. Egyptian-American Suehyla El-Attar was invited to join the Alliance Theatre's first Atlanta Playwrights Lab in 2006; her plays have been produced in Atlanta and Alaska. The Minneapolis-based journal and cultural center Mizna presented works by Iranian-American Layla Dowlatshahi (*The Elevator*) along with Algerian-American Taous Khazem (*Tizi Ouzou*) in 2007; both writers were recipients of Mizna's first granting program. Also in Minneapolis, Pangea World Theater has presented Ismail Khalidi and Bassam Jarbawi's *Truth Serum Blues*. Seema Sueko, a Muslim of Pakistani-Japanese heritage and Co-Founder and Artistic Director of San Diego's new Mo`olelo Performing Arts Company, wrote *remains* for its opening and has received two commissions from Mixed Blood in Minneapolis.

Looking toward the future, Silk Road in Chicago, Golden Thread in San Francisco and the Lark Play Development Center in New York City have together established an initiative called Middle East America: A National New Play Initiative, which will grant a ten-thousand-dollar commission to a Middle Eastern–American playwright for a work that would be developed at the Lark, given staged readings at Silk Road and Golden Thread and, ideally, a full production at one or both theatres. The award would include travel expenses so that the playwright could be present at all stages of development. The first winner was announced in November 2008: Adriana Sevan, an American artist of Armenian, Dominan and Basque ancestry. Leila Buck and Turkish-American playwright Sinan Ünel were each honored with a Special Jury Prize.

Also at Silk Road, relates Kurup (whose *Merchant on Venice* was a 2007 production of the Chicago company), "Jamil has come up with this amazing idea: playwrights from Silk Road backgrounds are going to send in our DNA to be tested. We'll get the results back, ponder what we learn from that, and get together in Chicago. We'll talk about it, workshop it with each other, go home and write twelve-minute plays. Six months later, we'll come back, workshop the plays and put them on in one evening. Who knows what we'll come up with?" *The DNA Trail* is scheduled for a spring 2010 production at Silk Road.

It has been a great privilege for Dina Amin and me to work with Theatre Communications Group on the first collection to recognize and honor the plays of Middle Eastern–American artists. May they, their colleagues and their successors thrive.

Lebanese-American poet Kahlil Gibran wrote to his fellow émigrés:

I believe in you, and I believe in your destiny.
I believe that you are contributors to this new civilization.
I believe that you have inherited from your forefathers an ancient
    dream, a song, a prophecy, which you can proudly lay as a gift
    of gratitude upon the lap of America.

The gratitude, through the publication of this anthology, goes both ways.
    Salaam.Peace.

Readers who would like to know more about Middle Eastern–American theatre can refer to inclusioninthearts.org. The Alliance for Inclusion in the Arts website includes an expanded version of this essay with footnoted references, bios of Middle Eastern–American authors (including many not in this anthology) and annotated lists of their plays. I am grateful to Alliance Executive Director Sharon Jensen and her colleagues for creating a special website section on Middle Eastern–American theatre.

Ten Acrobats in an Amazing Leap of Faith

Yussef El Guindi

Author's Statement

It's a little troubling when depicting an ordinary Arab-American Muslim family, going about their ordinary day, getting involved in regular family mishaps and melodramas, seems like such a radical thing to do. In writing this play and trying to sidestep the stereotypes that attend Arabs and Muslims, and to simply present these characters as regular folk—not as wife-beating, bomb-strapping, terrorist-inclined fanatics with a thing for barring little girls from school and enjoying a good mob scene that ends in many deaths—I didn't quite realize how unexpected that would seem to an audience, given the fact that I was trying to write an accessible, family melodrama.

Such was (is) the misapprehension of Arabs and Muslims in mainstream American culture that just to show this Arab Muslim family as regular people would come as a surprise to some in the audience. I was of course grateful that those connections were being made ("they're just like my family"), but at the same time I was a little dismayed that that was even a question in the first place.

But then such is the power of repeating the same half truths and outright lies about a people. Eventually, some (or most) of it sticks.

Indeed, beyond the understandable fears that arose after 9/11, it felt like Arabs and Muslims had become the screen onto which everyone could project their worst traits, or *shadows*. There is apparently something almost irresistible in finding a group to rail against. Dividing the world into "us" and "them" is psychologically very satisfying for some. It puts aside all that emasculating ambiguity and compromising that one has to do most of the time, and empowers one. Scapegoating is a guilty pleasure. Feeling right and moral and virtuous and better (much, much better than someone else) and feeling those things as a community under the banner of flag-waving leaders with a war agenda, sometimes, well, it just hits the spot.

After 9/11, there was a feeling within the Arab and Muslim community that we had been placed beyond the pale. Though, in truth, we had never really found our way into the cultural conversation even before 9/11. And now that we had been shoved into that conversation, it was not in a good way. At all. And so I had in mind to write the most ordinary of plays to get us—I can't say "back in the conversation"—but at least to within hailing distance of starting a whole new one.

When Cornerstone Theater Company (whose mandate is to involve the different communities they reach out to in the shaping of a project) commissioned me as part of their cycle of religious-themed plays, I thought I would take the opportunity to reinstate that share of humanity that had been sucked out of us by some observers after 9/11. Nothing over the top, mind you (I enjoy characters with their fair share of flaws and warts), but enough humanizing to allow audiences who only hear terrible things about Muslims and Arabs to go, "Oh, they're not the monsters we thought they were." Nothing too mawkish and sentimental, but something with a little heart. (From this vantage point, several years later, it feels somewhat depressing that I felt the need to do this. It's startling how susceptible we are to dehumanizing propaganda.)

That was my intent. (As well as to use the opportunity to explore other issues facing a fair number of immigrant families.) But such is the psychology of any group that has been consistently portrayed in a negative light and feels under siege, that when a project comes along that aims to construct a narrative around them, the defenses of that group instinctively go up. Mine go up, too. One's immediate thought is, Here we go again. We're going to get trashed. And one's fears aren't necessarily allayed when the writer of the project comes from that same race or religion. It's often the case that the rare Arab or Muslim voice that makes it to the mainstream, or something approximating it, does so because it reflects the mainstream's negative view of the Arab and Muslim cultures. Thus, my coming from that group was no guarantee of anything.

So there was wariness. In addition, there was an understandable desire for a sympathetic and positive portrayal for once—if Cornerstone was indeed sincere in reaching out to the Muslim community. Given the years of being battered by mainstream culture, I was definitely onboard with that.

But when sections of the play were presented to a gathering of people from the Muslim community in Los Angeles, those sections were met with some resistance. Even though I felt the play was conveying the sympathy and love I felt for the characters, and the cultures from which they emerged, certain conservative elements objected to aspects of the play. They wondered why I had decided to include particular conflicts and issues, when so much else could have been included. In retrospect, I think it was a mistake not to present the whole play and put the things some people took issue with in context.

When Cornerstone Theater Company, ever mindful of its mandate to listen and to collaborate with the community they're engaging, asked me to make changes to address the concerns of those conservative elements (like, for instance, their concern over one character's struggle with his sexuality) I balked. As a consequence, Cornerstone felt it had to pass on the play. A decision I understood. I'm very thankful to the theatre for wanting to do this project in the first place, and for doing so with the sincerity and heart they approach all their projects. I was simply a tad stubborn at the time and didn't want to accommodate what I felt were the conservative voices coming from the community. (There were liberal Muslim voices who were supportive of the play.)

A few months later, Jamil Khoury and Malik Gillani of Silk Road Theatre Project in Chicago stepped in and staged *Ten Acrobats*. They, and director Stuart Carden and the wonderful cast assembled, did an amazing job of getting the play up on its feet and giving it a life. And the Muslims who came to see it did not raise objections. The controversy that preceded the presentation of the play melted away. I think people just had to see the play fully realized on stage to understand my intent, and hopefully to see the heart I wanted to place center stage with this play.

Part of the problem at the time, I sense, was that people were just overly sensitized and even traumatized by what was going on around them. And since writing an Arab-/Muslim-themed play was unfortunately more of a singular occurrence, at least in the States, then there was bound to be extra scrutiny directed at any Arab-/Muslim-themed play that came along. As more plays are written by Arabs and Muslims, then no one play will have to carry the burden of having to get it "just right." Any drama by its nature is going to go into uncomfortable territory. As more plays are written, I hope future Arab- and Muslim-American playwrights will wade deep into that uncomfortable territory and create an engaging body of work that wider audiences will want to see.

Production History

Ten Acrobats in an Amazing Leap of Faith premiered at the Silk Road Theatre Project in Chicago in 2006. It was directed by Stuart Garden. Set design was by Matthew Morton. Lighting design was by Kurt Ottinger. Sound design and original music were by Robert Steele. Costume design was by Aly Greaves. The stage manager was Alexandra Herryman. The cast was as follows:

KAMAL	Vincent P. Mahler
MONA	Irit Levit
TAWFIQ	Kareem Bandealy
HAMZA	Anil Hurkadli
HUWAIDA	Monica Lopez
MURAD	Peter Nicholas
AZIZ	Frank Platis
PAULINE	Mary Ann de la Cruz
H.D.	Jen Albert
KEVIN	Steven Gilpin

Characters

KAMAL, the father of the family
MONA, the mother of the family
TAWFIQ, their son
HAMZA, their other son
HUWAIDA, their daughter
MURAD, Huwaida's fiancé
AZIZ, Murad's father
PAULINE, Huwaida's psychologist
H.D., Huwaida's dream-double
KEVIN, a student

(The cast above can double for the following characters:)

VEILED FIGURES, PILOT'S VOICE, CUSTOMS OFFICER, BOMB EXPERTS

Setting

Los Angeles.

Place

The present.

Note

A glossary of select terms appears at the end of the play.

For my family: Fatma, Zein, Zaki, Amal and Ahmed.

·❖❈❖·

Scene 1

The sound of an oud, played offstage. The sounds are occasionally halting, discordant, even painful to hear.

    Kamal and Tawfiq are in the living room, which is bare of furniture. Both men are polishing the floor. Kamal is shuffling along, a rag under his bare feet. Tawfiq is pushing a mop before him. He is barefooted or in socks.

    This goes on for a few beats before Tawfiq stops what he's doing, looks at his father and addresses him with some resolve.

TAWFIQ: *Ba-ba.*

    (Kamal doesn't seem to hear him and continues to clean.)

    Ba-ba.

    (Again, no response.)

    Ba-ba!

    (Kamal turns to his son just as Mona appears in the doorway.)

KAMAL: What? *(He remembers to take his earplugs out)* What is the matter?

MONA: Who's going to speak to him, you or me?

KAMAL: What are you talking about?

(A particularly painful sound from the oud is heard.)

MONA: You're his father. He'll listen.

KAMAL: He's getting in touch with his roots.

MONA: What roots? These sounds come from a country that is not on the map.

KAMAL: He's better.

MONA: In theory. In practice, he is killing us today.

KAMAL: It takes time.

MONA: A little too long.

KAMAL: There are no shortcuts to learning a musical instrument. There is agony and then there are the sweet sounds of someone who has not given up. Who continues in spite of the problems. Who refuses to rest until his passion is answered by the sounds he knows his beloved instrument possesses.

(Another particularly harsh sound from the oud.)

I'll go speak to him. *(He starts for the door)* He doesn't have to practice all day.

MONA: He can go to the park. Perhaps nature will inspire him.

KAMAL *(Taking her face in his hands)*: Did I mention how beautiful you are today?

MONA: Yes, but you can tell me again.

KAMAL: You are the light on my dark nights.

MONA: Mmm.

KAMAL: You are the blue in my morning skies.

MONA: More.

KAMAL: You are the water that brings back to life my dry heart and makes it speak in little cooing sounds.

TAWFIQ: Excuse me. Would you like me to leave?

KAMAL: Why? Would you prefer to watch us argue instead?

TAWFIQ: No. But . . . never mind.

(Tawfiq starts mopping again.)

KAMAL *(To Mona)*: It is not cool to be in love.

MONA: At our age, he has a point.

KAMAL: We'd better quarrel for the sake of our son. Any particular quarrel you would like?

MONA: You choose.

KAMAL: I'm in too good a mood, you begin.

MONA: I am afraid they will start soon enough without my help.

KAMAL: In that case let us say we quarreled and make up.

MONA: Agreed.

KAMAL: That was quick. You know, in this country, married people sometimes marry each other again. Renewing their vows they call it. When our daughter gets engaged, why not we make it a double ceremony? I feel like taking a second wife. I would like my second wife to be you.

MONA: As your first wife, I second that. For the sake of your health. You wouldn't live long enough to enjoy another woman.

KAMAL: We do it then? *(To Tawfiq)* Tawfiq: You never saw us get married, did you.

MONA: He wouldn't have.

KAMAL *(To Tawfiq)*: Would you like that? How often do children see their parents marrying? One good thing about this country is that old people don't have to act old if they don't want to. They can be as young as they want to be.

MONA: Go ask your son first to take a break. Then I can feel romantic again—but be kind, don't discourage him.

KAMAL *(As he exits)*: He can bring the oud with him and practice after prayers. The pigeons can be his audience for a change.

(Kamal exits. Tawfiq continues to mop.)

TAWFIQ: I wouldn't put him off it. It's the one thing he enjoys.

MONA: I want him to continue. He *is* getting better . . . I needed to talk to you. *(Takes a breath)* Tawfiq . . . I would like to know what is going on.

TAWFIQ: What do you mean?

MONA: Tawfiq, please.

TAWFIQ: Can we leave it alone?

MONA: That is not possible with me, you know that.

TAWFIQ: There's nothing more to say. I've told you. It's not a big deal.

MONA: Are you still going to tell him? . . . If it's not a big thing, then you don't have to tell him.

TAWFIQ: And you want me to do what? Lie?

MONA: It's not a lie if you don't say anything. Nobody asked you a question.

TAWFIQ: And when I go pray with him, what is that?

MONA: It's being a good son.

TAWFIQ: You brought me up better than that.

MONA: Then tell him next week. After the engagement. Why tell him today?

TAWFIQ: Someone needs to stop that; I mean it. She doesn't know what she's doing.

MONA: Do not concern yourself with that, it's none of your business.

TAWFIQ: It is my business when I see my sister walking into something this stupid.

MONA: Worry about your own life, it's her choice.

TAWFIQ: Oh, bull. She may think it's her choice but it's not.

MONA: What's gotten into you—when did you become so hard? That you think you can speak to me like that. And your father, to want to tell him this. Really, what is happening? You're short tempered. You don't sit with us. You used to laugh. What happened to my son who used to laugh?

TAWFIQ: I just don't want to pretend anymore.

MONA: Why not, it's easy. You keep it to yourself until this nonsense you are in passes.

TAWFIQ: It's not nonsense.

MONA: It's not necessary.

TAWFIQ: Didn't you both bring me up to always tell the truth?

MONA: The truth is not a knife you stab someone with. What do you achieve by telling him? Is it fasting you're fed up with?

TAWFIQ: Oh, Mum, stop.

MONA: Because it's not everything; we'll make up some excuse to your father.

TAWFIQ (Overlapping last few words): It has nothing to do with that.

MONA: Is it some course you're taking in college?

TAWFIQ: *No.*

MONA: *Then what?* One day you're a Muslim and the next you decide everything you grew up believing is now meaningless? A joke?

TAWFIQ: I didn't say that. I just said . . . I don't want to be a part of something that doesn't make sense to me anymore.

(At some point during the above exchange, the sound of the oud has stopped.)

MONA: Then don't. No one is forcing you to. But you don't have to tell your father, and you don't have to tell him today.

TAWFIQ: I don't want to go to prayers with him.

MONA: Okay, we'll make up some excuse.

TAWFIQ: I don't want to lie to him.

MONA: Instead you just want to twist his heart and break it.

TAWFIQ: Thinking God is a fairy tale is not a crime.

MONA: I'm not talking about you or what you believe. Believe what you want. But you don't have to drag it in here and hit us over the head with it.

TAWFIQ: What do you think you've been doing with me? *With all of us? For all these years?*

(Slight beat. For a second, it looks like Mona might slap him. But she doesn't.)

MONA: Is that what we've been doing? And what you want to do helps you how?

TAWFIQ: I get to breathe . . . I finally get to breathe.

(Kamal enters and stops for a moment as he notes the mood change in the room.)

KAMAL: I was gentle. I told him the house wasn't big enough to hold his musical ambitions. We should look into renting him a studio. *(He takes a second mop leaning against a wall)* Are we finished here, or . . . shall we wait until after we return? *(Regarding the heavy mood)* What did I miss? . . . What did you say to upset your mother?

MONA: Nothing. Tawfiq can't come with you and Hamza today.

KAMAL: Why not? We were going to call on Am Aziz afterwards.

MONA: He has a meeting with a college professor.

KAMAL: Oh? Is everything okay?

MONA: It's just about a project he's working on.

KAMAL: Why are you talking for him? *(To Tawfiq)* Is everything okay?

TAWFIQ: Yes, everything's fine.

KAMAL: No problems at university?

TAWFIQ: No.

KAMAL: Then I can meet this professor. *(Calling out)* Hamza. Get ready. We're leaving now.

TAWFIQ: It's okay, we don't have to meet him today.

KAMAL: Why not? It's about time I met one of your teachers.

TAWFIQ: We can do it later.

KAMAL: If we're dropping you off, I might as well.

TAWFIQ: It's not like high school, you don't have to.

KAMAL: Are you embarrassed to introduce me?

TAWFIQ: *No.* Look—never mind the meeting. I'll reschedule it for later. *(He starts heading for an exit)* We can just go straight to the *masjid.*

(Tawfiq exits. Kamal turns to his wife.)

KAMAL: What's going on?
MONA: Nothing. It was a drama professor. Not engineering.
KAMAL: Drama? I'm paying for drama?
MONA: He's thinking of taking a course. It's a phase.
KAMAL: Life is drama enough; why take a course in it?

(Mona goes up to Kamal.)

He wants to be an actor?
MONA: No.
KAMAL: He'll starve. He'll never get cast.
MONA: Whatever he says to you—be patient. Don't explode.
KAMAL: I never explode. I just speak clearly.
MONA: He doesn't know what he wants right now. Don't push him into making a decision he'll regret.
KAMAL: What are you hiding? I know when you're hiding something you don't want me to hear.

(Mona makes a mollifying gesture, such as taking her husband's face in her hands, or touching his arm.)

MONA: We've done well so far, haven't we? . . . Let's be thankful for what we have. Okay?
KAMAL: I am not going to like this, am I.
MONA: No . . . I don't think you will.

(Blackout.)

Scene 2

Lights are dim. Several Veiled Figures enter wearing some variation of extremely conservative veiling, where, in addition to the flowing robes, the faces are covered.

Two chairs are placed on one side of the stage as Huwaida and Pauline enter. A spot comes up on them. Pauline sits. Huwaida stands. Huwaida is veiled but in a much more relaxed way. Her face is exposed and perhaps she wears jeans.

HUWAIDA: Okay. So this is the dream. It's a dream, okay, so it's going to sound really, really weird.

PAULINE: That's all right. Go on. You've had this dream before?

HUWAIDA: Yes, and I'm sick of it and I want to answer it back. I mean I want to figure out what it wants to tell me, so maybe it will go away. It's obvious to me on one level, but . . . do you believe dreams try to teach us things?

PAULINE: Sometimes—why don't you tell me about it.

HUWAIDA: This is my first time with a psychologist.

PAULINE: I'm glad you came.

HUWAIDA: Just so you know. I'm not having a breakdown. I need someone to help me figure this out, that's all. Is this going in some record?

PAULINE: Everything said here is kept in strict confidence.

HUWAIDA: I don't want my parents to know.

PAULINE: They won't. You're perfectly safe here. Why don't you tell me about the dream.

HUWAIDA: Okay. *(Takes a breath)* So . . . there are these veiled figures.

(Lights up on the Veiled Figures.)

Around five or six of them. Sometimes more. Sometimes it's a whole crowd. And they're just standing there, very still. And then I realize what they're doing. They're . . . watching television. On a big screen.

(Perhaps a flickering light is shone on the figures to suggest a television set playing offstage.)

And what they're watching is the Miss America contest. They're glued to the screen watching this . . . Miss America contest. And there's this feeling in the room that something terrible is about to happen. And then it does. And what happens is me. I'm in the contest. I'm a contestant in this beauty pageant. And for some reason it always begins in the swimsuit section. And it's like I'm both in the room watching, and on the screen waiting to come on. And I realize now these figures are not strangers, but—my friends and relatives, people from the community. They've all gathered to watch me come out. And I do—I'm standing there, horrified, as I watch myself come out in a swimsuit.

(A spotlight comes up on Huwaida's Double, H.D., as she enters dressed in a one-piece swimsuit, carrying a beach ball. She wears a scarf that leaves her face exposed.)

And I'm veiled. It's bad enough I'm in a swimsuit. But on top of that I'm also veiled. Like I have to humiliate myself in front of Muslims and non-Muslims alike, like I'm a circus freak.

PAULINE: When you say veiled—

HUWAIDA: Just my head. The rest of me is barely covered. Though I have to say, I look very good. The swimsuit fits fantastically on me. I mean I'm mortified but a part of me takes note of, wow: I'm not bad. That diet really worked. I should say of course that this woman, though I know it's me, looks nothing like me. Only it is me in the way you know it is in dreams. Anyway, I come out . . . and stand there with this stupid beach ball and smile. One of those smiles only beauty contestants can get away with.

PAULINE: How do these figures react?

(The Veiled Figures gasp in unison.)

HUWAIDA: The expression "cut the air with a knife" comes to mind. There's enough outrage in the room to start a bonfire. And then out of nowhere a microphone is placed in front of me.

(A microphone on a stand is placed before H.D.)

VEILED FIGURE 1: Oh no. She's going to speak.

H.D.: What did you think: I was just going to come out here and look beautiful?

HUWAIDA: And there's nothing I can do to shut myself up.

H.D.: I would like to dedicate this moment to all my Muslim sisters around the world.

HUWAIDA: Oh no.

H.D.: And to all my Muslim brothers, I say *assalam alaykum*, and please hold off on your objections until after you see me in the talent section.

HUWAIDA: I get nauseous just telling you about it.

VEILED FIGURES *(In unison, to Huwaida)*: How could you do this to us?

HUWAIDA *(To the Veiled Figures)*: I had no idea I'd be in this contest, I swear to God.

H.D.: I think it's time we Muslims stepped out into the light and made a big splash. For too long we have let others misrepresent us, mock our ways and call us everything under the sun. Well I say, enough of that. We're here, we're proud, and by golly we can kick ass along with the best of them.

HUWAIDA *(To H.D.)*: But you're in the swimsuit section, for crying out loud. What are you talking about?

H.D.: And another thing.

HUWAIDA: Oh no, please shut up.

H.D.: I am tired of being told that I have no modesty in coming out like this. I do have modesty. I was actually thinking about coming out in a bikini. Unfortunately, I couldn't find one in the color I wanted. But isn't this great? *(Refers to the one-piece she's wearing)* My auntie made it for me. Auntie?

(H.D. turns around to one of the Veiled Figures in the room.)

Would you like to take a bow.

(No one moves.)

Go on. Don't be shy. Your work deserves praise.

(The Veiled Figures turn to one of the Veiled Figures. The selected Veiled Figure hesitates, then shrugs.)

VEILED FIGURE 2: She's my niece. She asked. What could I say.

VEILED FIGURES *(In unison)*: *Shameless.*

HUWAIDA *(To Pauline)*: And that's the end of the dream.

H.D.: No it's not. I haven't sung yet.

HUWAIDA *(To H.D.)*: I'm sorry, you're done.

H.D.: And I haven't made my speech about making the world a better place.

HUWAIDA: Please get off the stage.

H.D.: Or the line of swimsuits I want to open up for Muslim ladies on Venice Beach.

HUWAIDA *(To offstage crew)*: Shut the microphone off right now. *(To the Veiled Figures)* That's all I'm telling about the dream. Get out. Please. Thank you.

(The Veiled Figures exit.)

H.D.: You are wound up way too tight.

HUWAIDA: That's why I'm here. Get out.

H.D.: Till tonight. And in the next dream, I'm singing. I'm thinking of doing the call to prayer in a funky pop tune with a good solid base.

HUWAIDA: Get out!

H.D. *(As she exits, under her breath)*: You're such a nutcase.

(She's gone. Spotlight goes out.)

HUWAIDA *(To Pauline)*: I wake up in a sweat. And afterwards I can't sleep. This has been going on for the past month and I'm fed up. I can't . . . It's like I can never grab a hold of it long enough to figure out what it wants.

PAULINE: You said it was obvious to you on one level, how?

HUWAIDA: Well . . . because . . . probably a part of me, even though I think it's a joke . . . maybe I'm a closet exhibitionist, or something, or vain, and this dream is acting out what I don't permit myself in real life.

PAULINE: What don't you permit yourself?

HUWAIDA: I'd never be that . . . in your face. Or dumb, for that matter. I'd never degrade myself in that way. I'm a bit of a feminist believe it or not.

PAULINE: But you take note in the dream that you look good.

HUWAIDA: Well heck, it's my dream, I might as well look good.

PAULINE: Why do you think you're also veiled?

HUWAIDA: Because it's still me, I suppose. I can't leave myself behind completely.

PAULINE: Is that how you identify yourself? As a veiled woman?

HUWAIDA: No. It's just what comes naturally. What makes sense.

PAULINE: Was veiling your choice?

HUWAIDA: You know, that's not relevant. What I want to know is—in your experienced, professional opinion, what comes to mind? What's up with this dream?

PAULINE: Huwaida, the question is what does it mean for you?

HUWAIDA: Oh no, don't do that. Don't throw it back to me. Is this what all psychologists do? Question your questions? So that you come out with more questions than you came in with?

PAULINE: Yes. And hopefully those additional inquiries help open up the problem that brought you in here. The idea being to leave you with a better grasp of what's going on . . . Can I ask what your major is?

HUWAIDA: Why? Mathematics.

PAULINE: Do you enjoy that?

HUWAIDA: I do. There are only so many interpretations you can make with numbers.

PAULINE: Was that your choice?

HUWAIDA: That's the second time you've asked me that. Yes it was. I'm also minoring in art.

PAULINE: Oh?

HUWAIDA: Yes. I come from a family of frustrated artists. My father was a calligrapher once. Now he sells carpets. I have to go. *(She moves to the chair to get her backpack and jacket)*

PAULINE: We still have the rest of the hour.

(Huwaida starts putting away her schedule book, water bottle and anything else she might have taken out.)

HUWAIDA: I have to get ready for class.

PAULINE: I'd like to help you.

HUWAIDA: If you're just going to ask me questions, I can puzzle through the dream on my own. I was hoping for something else. Something a little more concrete to make it stop.

PAULINE: Will you allow me one more question?

HUWAIDA: I really do need to go.

PAULINE: You said it was the Miss America contest? This will sound odd . . . but . . . do you know what state you were representing?

HUWAIDA *(A laugh)*: Excuse me?

PAULINE: On the sash. What did it say? California? New York?

HUWAIDA: What does that have to do with anything?

PAULINE: I was just wondering. Who were you representing?

(In spite of the perceived silliness of the question, Huwaida stops to recall.)

HUWAIDA: I . . . I didn't . . .

(H.D. comes out again and stands near the wings. As before, she isn't wearing a sash. She begins to bounce the beach ball. Huwaida looks at her.)

I don't remember. I wasn't wearing one.

PAULINE: Were you representing anything? If not a state, something else? A country? A religion? —I guess I'm suggesting, and it's only a suggestion, that maybe you're not wearing a sash because . . . in a sense . . . is the veil the sash? Do you think?

H.D. *(To Huwaida)*: You are so lame.

PAULINE: Does it stand in for the sash? In the dream it's clear who you address.

HUWAIDA: I knew you'd reduce it to that.

PAULINE: Reduce it to what?

HUWAIDA: "If she's having problems it has to be because she's veiled."

PAULINE: I don't know if it is. Is it?

H.D.: Something's going to break, Huwaida.

HUWAIDA: Maybe my dream is a celebration of being veiled. Inappropriate maybe, in the way dreams are, but a celebration nonetheless, a coming out.

PAULINE: How can it be a celebration if your reaction is one of embarrassment?

HUWAIDA: Well a part of me's enjoying it.

PAULINE: The other half is mortified.

HUWAIDA: Well I guess that's life. We're always splitting off into different people depending on the occasion.

PAULINE: Yes. And a healthy person is one who is able to integrate those various parts.

H.D.: Why don't you tell her what's going on?

PAULINE: Did you choose to be veiled?

HUWAIDA *(To H.D.)*: Would you stop bouncing that ball!

(H.D. stops.)

Look. I don't need to be liberated *or* saved. I just want this annoying character in my dream to go away.

PAULINE: Let's work on it.

HUWAIDA: I don't think so. I came to see a psychologist, not an anthropologist.

PAULINE: Are you sure it's not *you* who's starting to look at yourself in an awkward way?

HUWAIDA: Sorry, but you're way off. I have to go. *(She heads for the door)*

PAULINE: Huwaida.

H.D.: Huwaida! Catch.

(H.D. throws the beach ball to Huwaida. She catches it. Blackout.)

Scene 3

In the blackout we hear the call to prayer. Lights up on an area outside the mosque.

    Tawfiq enters holding his shoes. He stops at a spot and starts putting them on. Hamza also comes out of the mosque and starts putting on his shoes.

HAMZA: What happened?

(No response.)

What's up?

TAWFIQ: And you? How are you doing?

HAMZA: Why weren't you praying? . . . Why were you just standing there like that?

TAWFIQ: Well, let's see. I was just standing there, probably because I wasn't praying, or I wasn't praying because I couldn't figure out what I was doing standing there. What were you doing? As someone who *was* praying, perhaps you can clue me in.

HAMZA: What's up?

TAWFIQ: What's up? I guess that's what I can't figure out. Which takes me back to why I was just standing there.

HAMZA: Seriously, man, what's going on?

TAWFIQ: Why is it whenever anyone asks me that question and I tell them, it's as if they haven't heard me. *(Spelling it out)* I wasn't praying because I didn't want to. I do not want to pray. I did not want to come to the mosque. I chickened out and came anyway because God forbid we should upset Puppy. God forbid we should have our own opinions and beliefs.

HAMZA: What do you mean you don't want to pray?

TAWFIQ: It's just amazing how people can't get their minds around this. *Figure it out.*

(Slight beat.)

HAMZA: Why are you so pissed off? Really. You've been acting ticked off for weeks.

TAWFIQ: Yeah, well, things change.

HAMZA: Like what? . . . Talk to me, man.

TAWFIQ: Talk to you? You really want me to do that?

HAMZA: When did you . . . stop believing in God?

TAWFIQ: What are *you* doing in there?

HAMZA: I mean it, man. All of a sudden?

TAWFIQ: I'll tell you when. When I did what God commands all of us to do: to open our eyes and look around us. Investigate, question. I took those commands very seriously. I questioned, I looked. Unfortunately I questioned him right out of the equation.

HAMZA: Really. How'd you do that?

TAWFIQ: Have you even bothered to think about this? Or do you just go in there 'cause it's what our father does?

HAMZA: Are you embarrassed to be a Muslim now?

TAWFIQ: Oh, please. It has nothing to do with that.

HAMZA: Is all this crap they're saying about us getting to you?

TAWFIQ: That's not the reason; if anything, that's what's kept me a Muslim this long.

HAMZA: You're not going to change your name on us now are you?

TAWFIQ (Going up to his brother): You tell me something. Are you sure the God in there loves you?

HAMZA: What does that have to do with anything?

TAWFIQ: It's a pretty basic question, don't you think?

HAMZA: Yes, I know He does.

TAWFIQ: If you strictly follow certain things. Certain basic things.

HAMZA: That's right. As with every faith.

TAWFIQ: Like who you love, and how you love.

HAMZA: Among other things.

TAWFIQ: Conditional love. God's love is conditional. I love you unconditionally, and somehow God's love is less than mine. Does that make sense? That my love should be bigger than His?

HAMZA: No, what it says—it's repeated enough times—is the "All Merciful," the "Compassionate."

TAWFIQ: As long as you play by His rules.

HAMZA: That would follow, sure; why does that sound strange to you?

TAWFIQ: It just seems very petty. If you're going to be God, don't you think your capacity to love and forgive should be bigger than ours?

HAMZA: It is; the rules are guidelines, to support you.

TAWFIQ: They're more than guidelines. These are players' rules. Break one and you're that much closer to getting kicked out of the game permanently.

HAMZA: You don't think we need help? I'm not so arrogant as to believe I've got it all figured out. And the other way is what? No laws? We're too weak for that.

TAWFIQ: Yes, we're human. I don't want to be penalized for being human.

HAMZA: God allows for our weaknesses.

TAWFIQ: Up to a point, after that, it's: "Burn, baby, burn."

HAMZA: Why are you focusing on the negatives? It's such a small part.

TAWFIQ: People going to hell? That's a detail to you?

HAMZA: There have to be consequences, in everything. And the Qur'an repeatedly speaks of forgiving sins. And why would you cut yourself off from His blessings?

TAWFIQ: Because I don't believe He exists to give me any!

(Beat.)

HAMZA: When'd you start believing all this?
TAWFIQ: Is that how you classify it? A weakness?
HAMZA: What?
TAWFIQ: I'm just wondering . . . where you stand . . . Where, if something feels so right . . . and good . . . it makes you glow inside, and gives meaning to your life like nothing else does. And you know in your heart this can't be a sin . . . it can't be because it feels too necessary just to breathe. And it doesn't hurt anybody, and it *is* good and it just has to be. What if your faith forbids it? What then . . . What do you do then?
HAMZA: What are you talking about?

(Tawfiq looks at his brother for a moment, then turns and walks away.)

Where are you going? Tawfiq. Wait up.

(Tawfiq exits. Hamza stands there for a moment. Kamal enters carrying his shoes, the oud and a backpack.)

KAMAL: Did he leave?
HAMZA: He had a . . . he had an appointment.
KAMAL *(Referring to the backpack)*: He forgot this.
HAMZA: I can take it to him.
KAMAL: You go practice. When he remembers he'll come back for it.

(Kamal puts down the backpack. He hands the oud to Hamza.)

What's wrong with him?
HAMZA *(Shrugs)*: I don't know, he's . . . he seems to be . . . he didn't really say.

(Slight beat.)

KAMAL: So far everyone in this family knows what's going on except me. Why is that? Is it so difficult to tell me things? —Never mind. Go practice. I'll see you at *iftar*.
HAMZA: Do you want me to bring anything on the way back?

KAMAL: Call your mother, see if she needs anything.
HAMZA: Okay . . . I'll see you later.

(Hamza starts to walk off. Kamal sits to put on his shoes.)

KAMAL: Hamza.

(Hamza stops.)

Is everything all right?
HAMZA: Yes.
KAMAL: Don't you kiss your father good-bye anymore?
HAMZA: Oh. *(Goes over to his father)* Sorry.
KAMAL: You can't forget these things with me. I'm sensitive.

(Hamza leans down to kiss his father. Kamal holds him for a second and affectionately pats his cheek.)

I'm very proud of you.
HAMZA *(Feeling awkward)*: Thanks.
KAMAL: If you see people around you doing this . . . *(He puts his fingers in his ears)* . . . come home. *(Takes his fingers out)* We understand your sounds better than they do.
HAMZA *(Smiling)*: I'll do that. I'll see you later.

(Hamza starts to exit. Kamal continues tying up his shoes.)

KAMAL: You'll be a good musician one day. Don't give up.
HAMZA: I won't. *(He goes)*
KAMAL *(To himself)*: Inshallah . . . Inshallah.

(Tawfiq enters. Sees his father, hesitates, then comes forward.)

TAWFIQ: Hi.
KAMAL: *Assalam alaykum.*
TAWFIQ: Forgot my bag.
KAMAL: Yes you did.

(Tawfiq picks up his backpack, but Kamal grabs hold of the other end.)

You also forgot to say good-bye.
TAWFIQ: I'm late for a meeting.
KAMAL: Your teacher?

TAWFIQ: No; someone else.

KAMAL: Are you not feeling well?

TAWFIQ: I'm fine.

KAMAL: So you behaved that way inside why? . . . We can have this conversation now, or we can have it later—but open your mouth to me you will. *(He lets go of the backpack)* Your mother thinks I will be upset with your news. What upsets me is being treated like I can't handle the problems of my children. Like I'm a guest in my own family who mustn't be allowed to know too much. *(He finishes tying his shoes, and stands)* If it is bad news, it is better said than left to stay secret and become something it needn't be, no?

TAWFIQ: I don't want to come to the mosque again.

(Slight beat.)

KAMAL: That's the big news?

TAWFIQ: Yes.

KAMAL: No problem. Is that all?

TAWFIQ: And I don't consider myself a Muslim anymore.

KAMAL: Oh . . . Okay.

TAWFIQ: I think God's a joke . . . I mean . . . you're welcome to believe in Him . . . but I don't.

(Slight beat.)

KAMAL: Uh-huh . . . Is there more?

(Tawfiq shakes his head.)

Will you be joining us for *iftar?*

TAWFIQ: I don't know yet.

(Slight beat.)

KAMAL: Anything else?

TAWFIQ: No.

(Slight beat.)

KAMAL: Can we still hug? Or don't you believe in that anymore?

TAWFIQ: This isn't a phase. I'm not just going through something and will come to my senses later; it's what I believe.

KAMAL: Did I say anything? You are free to believe what you want. I am just asking for a hug.

TAWFIQ: You want to dismiss what I just said.

KAMAL: What do you want me to do? Get angry?

(Tawfiq turns away from him and starts to leave.)

(Quiet) You do not walk away from me like that. Ever.

(Tawfiq turns to look at his father.)

TAWFIQ: I'm late. I'm sorry.

(Tawfiq turns and exits.)

KAMAL: Tawfiq . . . Tawfiq!

(Blackout.)

Scene 4

Lights up on the living room. Kamal, his shoes off, walks in. The space is still empty of furniture. There are scuff marks on the floor, as if people have been walking all over it. Kamal stares at the floor for a few moments.

KAMAL: Anyone home? *(Louder)* Mona?

MONA *(Offstage)*: I'm in the kitchen.

KAMAL: Please come out here.

MONA: I'm busy.

KAMAL: Mona!

(Slight beat, then Mona appears at the doorway.)

MONA: I didn't hear you come in. *(Sees the floor, gasps)* What did you do?

KAMAL: What did *I* do?

MONA: It was drying.

KAMAL: I just got here. I found it like this.

MONA: You didn't do this?

KAMAL: No. I just got here. Doesn't anyone have any sense around here? Who did this?

MONA: It doesn't matter. Let's just clean it up.

(She exits.)

KAMAL: Of course it matters. It matters if our children have become so irresponsible they don't know how to behave.

MONA *(Offstage)*: Kamal, it's the floor, it's dirt, it's not a crisis.

(She reenters with a mop.)

KAMAL: It tells me they have no respect for anything anymore. Were you here the entire time?

MONA: Forget about it.

KAMAL: Why should you mop the floor? Leave it. It's not your mess.

MONA: I want to do it.

KAMAL: Let one of them do it.

MONA: I've already started.

(He moves to take the mop away from her.)

KAMAL: I'm fed up of you making excuses for them all the time.

MONA: And I'm tired of not having any furniture to sit on!

(Slight beat as they both hold onto the mop.)

Let me just finish.

KAMAL: I'll do it.

MONA: As you wish.

(He takes the mop from her and starts cleaning the floor for a few moments, before throwing down the mop. They stand there for a moment.)

KAMAL: It was a mistake coming to this country.

MONA: Twenty-five years later, this is the conclusion you come to?

(Slight beat.)

KAMAL: Why did we come? So I could sell carpets? This is my great accomplishment?

(Slight beat.)

MONA: They're beautiful carpets.

KAMAL: They're carpets.

MONA: They bought this house.

KAMAL: They're still carpets.

MONA: They put our children through school. Good schools.

KAMAL: Not good enough.

MONA: He spoke to you?

KAMAL: It would never have happened if we'd stayed.

MONA: What did he say?

KAMAL: We have a responsibility for what goes inside here also. *(Presses his hand against his chest)*

MONA: What did he say?

KAMAL: He didn't want to . . . didn't want to hug me. His own father.

MONA: What do you mean?

KAMAL: I opened my arms to him and he refused them.

(Slight beat.)

MONA: How did you do it?

KAMAL: What do you mean, how did I do it?

MONA: How'd you do it?

KAMAL: How? Like this.

(He opens his arms as if for an embrace.)

MONA: Are you sure it wasn't like that?

(She also opens her arms for an embrace but with a slightly more aggressive stance.)

KAMAL: What is that?

MONA: This is "hug me or else."

KAMAL: I don't do that. That's you.

MONA: I'm your wife, I like them. But maybe your children find it too much.

KAMAL: Oh, this is when you become impossible, when you defend your children to a ridiculous point.

MONA: He's trying to grow up.

KAMAL: Being disrespectful and rude is growing up? Or is that what growing up means in this country. Treating your parents like they are something that has fallen out of fashion. Disposable. *(Mona starts mopping)* And while we're about it, let's throw God out, too, because He doesn't go with all the latest trends either. He isn't cool enough. Isn't hip enough. He asks too much, demands too much. Takes away from one's busy schedule of shopping and buying and watching more TV, and everything else people feel they must do to function—to be considered a healthy member of this society. *That's what being healthy means here.* And God has no place in it. This is the environment we brought Tawfiq up in—we should've stayed put!

MONA: Kamal, he turned out fine. They all did, *Hamdu'lillah.* He's just trying to assert himself. You did it when you went against your father's wishes and came here.

KAMAL: And look at the good it did me; I should've listened.

MONA: Yes, look at the good, let us be thankful.

KAMAL: And I did not part on bad terms. I came to him and talked about it. I treated him with respect, in the way parents everywhere are treated, except here.

MONA: Kamal, please, it's not the end of the world. He's free to see things the way he wants to. Let him stumble forward on his own.

KAMAL: And if his stumbling leads him to the edge of a cliff, are we supposed to stand back and watch him fall? Don't we have a responsibility for his soul? And what if it's not a phase and he has stopped believing?

MONA: Then he has stopped believing. What are we supposed to do, shove God down his throat? He doesn't believe in Him, and that's that. He knows where He is if he changes his mind.

KAMAL: This doesn't sadden you?

(Mona stops mopping.)

MONA: Why? I have no reason to be sad. I have a beautiful daughter who is getting engaged tomorrow, who has no problem being a Muslim and fitting into this country. I have a son who is more curious about the country we came from than we ever were. And, yes, we have a son who has decided he can live just fine without being a Muslim, and so what? He's not an addict, he's not lazy; it's not because he wants to live a crazy life and do depraved things.

KAMAL: We don't know that.

MONA: Oh stop.

KAMAL: We may yet find this out.

MONA: Whatever else he is, he is responsible and wants to make something of himself. I have a hundred reasons to be thankful, and so do you. Here, finish please. *(Holds out the mop)* I have to start the soup for Aziz. Was Murad there?

KAMAL *(Takes the mop)*: This is like Afifi. Exactly. Becoming a Christian. Wanting to call herself Sandra.

MONA: That was different. She was getting married.

KAMAL: But why become a Christian? Her husband didn't care. He would've converted.

MONA: Because it's Afifi. She likes to be dramatic.

KAMAL: *Because it was an easy way out.* Being a Muslim in this country has become too difficult now. Too many complications. Nobody wants to take the trouble to actually live their faith.

MONA: Forget Afifi and finish the floor.

(She starts to exit.)

KAMAL: It's Sandra not Afifi. And when Tawfiq becomes Tom, will that be all right with you? Will we lose him piece by piece?

MONA *(Faces Kamal; firm)*: When he comes home tonight, please—I don't want to argue about this, or even talk about it. If you start, it will explode, you know it will. Tomorrow is a special day. Please, let's have peace in this house. Promise me this won't become something it doesn't have to be.

(Kamal begins mopping.)

Kamal, promise me.

KAMAL: I heard you . . . Go finish what you were doing.

(Mona remains where she is.)

I heard you!

(Slight beat. Mona turns and exits. Kamal continues mopping. Then, suddenly, he hurls the mop away. He stands there as the lights quickly fade to black.)

Scene 5

Secluded courtyard on campus. Lights up on Tawfiq standing, waiting, his backpack at his feet. Huwaida enters carrying her backpack. Tawfiq turns and sees her.

HUWAIDA: What is so important I have to be late for my class?

TAWFIQ: You hate that class. You should thank me.

HUWAIDA: I still have to pass it.

TAWFIQ: What's to learn? It's an art class.

HUWAIDA: What do you want, Tawfiq?

TAWFIQ: To say hi . . . We haven't said hi in weeks.

HUWAIDA: Bye.

(She starts to leave.)

TAWFIQ: Huwaida.

HUWAIDA: I have work to do.

TAWFIQ: I want to talk to you.

HUWAIDA: What about? You've made yourself so very clear on every subject.

TAWFIQ: We're not on speaking terms now?

HUWAIDA: You? Mr. Sphinx? Mr. Don't-Talk-To-Me-I'm-Too-Busy-Being-Special? You're such a hypocrite.

TAWFIQ: I told Puppy.

(Slight beat.)

I told him.

HUWAIDA: Told him what?

TAWFIQ: You know . . . about . . . not being a Muslim anymore.

(Slight beat as Huwaida stares at her brother.)

HUWAIDA: When?

TAWFIQ: A little while ago. At the mosque.

HUWAIDA: You told him?

TAWFIQ: Yes. I finally had the guts to say it the way I feel it.

(Slight beat.)

HUWAIDA: You asshole.

TAWFIQ: Thanks.

HUWAIDA: How did he react?

TAWFIQ: I don't know that he believes me.

HUWAIDA: Good, that's the way it'll stay.

TAWFIQ: No, it needs to be made very clear.

HUWAIDA: You promised you weren't going to bring this up until after the engagement. Now he's going to be ticked off, you little shit. Why did you tell him?

TAWFIQ: It came up.

HUWAIDA: Oh, crap, you deliberately told him.

TAWFIQ: I don't want to walk around like I'm a criminal in my own home.

HUWAIDA: You can be so destructive.

TAWFIQ: What is wrong with being honest?

HUWAIDA: That's not being honest. That's wanting everyone to stop and pay attention to you. Well, congratulations, you've soured everything.

TAWFIQ: I'm looking out for you, Huwaida, believe it or not. I want what's best.

HUWAIDA: Precisely. Thank you. That's why you told him. You want to screw up the engagement. Well, give up. It's going to happen.

TAWFIQ: Huwaida, I really want you to think about what you're doing. I'm not going to stand by and watch you do something I know you'll regret.

HUWAIDA: You know what really ticks me off about atheists, if that's what you are. They make the worst zealots. They walk around with contempt for anyone who might be stupid enough to believe something they don't. Like suddenly you're plugged into something we mere mortals struggling in the dark could never imagine. And it is your duty to enlighten us and you won't stop until we bow before your own private temple of reason and give up our stupid beliefs. You're worse than the fanatics. You and all fundamentalists should find yourselves a nice little island and preach yourselves to death.

TAWFIQ: You think what you're doing is enlightened?

HUWAIDA: Are you going to live my life for me?

TAWFIQ: Don't do this to please Mum and Dad.

HUWAIDA: They're the ones who argued against it!

TAWFIQ: Oh, come on, you know they were thrilled, in spite of what they said. Mother's been pushing this guy on you for years.

HUWAIDA: *Just stay out of it.*

TAWFIQ: I know you're having second thoughts about this and don't want to admit it.

HUWAIDA: Oh *now* you know what goes on in my head? Are those special powers that come with being an atheist?

TAWFIQ: Stand outside of this for one second: Don't you think what you're doing is bizarre? By any standards?

HUWAIDA: Are you aware that over half the marriages in this country fail, leaving a miserable trail of stepparents and screwed-up kids? As opposed to arranged marriages that have a much higher success rate.

TAWFIQ: Tell me you're happy going into this.

HUWAIDA: You wouldn't believe me if I said yes.

TAWFIQ: Because I don't believe *you* believe it. You're so stubborn you'd rather plow on ahead than admit you've made a huge mistake.

HUWAIDA: I want to get married! How much clearer do I have to be?

TAWFIQ: Fine. But at least meet the man you're going to marry!

HUWAIDA: I will be meeting him! I'll have the rest of my life to meet him and get to know him!

(Slight beat.)

TAWFIQ: This is just too crazy. Nobody does this anymore. Not even in Egypt.

HUWAIDA: Sure they do. It's a lot saner than strangers hooking up through the internet, which you have no problem with.

TAWFIQ: What are you trying to prove? How pious you are?

HUWAIDA: Tawfiq . . . I can't explain it further. I just know this is the best thing for me. I really do—I know it in my bones.

(Slight beat.)

TAWFIQ: Aren't you nervous?

HUWAIDA: *Yes.* Of course I'm nervous. I'm . . . a part of me's petrified.

TAWFIQ: Why not listen to that part of you?

HUWAIDA: Because I *know*— Yes, even in my heart I know.

(Slight beat.)

TAWFIQ: You grew up to be very odd, you know that.

(Huwaida picks up her backpack as she gets ready to leave.)

HUWAIDA: If you're not going to support me, at least . . . don't interfere . . . Besides, he's not a stranger—I've spoken to him enough times on the phone.

TAWFIQ: Huwaida. Promise me one thing. *(Looks into the distance, he waves his arms)* If you see him and don't like him, don't go through with it.

HUWAIDA: What are you doing?

TAWFIQ: Get his vibe, talk to him, and if anything seems odd, cancel it. I'll back you up.

HUWAIDA: Who are you waving to?

TAWFIQ: I invited him here.

HUWAIDA: Who?

TAWFIQ: Murad.

HUWAIDA: You invited him?

TAWFIQ: He wants to meet you.

HUWAIDA: You invited him here? *(Looks in the direction Tawfiq waved)* You shit. Why'd you do that?

TAWFIQ: So if a face-to-face meeting bombs, you don't have to go through with it.

HUWAIDA: You are such an asshole.

TAWFIQ: Related to you by blood, which makes me a special asshole.

HUWAIDA: I'm not dressed.

TAWFIQ: You're gorgeous.

HUWAIDA: I don't want him to see me like this. I swear to God I'm going to kill you.

TAWFIQ: Thou shalt not kill your sibling, especially when he's trying to help you.

(Huwaida tries to bolt; Tawfiq blocks her way.)

What are you afraid you of? That you'll see him and not like him? Good. There's every chance you won't. He doesn't have a clue about your life here.

(Murad appears. The brother and sister turn to him. Tawfiq speaks to Huwaida, not caring if Murad overhears.)

MURAD: You don't have to do this—any of it.

(He turns to Murad, nods his head.)

(To Huwaida) I'll see you later.

(Tawfiq exits. Huwaida stares at Murad, looking somewhat paralyzed. When Murad speaks, it is with an accent—though not too heavy.)

MURAD: Your brother . . . phoned me . . . He said . . . that you wanted to see me?

(Slight beat.)

HUWAIDA: No . . . I don't.

(Slight beat.)

MURAD: Oh.

HUWAIDA: I mean . . . this is fine . . . I just didn't know you were coming.

MURAD: You would like me to leave?

HUWAIDA: Would you mind?

(Slight beat.)

MURAD: You . . . *do* want me to . . . ?

HUWAIDA: Unless you want to stay; I could go.

MURAD: No, I will go.

HUWAIDA: No, since my brother dragged you here, you should stay.

MURAD: Not at all. I will find my way back.

HUWAIDA: I insist; it's a nice campus, walk around. I have a class.

MURAD: Ah.

HUWAIDA: Yes, I have an art class. Otherwise I'd stay.

(Beat.)

MURAD: I am happy we finally . . .

HUWAIDA: Yes . . . Nice to meet you, too. *(She goes up to him and shakes his hand)* Welcome to the States. I'm sorry for the misunderstanding.

MURAD: It is not a problem.

HUWAIDA: Plus I'm very sweaty.

MURAD: Excuse me?

HUWAIDA: The, um. I'm not—. These are pretty ratty clothes. I didn't want you to—. This really wasn't how I wanted our first meeting to go.

MURAD *(Not getting what she means)*: I . . .

HUWAIDA *(Points to a hole in her clothing)*: Look. It has a hole. In case you've seen it and think, Gee, that says a lot. I'm aware of it. In case you think I walk around not knowing these things. And the sneakers have clearly died on me, I know that, too, except I haven't had time to go shopping, and I know my face must look all puffed up, because when I run around, that's what happens, I puff up . . . How's your father?

MURAD: He is better, thank you.

HUWAIDA: Will he be coming tomorrow?

MURAD: *Inshallah.*

HUWAIDA: *Inshallah.*

(Slight beat.)

I'm . . . sorry we haven't been able to meet.

MURAD: You have exams?

HUWAIDA: Well, between classes and Ramadan—and running around, it's been . . . hectic.

MURAD: Yes.

(Slight beat.)

HUWAIDA: Did it seem weird to you that I didn't call?

MURAD *(Smiles, shrugs):* I . . .

HUWAIDA: Did you want to see me?

MURAD: Of course.

HUWAIDA: Why?

MURAD: Because . . . we're getting engaged?

HUWAIDA: Right.

(Slight beat.)

You'd have preferred to spend some time together before?

MURAD: A walk or two would be nice.

(Slight beat.)

HUWAIDA: And yet you got on the plane and came all the way here to get engaged to a woman you barely know.

MURAD: Our families know each other.

HUWAIDA: But . . . you don't know me.

MURAD: I remember your visits.

HUWAIDA: I was six and thirteen. I've changed.

MURAD: Yes. You have. And yet . . . as it is said . . . the child is a parent to the adult that follows, no?

HUWAIDA: I've really changed.

MURAD: And you? It is a gamble for you, too. To say yes to a man you know only through the phone. A picture.

HUWAIDA: True . . . But in practice, it never seems to work out, does it? Getting to know the other person beforehand. You hear of people spending years together before they marry and then they do and it all falls apart. So what advantages did they have in getting to know each other? Perhaps that was the problem. They entered the marriage with nothing to give to each other by way of discovery. There was no mystery.

MURAD: You like mystery?

HUWAIDA: It's not that. It's just that I feel dating is overrated. It gives you a false impression of knowing the other person, before entering into a commitment that by its nature changes the people who enter into it . . . which is to say you can't really know the person until you enter into that very thing that changes the both of you. That's when you really begin to see the other person. Do you see what I'm saying?

(Murad looks confused.)

Which is why some people never get married, because they know it changes everything.

MURAD: The two people who marry will know each other soon enough. The mystery is soon over.

HUWAIDA: Replaced by respect, hopefully. What you show of yourself in marriage, under the sacredness of those vows taken, and what you learn of the other person, acquire different meanings . . . And the difficulties that naturally arise, which, obviously there are always problems—these are handled with your vows in mind. Those vows become the third party in any dispute, so to speak. The sacredness of your commitment becomes—that becomes the mystery.

(Slight beat.)

Do you . . . *(Seeing that he might not understand)* Do you see what I'm saying?

MURAD: Yes . . . It is very interesting what you say.

HUWAIDA: Interesting?

MURAD: It is, yes.

HUWAIDA: But what do you think about what I just said—you must have an opinion.

MURAD: I do.

HUWAIDA: Can I hear it?

MURAD: Wouldn't you prefer to wait until we get married?

(Huwaida is not amused.)

HUWAIDA: In other words you think what I was saying is stupid.

MURAD: Not at all. No. I have just not—I have never thought of it in this way.

HUWAIDA: You must share a similar viewpoint, or you wouldn't be here.

MURAD: I am here . . . because of you.

HUWAIDA: What do you mean? —Yes, me. And what I believe, and what you believe. We've talked enough on the phone to know we at least share the same beliefs; care about the same things. You hear of people meeting, the chemistry's great and then after six months they break up. They discover they don't agree on anything beyond the basic, "Do you find each other attractive," and you're not too far from the pictures you sent me. So no shock there. Am I?

MURAD *(Not following)*: Are you what?

HUWAIDA: Am I like my photos?

MURAD: No.

HUWAIDA: I'm not?

MURAD: You are more beautiful . . . Many times more attractive.

(Slight beat.)

HUWAIDA: I paid three hundred dollars for those photos.

MURAD: I apologize if I prefer the real person.

(Slight beat.)

HUWAIDA: I look horrible.

MURAD: Even better. Now I know when you look horrible, you are also beautiful.

HUWAIDA: Please don't feel you have to say these things.

MURAD: I want to say them.

HUWAIDA: Because one of the things that gets my goat is friends will go on about how their boyfriends said this and that to them and then later finding out these wonderful guys with their wonderful words were dishonest cheats. One of the benefits of doing this is not having to go through *that*. Pass stops A through Z and all the bull that goes with it . . . Why are you looking at me like that?

MURAD *(Not grasping the question)*: Excuse me?

HUWAIDA: Why are you . . . staring at me like that?

MURAD: We are . . . meeting finally? I'm sorry if my looking offends you.

HUWAIDA: It's not that. I'd just . . . I would prefer it if you'd please respond to what I've been saying.

MURAD: Which part?

HUWAIDA: Any part. Pick something.

MURAD: Yes. I see. I will tell you then . . . I believe in mystery, too . . . like you do . . . I believe in love. Like you must do. I believe if it is there, you do not need much to know it. A look. A photo. Even a cheap one. A phone call. I believe the mystery never disappears, if you don't want it to. And when people get bored it is by nothing that matters. By habits, things that make them go to sleep by the person they care about. And to change this they only have to wake up and see again to remember this puzzle, that also comes with its own solution, yes? And if it is there, this mystery, respect follows. How can you not respect someone who opens your eyes to something this good; especially someone who draws it out of you so easily? This is the wedding gift, no? This is the contract. What we give to each other. It is the only gift that matters.

(Slight beat.)

HUWAIDA: Please don't take this the wrong way. But I have to ask. So it's not this thing floating in the back of my mind . . . Are you doing this to get a green card?

(Slight beat.)

Obviously the thought's occurred to me. Not that I believe it is, but I have to get it out of the way . . . There's no polite way of asking.

(Slight beat.)

MURAD: No. One of the obstacles to this union . . . was that I might have to live here.

HUWAIDA: We *are* going to live here.

MURAD: I understand. But what I am saying—living here is not the prize you think it is. You should also know I'm not going to pursue my medical studies.

HUWAIDA: Oh? . . . What are you thinking of doing?

MURAD: I have not decided yet. I'm sorry you will not be marrying a doctor.

HUWAIDA: I don't care about that.

MURAD: And I do not care about a green card.

HUWAIDA: But you have me worried now: Can you see yourself living here?

MURAD: Yes; it is all the same.

HUWAIDA: No it's not.

MURAD: If I am comfortable with you, I will be comfortable wherever I live.

HUWAIDA: I don't know if that follows . . . Are we crazy for doing this?

MURAD: It is natural to be scared. I am a little scared, too.

HUWAIDA: What if it's too much of a shock to all you're used to?

MURAD: I am marrying *you*, Huwaida. It is you I see.

HUWAIDA: But you don't know me. *How do you know?*

(He holds out his hand.)

MURAD: For the same reason you do.

HUWAIDA: What if *I* don't know anymore.

MURAD: Let us see.

(She doesn't take his hand. Slight beat.)

HUWAIDA: I really have to go.

(She starts to go.)

MURAD: Wait, please.

(Huwaida stops.)

I will go . . . It's all right. *(He takes a few steps toward her)* I am sorry to have surprised you today . . . but . . . perhaps it is best I did. Do not worry . . . if it's God's will . . . it will happen . . . Remember the thing that made you say yes to this . . . perhaps it is a good voice that whispered to you.

(Slight beat.)

Enjoy your class.

(He exits. Huwaida remains where she is.)

HUWAIDA *(To herself)*: Shit. *Shit.*

(Blackout.)

Scene 6

In the blackout, we begin to hear the strains of the oud. The sounds are a little more coherent and recognizable than they were before.

Lights up on a park area. Hamza, wearing his skull-cap, is sitting on the park bench, practicing his oud. He stops and starts on a tune, trying to get it just right. (Or, if the actor happens to know how to play the oud, perhaps the tune is played right through to the end.) Also, the tune attempted is a recognizable classic. Something from Cole Porter or Gershwin or some other American standard.

During the playing, Kevin enters as if having heard the music from another area of the park. He hangs back, listening. When the tune ends, he claps. Hamza turns, startled. Kevin continues clapping as he approaches.

KEVIN: Not bad . . . Not bad at all.

HAMZA *(Embarrassed)*: No. Not really.

KEVIN: It was good.

HAMZA: Thanks, but—

KEVIN: I know that tune. What was it?

HAMZA: I don't think you could call that a tune. It was more like a bad pile up.

KEVIN: Was that Cole Porter?

HAMZA: You actually heard a melody?

KEVIN: Where did you learn that?

HAMZA: Nowhere. Myself. If that isn't obvious.

KEVIN: Cole Porter on a oud. That's a first. I'm impressed.

HAMZA: You know ouds?

KEVIN: I'm a big fan of the oud.

HAMZA: Yeah? How come? They're not exactly popular.

KEVIN: I like mandolins. The oud gave birth to the mandolin—and lutes.

HAMZA: What's a lute?

KEVIN: It's sort of like that. A renaissance instrument. It's what the Europeans picked up from the Arabs. Among other things.

HAMZA: You know how to play?

KEVIN: Strictly an admirer. I like musical instruments in general. I find them fascinating.

HAMZA: If I could learn just one I'd be happy.

KEVIN: Why did you pick that?

HAMZA: It was in our basement. It belonged to my grandfather. I just started playing it one day. And drove my family nuts.

KEVIN: Hey, it could've been worse. Your grandfather could've played the drums.

HAMZA: I think that's what they hear when I play.

KEVIN: Where are you from?

HAMZA: Originally? San Diego.

KEVIN: I mean—where's your family from?

HAMZA: Oh. Egypt.

KEVIN: Wow. Always wanted to go . . . I'd definitely buy a oud from there. Though I hear the best ones are found in Turkey. They use a different quality string, apparently.

HAMZA: You do know about ouds.

KEVIN: You like Cole Porter?

HAMZA: I can't say I know him. It's a tune I hear playing in my advisor's office, every time I go see her.

KEVIN: Then you have a good ear; if you picked it up just like that.

(Slight beat.)

Can I . . . can I hold it?

HAMZA: Er . . . sure. If you want.

KEVIN *(Approaching)*: I just love the way they look. And the feel of them. *(He takes the oud and positions it as if to play)* They're so unique—I wish I could play.

HAMZA: Go ahead.

KEVIN: I respect music too much to butcher it.

HAMZA: It doesn't stop me.

KEVIN: That's why you're a musician and I'm not. I couldn't put up with the mistakes I'd have to make to become good. I just find it so bizarre how we decide what is music and what isn't. I mean why isn't this pleasing? *(He randomly strums the oud)* Why not? Why is that noise, and something else a tune? What makes us know that this note, and not that one, needs to follow in order to make pleasing sounds? So even if it's a tune from another country and it sounds foreign, we can still recognize it as having—as being melodic.

(Slight beat.)

HAMZA: Are you in the music business?

KEVIN: Nope. Studying law. No music there. Just arguments. And you?

HAMZA: I'm . . . I'm also a student.

KEVIN: Where?

HAMZA: At USC.

KEVIN: What are you studying?

HAMZA: Computer science.

KEVIN: Do you play here often?

HAMZA: No. It just seemed a quiet place. To practice.

(Slight beat.)

KEVIN: Practice what?

HAMZA: Can I have my oud back?

(Slight beat.)

KEVIN *(Holds out the oud)*: You know, there's a funny myth attached to the invention of the oud. Do you know it?

HAMZA *(Takes the oud)*: No.

KEVIN: Well . . . it is said . . . the myth goes that the oud was invented by Lamak, a direct descendant of Cain, the sixth grandson of Adam. And when Lamak's son died, he hung his remains on a tree, for some reason. And when the remains dried out, when they were completely desiccated, the skeleton suggested the form of the oud . . . And from that moment on, God gave the sons of Cain the know-how to make musical instruments . . . and so . . . they did. Lamak invented the oud, the drum and the harp. And these instruments became celebrated for treating illnesses. For reviving the heart and invigorating the body. Creating balance . . . Fascinating, huh? *(Extends his hand)* Kevin.

HAMZA *(Hesitates)*: Hamza.

(Hamza shakes Kevin's hand.)

KEVIN: You keep practicing.

HAMZA: I will.

KEVIN: Don't let your parents discourage you.

HAMZA: They don't.

KEVIN: I hear a musician struggling to get out.

HAMZA: Yeah, well, we'll see.

KEVIN: He's halfway out already.

HAMZA: I hope so.

KEVIN: I know so . . . The music isn't far behind either.

(Slight beat. Kevin leans forward and tries to kiss Hamza. Hamza pulls back. A quick beat as Kevin tries to get a reading on Hamza.)

Sorry. I thought . . .

(Hamza's manner suggests his pulling back was more reaction than response. Kevin leans in to try and kiss him again. Again Hamza pulls back.)

HAMZA: I can't.

KEVIN: Okay.

HAMZA: I . . . I can't.

KEVIN: That's fine. No problem. You have a nice day. I thought—

HAMZA: No.

KEVIN: Okay. Most times . . . this area . . . You didn't know?

HAMZA: It's not a good idea.

KEVIN: What isn't? Why not, we're safe. Nothing unsafe will happen . . . I like you.

HAMZA: I don't do that—I don't . . . I don't do that.

KEVIN: What?

HAMZA: This.

KEVIN: What this?

HAMZA: I can't.

KEVIN: You keep saying that, but you're not leaving . . . Not that you have to. You don't have to budge an inch. There's enough room in whatever you're feeling to . . . to relax.

HAMZA *(More excuse than explanation)*: I'm fasting.

KEVIN *(A laugh)*: What?

HAMZA: I'm . . . fasting. I can't do this.

KEVIN: Oh. Right. Fasting. What's it called? I know that. Until the sun goes down, right. *(Looks toward the sunset)* It's almost down.

(The lights are indeed changing and have been changing throughout the scene.)

HAMZA: I have to go home.

KEVIN: Is it a high? Fasting? I'd love to try it one day. I find so much of that culture intriguing. I wish I was a Muslim.

HAMZA: Why?

KEVIN: I don't know. I just think I'd take to it.

HAMZA: Muslims don't do this.

KEVIN: Sure they do. One of my best lovers was a Muslim.

HAMZA: He wasn't a real Muslim then.

KEVIN: He thought he was. Is that what's troubling you? —Not what a devout Muslim does? Is a devout Muslim and a devout human being two different things? It's a shame how so many religions end up being such killjoys.

HAMZA: My religion isn't that.

KEVIN: I can relate. I was a Catholic. I loved the whole thing. Loved the saints, loved praying to Mary. I just couldn't take being called a perpetual sinner.

HAMZA: You don't believe in God?

KEVIN: Sure I do. After that I joined the Pentecostals. Something about speaking in tongues and handling snakes appealed to my lawyer nature. —I'm kidding. Don't be scared. Nothing is going to happen if you don't want it to.

HAMZA: So you *don't* believe in God?

KEVIN: I do. Very much so.

HAMZA: How can you be doing this then?

KEVIN: Because in my universe God is gay. What, you think He's straight? Isn't that just as dumb as thinking God is gay? I don't think He gives a damn. I don't think He has sex. I don't think He's as sex-obsessed as the people who speak on His behalf are.

HAMZA: I need to get home.

KEVIN: What really pisses me off is how religion screws people like you up. Don't waste these years like I almost did. Never mind what's *not* going to happen between us. Nothing will. But don't . . . don't get all twisted up inside about this.

HAMZA: About what? Nothing's happened. I don't know what you're talking about.

(Slight beat.)

KEVIN: Okay . . . whatever . . . it's your life. But just . . .

(Slight beat.)

What if it's not a flaw that you have to struggle against? What if it's a way for you to open up to the world. A blessing. A blessing even . . . Think about that.

(Slight beat.)

HAMZA: You're a lawyer. They make arguments. Not music.

KEVIN: That's right . . . and I wasn't just flattering you up about being good either. Keep playing.

(Slight beat.)

And maybe I'll see you around.

(Hamza doesn't move. Kevin turns to look at the last light of day. Hamza also turns to look.)

The sun's going down.

(A park light goes on, throwing a spot on them.)

Just in time. You're on. Your very own spotlight. It's calling out for one last tune.

(Slight beat.)

Go on . . . play something.

(Slight beat.)

Play me something.

(Beat. Blackout.)

Scene 7

Living room. The room is still empty. We hear the sound of a sewing machine. The front door is heard opening and shutting offstage.

KAMAL *(Offstage)*: Huwaida? . . . Hamza?

(Kamal appears at the doorway carrying a soup container in a plastic bag.)

Where's the furniture? Mona? Where is everyone? *Mona?*

(He sees footprints on the floor. He quickly slips out of his shoes and walks in.)

Are they doing this on purpose?

(Mona appears at another doorway, unwinding thread from a spool.)

MONA: How's Aziz?
KAMAL *(Pointing to the floor)*: What is that?

MONA: It's the jinn, my love. They're coming out to celebrate the engagement. They've been dancing. Dancing and jumping and having a good time, as we should.

KAMAL: Jinn don't wear sneakers.

MONA: Come on, let's dance.

(She moves toward him and takes him in her arms.)

KAMAL *(Breaking away from her)*: It's as if my word means nothing anymore. And where's the furniture? It's *iftar* already.

MONA *(Looking at her watch)*: So it is. I forgot the time. I'll go heat the food.

(She starts to exit to the kitchen.)

KAMAL: Where are they? And where are we going to eat? They said they'd put the furniture back.

MONA: We'll do it after dinner; we'll bring out the table for now.

KAMAL: On this? *(Pointing to the floor)* I'm not cleaning this up.

MONA *(Stopping at the doorway)*: Don't. I think we should draw a chalk outline around the dirt as evidence.

(Offstage, the front door shuts rather loudly.)

KAMAL: This has become the sound of our children.

MONA: Tawfiq?

(Huwaida comes in, carrying her backpack, removing her veil. She drops her backpack on the floor. Kamal puts his hand out for her to stop. Huwaida stops.)

Help your father roll the carpets out, and clean that up, please. And I want to measure the sleeves again.

(She exits, then speaks from offstage:)

And bring out the table.

HUWAIDA *(Slipping out of her shoes)*: Why hasn't the furniture been put back?

KAMAL: You and your brothers were supposed to do it.

HUWAIDA: They said they'd take care of it.

KAMAL: Well they didn't. *(Reining in his irritation)* Never mind—you have special exemption. How are you?

HUWAIDA: I'm . . . okay. *(She takes the mop from the corner)*
KAMAL: That's all. Aren't you excited?
HUWAIDA: About what?
KAMAL: "About what," she says. Is this how the next generation views marriage? About the next big step in your life.
HUWAIDA: Where's the dirt?

(Kamal hugs her.)

KAMAL: *Habibti.* My darling girl. Look at you now. Look how far you've come. You could've turned out so many different ways, but here you are: a jewel, a pleasure and a wonderful daughter.
HUWAIDA: I can't breathe.
KAMAL: Don't move to a different state.
HUWAIDA: It's an engagement not a marriage.
KAMAL: I am so proud of you.
HUWAIDA: If you squeeze any harder I'm going to faint.

(Mona enters carrying two sleeves of a dress, one of them draped across her shoulder. Kamal eases up on his hug, but continues to hold Huwaida.)

KAMAL *(To Mona, about Huwaida)*: Look at her. Look at this woman. When did she become a woman?
HUWAIDA: Can I clean this up so we can eat?

(Mona measures the sleeves out against each of Huwaida's arms, marking it with chalk, doing so even when Huwaida mops.)

KAMAL: We have a woman for a daughter. Full grown. Able to walk. And go to university and get married. Yesterday we were cleaning your ka-ka, tomorrow you might run for congress.
HUWAIDA *(Sarcastic)*: Right. Why not run for president.

(She steps back from her father and starts mopping.)

KAMAL: You can. You were born here. You have the right. *(To Mona)* Think of that. Our children can become presidents.
HUWAIDA: The first veiled President of the United States. That I'd like to see.
KAMAL: Why not? They've elected a lot stranger.
MONA: Hold still.
KAMAL: Everything is possible.

MONA *(To Kamal)*: Is Aziz well enough to come?

KAMAL: He'll be here. It was just jet lag. What a wonderful boy Murad is. He's grown up to be a real man.

HUWAIDA: So I hear.

KAMAL: As nice in person as he is over the phone.

MONA: And if you don't like him, we can call it off.

KAMAL: Of course, of course. You are not committed to anything yet. Nothing has been signed and no prayers uttered. You are free to walk away. Like everyone else does in this country when they're not in the mood anymore. When it upsets their precious little freedoms.

MONA *(To Kamal)*: Why don't you get the carpets out.

KAMAL: Did you hear about your brother? He has made a great discovery: There is no God.

HUWAIDA: I heard.

KAMAL *(To Mona)*: You must remind me to ask him for his proof of this.

MONA *(To Huwaida)*: Go bring in the small carpet.

(Huwaida gives her mother the mop and exits. Kamal continues talking.)

KAMAL: It's a pity he didn't discover this in high school, he could've made it his science project.

MONA: Kamal.

(Mona deposits the mop in an offstage area. If she exits, it is only for a few seconds.)

KAMAL: I wanted to bring it up with Aziz; to warn him, just in case. His father was a *shaykh* in Al-Azhar, he might take offence. I wanted to make a joke of it and say, "See how crazy this country can make you." But I couldn't. I couldn't laugh about it. I find no place in my heart for this thing to settle.

MONA: And if tomorrow I said I was an atheist, would it change anything? Would it make a difference in our relationship?

KAMAL: Yes. I would seek medical advice. I'd be worried this was a sign of menopause, or you were losing your mind.

MONA: And I would seek a divorce because you were acting so stupid.

KAMAL: Mona—careful. I have only so much humor today and I am very upset.

MONA: It's not about *you*, Kamal.

KAMAL: It's about *us*—our family, the ground upon which we raised our children and everything else that has kept us together.

MONA: He's a grown man; he's free to believe what he wants.

(Huwaida enters dragging in a carpet. Mona goes to help her, followed by Kamal.)

KAMAL *(To Huwaida)*: Your mother has become an atheist. Say something. Your religion is being challenged.

MONA *(To Huwaida)*: What's wrong? You look like you're coming down with a cold.

(She places her hand on Huwaida's forehead.)

HUWAIDA: I don't want to get engaged tomorrow.

(The other two stop what they're doing. Beat.)

That was a joke. I wanted to see what your reaction would be.

(The front door is heard slamming loudly offstage.)

I'll get the other carpet.

(Huwaida exits. Kamal and Mona look at each other. Tawfiq appears in the doorway.)

KAMAL: Where were you?

TAWFIQ: I'm sorry, I was—I got held up.

KAMAL: You said you would help us.

TAWFIQ *(Slipping out of his shoes)*: I'll do it right now.

KAMAL: Thank you for gracing us with your presence. I understand how difficult it must be to mix with people who have such primitive beliefs.

MONA: Kamal.

KAMAL: Poor God: To have become a figment of our imagination. And us poor savages for building civilizations around this figment.

(Tawfiq crosses the room and exits.)

MONA: I beg you . . . don't push this. Don't drive him away.

KAMAL: I will speak to my son any way I wish.

MONA: If he leaves, I will leave with him.

KAMAL: Do as you wish. I can book you in the same motel as Aziz right now.

MONA: Can't you *please* leave it alone?

KAMAL: No! It is like a chicken bone stuck in my throat and I will have any conversation I want in my own home!

MONA: Perhaps it is about you after all. You make believing in God such a pain in the ass.

KAMAL: Go get the food ready. And find out what your daughter just said. What kind of joke is that? Is everyone losing their minds?

(Mona exits into the kitchen. Slight beat.)

This is my house! I will speak any way I choose!

(Huwaida and Tawfiq enter carrying the big carpet.)

(To Huwaida) What was that? —You were being funny? What kind of humor is that? Are you getting engaged to this boy or what?

HUWAIDA: Yes.

KAMAL: Then why did you say that?

HUWAIDA: I was just . . . I didn't mean anything by it.

KAMAL: Huwaida . . . I am in no mood for jokes. Save that for your brothers. *(To Tawfiq)* And where is Hamza? Where is he?

TAWFIQ: I don't know.

KAMAL *(About to launch into something, but interrupts himself)*: I will tell you both now I have only this much patience for your nonsense. Our house is not a circus for your silly behavior. You will leave that rubbish outside when you come in here. *(Considers going on, but instead)* What is wrong with people today?

(He exits. Huwaida and Tawfiq have been in the process of unrolling the big carpet.)

TAWFIQ: You *have* changed your mind.

HUWAIDA: I was joking, didn't you hear?

TAWFIQ: You don't want to go through with it.

HUWAIDA: You'd love that wouldn't you.

TAWFIQ: *Tell* them.

HUWAIDA: I don't want to talk to you, Tawfiq.

TAWFIQ: I'll back you up all the way.

HUWAIDA: Thanks, you'd be a great advocate to have.

TAWFIQ: You're going to do it just to *please them*? To spite me?

HUWAIDA: Oh, get a grip; you have such an inflated sense of yourself.

TAWFIQ: And you're pig-headed enough to do it.

(Huwaida gets ready to exit, Tawfiq stops her.)

What happened with Murad? What did he say?

HUWAIDA *(Facing him)*: You were right. He's a hick. He spoke of nothing but love. How backward is that?

(She exits. Kamal enters carrying a dining room chair and half a table for assembly. Tawfiq exits.)

KAMAL *(Deposits the furniture and stands for a moment)*: This should have been done already! I don't want to assemble the table now!

MONA *(Offstage)*: Tawfiq. Bring in the coffee table. Never mind the dining room set. Let's eat first. Did you hear me?

TAWFIQ *(Offstage)*: Yes!

(Kamal sits on the chair, exhausted. Huwaida enters carrying two more chairs. She puts them down.)

KAMAL *(Calmly, without threat)*: You do want this boy, don't you?

HUWAIDA: Yes, Puppy.

KAMAL: I don't want to force him on you. It's the last thing we want to do.

HUWAIDA: It's my decision.

KAMAL: I have no interest in losing you. I would love for my favorite girl to live with me for many more years.

HUWAIDA: I'm not going anywhere. I'll still be here.

(Whether or not he extends his arm for her to come, his manner beckons for her to draw close. She does so. He hugs her, still sitting down.)

KAMAL: I want what will make you happy . . . only that.

(Tawfiq enters carrying a coffee table. Mona enters carrying a large soup bowl, ladle and cutlery.)

MONA *(To Tawfiq)*: Put it right here.

(Tawfiq deposits the coffee table where indicated. Mona puts down the soup bowl.)

Someone bring in the bowls. And the bread. And bring in the fruit.

(Tawfiq and Huwaida exit into the kitchen.)

We can start with the *ats* and bring out the rest later, when Hamza comes.

KAMAL: This is not like him.

MONA: It's probably traffic.

KAMAL: Did he tell you he'd be late?

MONA: No. There's a good reason, I'm sure. *(She lays out the cutlery)*

KAMAL: I apologize if I was . . . unpleasant . . . even though everything I said was right.

MONA: Of course it was. You'd stop breathing if you were proven wrong.

KAMAL: Can we still get married again tomorrow?

MONA: No. I'd rather not do anything to remind me I am married to you already. You can be horrible, you know that?

KAMAL: No. I can be right in a way that pleases no one. That is not the same thing.

MONA: And the rest of us are stupid?

KAMAL: I didn't say that, I am speaking of things we have all agreed on.

MONA *(Avoiding an argument)*: Let's just eat; everyone's nerves have had enough.

KAMAL: Where are we going to sit?

MONA: On your precious carpets. *(To offstage)* Huwaida?

(Huwaida enters with plates of bread and fruit, soon followed by Tawfiq, carrying a pitcher of water and glasses. They set them on the coffee table.)

We're going to start.

HUWAIDA: We're not waiting?

MONA: Didn't any of you speak with Hamza?

TAWFIQ: I think he was going to practice.

MONA: Maybe he's breaking his fast elsewhere. I'm sure he's fine.

HUWAIDA: Where are we going to sit?

MONA: Hasn't anyone heard of the floor? We wouldn't have to be sitting on it if you'd come home sooner.

(They stand there for a moment.)

Are we going to eat or not?

(Kamal descends from his chair to the floor. The others, each in turn, sit down on the floor around the coffee table. Mona starts pouring water into the glasses. They all sit there for a moment. Perhaps Kamal looks toward the door.)

KAMAL: This is not like him . . . He would've called.

HUWAIDA: Maybe he finally figured out how to play and lost track of the time.

MONA: Let's just start.

(Kamal raises his palms in prayer. Slight beat.)

KAMAL: *En el nombre de Allah, El Clemente, El Misercordioso . . . (In the name of God, the Merciful, the Compassionate . . .) . . .* that's all I know.

HUWAIDA: Where did you learn that?

KAMAL: Luis. He invited us for *iftar* next week.

(Kamal drinks. Huwaida passes a bowl to her mother to start ladling the ats.*)*

TAWFIQ *(To his mother)*: I can do that.

(He takes the ladle from his mother. Huwaida passes the bowls to her brother. Mona passes the bread around.)

KAMAL: He promised us tamales if we come. Rice with frijoles. And those fried banana things. *(To Mona)* I have a special request. Would it be too much if we skipped *ats* for one day. As lovely as you make them, I'd be happy if I never saw lentils again for the rest of Ramadan. Anything that does not look like a bean would be appreciated.

TAWFIQ: Let us thank God and be grateful for the bounty He provides.

(The two women tense up in anticipation of Kamal's reaction. Kamal looks at Tawfiq.)

KAMAL: What?

TAWFIQ *(Continuing to ladle; hesitates)*: Let's be thankful for . . . for what we have.

(Slight beat.)

KAMAL: Are you being funny with us?

TAWFIQ: No. I was—

KAMAL: Are you being sarcastic with me?

TAWFIQ: No, I'm just saying, let's be thankful for what we—

KAMAL: What is the word "God" doing in your mouth if you don't believe in Him?

TAWFIQ: It's a . . . it's an expression.

KAMAL: An expression? . . . Are you *mocking* us?

MONA: Kamal.

KAMAL *(Continuing)*: Spitting our religion back in our face? What are you even doing here if you're not fasting anymore?

TAWFIQ: I *am* fasting.

KAMAL: Why? If not to remember God for what reason?

TAWFIQ: To keep you company.

KAMAL: Thank you, we'll do without. It is no company to have someone who mocks us sitting at our table.

MONA: *Please.* Let us eat and have this discussion later. We need to put *something* in our stomachs before we say another word.

(Silence. Kamal fumes. People hesitantly begin to eat. Then:)

KAMAL: "An expression."

TAWFIQ: I was trying to say we should be grateful for whatever mother cooks for us.

(Kamal slams his bowl and spoon down.)

KAMAL: Get out!

TAWFIQ: Why?

MONA: Stop it!

KAMAL: Get out!

TAWFIQ: I was just saying we have no reason to complain.

KAMAL: Are you now telling me how I should speak to my wife?

TAWFIQ: *No.*

MONA: Kamal!

(The telephone rings offstage. Slight beat.)

(To Tawfiq) Go see who it is. It's probably Hamza.

(Tawfiq rises and exits. Beat. Then:)

HUWAIDA: Mummy. Puppy. There's probably not a good time to tell you this. And I am actually not one hundred per cent sure if I should . . . tell you; or, if I didn't, whether I should go ahead anyway because I'm not, as I said, certain, and I guess you're not in the mood to hear this now, but . . . what I said earlier was probably accurate. In regards to the engagement. And while it's possible I was joking when I said it to hear how it sounded, I was most likely telling the truth. About not wanting to get engaged. I think—in thinking about it—I was telling the truth.

(Slight beat.)

That's . . . that's basically it.

MONA: I didn't understand a word you said.

(Tawfiq enters.)

TAWFIQ: It's Hamza . . . he's calling from—from jail. He's . . . he's in jail—he's been arrested.

(Beat. Blackout. Intermission.)

Scene 8

Spotlight on Pauline on another part of the stage. Her speech is addressed to the audience.

PAULINE: Huwaida . . . I know I may be overstepping a line . . . but I feel . . . I do feel I need to say something. Not as a psychologist—but as another person struggling to figure things out, like you. I feel now it would be wrong if I didn't. You wanted something definitive from me, something concrete, so . . . here it is. You were right . . . I do have a question about your veiling.—I do think the dream was speaking directly to it. It couldn't be any clearer to my mind. And I know you insist it shouldn't be reduced to that, and that it isn't about "liberating you from the veil," but, Huwaida, how liberating is something that prevents you from even questioning it? Which I think you're doing and are feeling distressed because you're not giving yourself permission to do so. And I can't imagine that's what any religion is supposed to do. Protect, yes, but imprison? —I *am* trying to be sensitive to your faith and I know I am woefully ignorant and God knows we could all do a little more to jump these abysses that separate us, but I do think . . . I just . . . I have to come right out and say that I think your religion is bad news for women. And I'm not sure it's right to be "culturally sensitive" when a system perpetuates injustices. And yes: I've heard how Islam was a great liberator of women and gave them rights that we in the West only began to get in the nineteenth century, but we're not living back then, and from what

I've seen, if that is true, your religion has stopped being a living, breathing support, and has become instead an excuse for men to put down women, keep them in their place. And, yes, we could get into a history lesson about how *all* religions have done that, but, again, we're not talking about that. You're making your life now, in America, and I honestly don't know if the two go well together. I'm sorry for being so blunt. But it was only after you left that I realized how offended I was by what your wearing of that veil meant to me. And the degree to which you'd been brainwashed into believing that was okay. It's not. It's not okay when we buy into our own oppressions. It's not okay that we take on the prejudices of one gender and make them our own. So that we women end up being the gatekeepers of our own oppression, to the point that we make of our manacles things of pride and even become vain about it. I don't know how you can call yourself a feminist and say that, and cover yourself as if you have something to be ashamed about, as if you have *anything* to apologize for.

(Huwaida enters. Lights up on her and Pauline. Huwaida has had a complete makeover. She wears a revealing, sexy dress, just shy of being gaudy, but clearly meant to be provocative. She wears makeup and her hair has been brushed out.)

HUWAIDA: How about now? . . . How do I look—liberated? Am I more pleasing to you? Am I the picture of mental health now? Is this what you're recommending?

PAULINE: Huwaida.

HUWAIDA: Too much? Less blush? Are my breasts showing too much? How would you have me?

PAULINE: This is not what I meant.

HUWAIDA: You obviously have a standard in mind. What is it? Is my lipstick too red?

PAULINE: It's not about any of that.

HUWAIDA: Yes it is, dress me. Unshackle me from my manacles. Help me be a better feminist. Or am I not a feminist wearing this? Should I let my underarm hair grow? Is that it? Let it all hang out. Burn my bra. Put a little jiggle in my breasts as I march down the street, declaring my womanhood. Is that the standard?

PAULINE: I'm talking about your emotional life. What we carry inside and how that expresses itself, either as a support or hindrance.

HUWAIDA *(Referring to her new style of dress)*: And what does this express? Freedom? The road to success as a woman?

PAULINE: I never said that.

HUWAIDA: Yes you did, if not the veil then this. Variations of this.

PAULINE: There are as many ways to dress as there are individuals.

HUWAIDA: Except it's funny how we all look the same from one fashion cycle to another. Gee, you might even call it a uniform.

PAULINE: Look, I understand the point you're making—

HUWAIDA: Is this not in fashion this season? Should I be mortified that I have no sense of "what's in" and waste a whole life jumping through *those* hoops?

PAULINE: I agree. We're always conforming to one standard or another, and they can be just as oppressive—

HUWAIDA: Yes, they can, so why not choose one based on the spirit and not on the meat market?

PAULINE: Because I don't see any signs of God in demanding women hide themselves. It seems to be the flip side of the meat market, seeing women as nothing but provocative creatures that have to be hidden away for everyone's protection. Which doesn't mean you have to jump to this.

HUWAIDA: What are you, the fashion police? Going around telling people what is and isn't appropriate? And what is your problem that you can't get beyond a frickin' headscarf? I come to you carrying a wealth of faith and you want to *cure* me of that?

PAULINE: Are you saying that Muslim women who don't wear the veil are any less religious?

HUWAIDA: It's how *I* choose to express it. Your receptionist is wearing a thumping big cross the size of her blouse, why is that all right? Why isn't she harassed or called brainwashed?

PAULINE: It doesn't prevent her from doing what she wants.

HUWAIDA: *Because it's accepted—she's not harassed about it and made to feel like a freak.*

PAULINE: Then perhaps you're experiencing the veil as a burden.

HUWAIDA: I never said that!

PAULINE: I think your dream did.

HUWAIDA: Oh screw my dream, that's your interpretation, I wish I'd never told you about it.

(Slight beat.)

PAULINE: And yet here you are . . . You came back.

HUWAIDA: I came back . . . because I was pissed off by what you said.— I wanted to come back wearing the conclusion that everything you said implied. I don't know what it is about women professors here that they feel impelled to save us—as if we needed your precious help when you spend most of your life agonizing over the dumbest, f'd-up things. Go crusade someone else's ass.

PAULINE: Did you come back just to tell me this?

HUWAIDA: You're not listening, are you?

PAULINE: I am. Very closely.

HUWAIDA: Then I guess your English is not the same as mine

(She starts to leave but stops when Pauline starts to speak.)

PAULINE: My door is always open.

HUWAIDA: No. It's not. It hasn't opened once.

(Blackout. We hear the sound of an airplane taking off.)

Scene 9

Lights up on a neutral area. Though it could be Murad's motel room, it's also his dreamscape. So it could also incorporate Huwaida's family living room, if that's simpler in terms of set transitions. Murad is asleep in a chair or on a couch.

Standing next to Murad is H.D. She is dressed in the hijab: long flowing dress, her face showing. The effect is elegant.

We hear the "ping" sound heard on airplanes.

PILOT *(Voice-over; through the "airplane speakers")*: Cross-check.

(Murad sits up. He sees H.D. and is startled.)

H.D.: Hi. I'm Huwaida's double. "H.D." for short. You're welcome to call me that, all my friends do, and I have a feeling we're going to be fast friends.

MURAD: Where . . .

H.D.: Where are you?

MURAD: Yes.

H.D.: Well, wouldn't you know we're in a dream. Your dream. And I thank you for hosting it as I needed a break from Huwaida. She's getting a little too frazzled for me and, though I am part of her unconscious and therefore responsible for helping her act out her issues, there's only so much chaos I can stand before I need the fresh air of someone else's dream-life.

MURAD: You . . . don't look anything like Huwaida.

H.D.: I know. There are some benefits to living in the dream world.

MURAD: I'm . . . *(Looking around, dazed)* I'm rather fond of the way she looks.

H.D.: Are you? I thought you might be. I caught that gleam in your eye when you were looking at her.

MURAD *(Looks at his watch)*: I have a flight to catch. I'm late.

(He stands up. The sound of the airplane "ping" is heard.)

PILOT *(Voice-over; through the "airplane speakers")*: Cross-check.

H.D.: Actually that's what I wanted to talk to you about.

(Murad starts looking around for his suitcase.)

MURAD: Where are my things?

H.D.: I think all in all it would be best if you didn't go.

MURAD: Where are all my things?

H.D.: If I could have your attention.

MURAD: She said no or haven't you heard.

H.D.: "No," "yes," when you're confused they mean the same thing.

MURAD: I have to go. Where's my suitcase?

PILOT *(Voice-over; through the "airplane speakers")*: You are now free to walk around the cabin.

H.D.: Murad, listen to me. It's a universal law of physics that you can't change directions in mid-jump. You'll spend the rest of your life wondering what might have happened. Finish the jump and then make your decision.

MURAD: I am finished, I'm going home.

H.D.: That's not the direction you took. You're leaping against the current.

MURAD: What concern is my business to you?

H.D.: Because Huwaida's jumping right there with you, and if she falls she's going to crash in on *my* head and right on through to parts of herself that even *I* don't go into. And I will not have her low-self-esteem demons messing me up when I'm this close to winning the pageant.

MURAD: What pageant?

PILOT *(Voice-over; through the "airplane speakers")*: We strongly recommend you keep your voices down as we need to hear the engines to fly this plane.

H.D. *(Referring to the Pilot)*: Okay, Murad. You need to take that out. I'm not competing with your unconscious. While I'm here, you need to clear the deck.

(A lunch box is slid out of the wings. Murad and H.D. see it.)

MURAD: Is that—? That can't be my suitcase.

(A Customs Officer enters.)

CUSTOMS OFFICER *(To H.D.)*: Is that your suitcase?
H.D.: Oh for godsakes.
CUSTOMS OFFICER *(To Murad)*: Is that your suitcase?
H.D. *(To Murad)*: Make him go away.
MURAD *(To H.D.)*: Please go away.
CUSTOMS OFFICER: Whose suitcase is this?
MURAD: I didn't come with that.
CUSTOMS OFFICER: Uh-huh. *(Into a walkie-talkie)* Bomb squad.
H.D.: Murad!
CUSTOMS OFFICER *(To Murad)*: Passport please.

(Murad searches his clothes for his passport.)

H.D. *(To Murad)*: You don't need a passport. This is your dream, you can travel anywhere you want.
MURAD: This is not my country; I don't belong here.
H.D.: Yes you do; you and this place are a perfect fit.
CUSTOMS OFFICER *(To Murad)*: I need to see your passport.
H.D. *(To Murad)*: You can always go back if it doesn't work out.
CUSTOMS OFFICER: Passport.
H.D. *(To Customs Officer)*: Shut up.
CUSTOMS OFFICER *(To H.D.)*: Yours as well, lady.
H.D. *(Giving him the finger)*: Stamp this, asshole.

(Three people in bomb-squad clothes enter, wearing head gear and dark visors that mask their faces. They are the Bomb Experts. The Customs Officer backs up, suddenly wary of the potential danger. Murad's attention turns to the lunch box. He starts approaching it, as do the Bomb Experts, staying a few steps behind him.)

MURAD *(To H.D.)*: You must go now—just go. Coming here, expecting things to magically work out, this was the crazy part. Neither of us were thinking.

H.D.: I wouldn't be here if you didn't secretly know something was up. I have no idea if you can work things out or if you two can live together. But your coming now was no arrangement; your parents didn't force this on you. Your dream lives have been working this out for years.

(Murad, now kneeling in front of the lunch box, opens it. The Bomb Experts gasp in fear. He takes out a photo.)

There! You see? It's Huwaida. What does that tell you?

BOMB EXPERT 1: False alarm.

MURAD: She canceled the engagement.

H.D.: Only because you turned out to be too real for her. She wasn't expecting an actual person to turn up. She still has to get used to you.

BOMB EXPERT 2: Wait! Maybe the photo is wired to explode.

BOMB EXPERT 1: Jesus Christ.

H.D. *(To the bomb squad)*: Oh, stop.

BOMB EXPERT 3: They're hiding explosives everywhere now.

BOMB EXPERT 1: Look at the smile, isn't that a detonator?

BOMB EXPERT 2: It's in the smile!

BOMB EXPERT 3: The whole goddamn face is wired.

BOMB EXPERT 2: Grab the photo!

(They push Murad aside and grab the photo. Perhaps they put it in a special container as they run off.)

BOMB EXPERT 3 *(Exiting)*: Duck! Duck! Get the disposal ready!

(The Bomb Experts are gone.)

MURAD: I'd never survive in America.

H.D.: It's a little whacky, yes, but that's what's so lovable about it.

MURAD *(Getting up)*: I don't want to live my life as a foreigner. I don't want to have that eating away at me. I can be of more value in my country.

H.D.: Fine. Run from your future. But I'm telling you this decision will bug you for the rest of your life.

(Murad takes a few steps in one direction.)

Egypt's that way, if you're leaving. *(She extends her hand)* Here. I'll take you. I swear to you you'll regret this. Ready?

(He takes her hand. The sound of the airplane "ping.")

PILOT *(Voice-over; through the "airplane speakers")*: Cross-check.

(Huwaida and Murad take a step forward. Lights change to something more mellow and peaceful. Murad lets go of her hand and walks around as if on familiar ground.)

H.D.: Happy now? . . . Don't let this mellow peaceful lighting fool you. It's just your memory doing a makeover.

MURAD: I would miss the skies over my city.

H.D.: What are you talking about? You can hardly see anything through the pollution.

MURAD: I would miss the streets. The broken pavements. The mess.

H.D.: You almost got killed crossing the road, remember?

MURAD: The faces. The look of the people. Knowing what gestures mean.

H.D.: People are strange and familiar everywhere. Even family members can become strangers to us sometimes.

MURAD: I would miss the language.

H.D.: Would you stop with these excuses before you bury yourself in them!

MURAD: I would miss the call to prayer most of all.

(We hear the call to prayer playing very faintly in the background.)

Hearing that in the morning. Waking up to it. The whole day waking up to those sounds . . . Like your whole family has come in to kiss you good morning. Calling on the best in you to meet the day . . . Yes . . . I would miss that most of all.

H.D.: You would carry that always. In your heart . . . But yours—you're losing yours.

MURAD: Who are you to judge me?

H.D.: Perhaps I am also calling on the best in you. I am not as beautiful as the call to prayer, but I am a call just the same. From a place messier and just as important. And if God is everywhere, might He not be in that place, too, and speak to us in many ways and guises. In impulses—and whims and crazy notions that might just turn out to be right. Why shut yourself off from that? You love mystery too much to do that . . . I can't promise you things will work out; no one can. But I do know you started something and you can't live like you didn't. Finish the jump. Fall if you have to, but finish it.

(She extends out her hand. Slight beat.)

MURAD: In dreams, when you fall from a great height, doesn't it hurt there as well?

H.D.: Only if you don't wake up.

(Slight beat. Her arm remains extended. Blackout.)

Scene 10

Family living room. Most of the furniture has been brought in. The furniture is at odd angles and positions, still waiting to be put in its proper place. The oud is on the coffee table. Kamal stands. Mona sits on a chair. Hamza is also seated, staring fixedly ahead.
   Silence.
   Tawfiq enters dragging in two more pieces of furniture. He pauses for a couple of beats, unsure of what to do next. He moves one of the pieces to its proper place. Then drags the coffee table a few feet to where it's supposed to be, beside Kamal. Kamal looks at the oud.

TAWFIQ *(To Mona)*: Want me to assemble the table now?

(Slight beat.)

MONA: What?

HAMZA: Can I go to my room, please?

KAMAL: No. *(He picks up the oud)*

(Beat.)

MONA: We should rest. We've been up too long . . . We can speak about this later.

(Slight beat. Tawfiq hesitantly sits next to Hamza. Perhaps he reaches out to touch his hand. Hamza stands abruptly and moves away. Kamal plucks on the oud.)

KAMAL *(To Hamza, but not directly)*: Did you even practice? *(Strumming a few strings)* My mother always thought it a vice of my father's, playing this . . . He would come home and get drunk on this instrument . . . Shut us out with the pleasure he found in it . . .

Sometimes making us be his audience. We would dutifully listen—and sometimes enjoy—but most times . . . I would grit my teeth and pray the song was short . . . He made it seem such a joy . . . I envied him his passion . . . I always wondered where he went in his head when he played.

MONA: *Allah yarhamuh* . . . He was a good man.

KAMAL: Yes . . . Perhaps it is best he is dead after all . . . He would have been upset that the grandson who continued his passion was caught with a man in the bushes, and that his beautiful oud was nearby. "What," he would have said, "You couldn't have left the oud behind. You had to drag it into your filthy habit."

(Hamza exits the room. Kamal shouts after him.)

"This, an inspired instrument, that calls out the best in us, this you had to have next to you while you were debasing yourself?"

MONA: I knew you could handle this properly. I was worried the wisdom of Solomon might be absent in this time when we need it most.

KAMAL: This will be in his record. This . . . stain. This . . . abomination. This is public record. You know this is public record? For everyone to see. This will spread like wildfire—in the community and back to Egypt. Oh they will love this. We will be the best show in town. We are supplying them with all the drama they need. Switch off your televisions and come see the Fawzi family as they explode. First, my son goes insane and becomes an atheist; then, my daughter goes insane and dumps the engagement, and now, my other son goes insane and goes fornicating in the bushes. What happened? Did they change the drinking water on us? Is there a virus going 'round that is affecting our ability to be sane? Decent? Oh. *(A short laugh)* We did a wonderful job. You especially, my dear, with your wonderful ability to damn your children to all the freedom they could ever want.

MONA: Enough.

KAMAL: Not enough. What's next? Suddenly I find myself in a new family with new rules and thinking. What is up next? Let it *all* happen. Bring it *all* on today.

TAWFIQ: You know . . . I just don't think we need to make a big deal about this. I really don't.

KAMAL: Yes! Listen to our son; he has the solution, of course. We, pitiful we, who were not born of this soil are behind the times. How could we not accept the right to fuck in the street.

MONA: Please stop with this language.

KAMAL: The *language* bothers you? After what's happened, this is what upsets you?

TAWFIQ: So what?

KAMAL: "So what?" Your solution is this?

TAWFIQ: No one was harmed. This isn't a crime.

KAMAL: Tell me: in your world, what is a big deal? Perhaps I missed something important growing up and need to go back to school.

(Agitated, Mona starts arranging the furniture, dragging pieces here and there. Kamal continues:)

Okay, let me understand . . . So, logically, according to you, for instance, since they tell us to be kind and treat animals nicely, when humans start behaving like animals and have sex in public, I should call the SPCA for guidance? I should call an animal rights group for moral guidance? Yes, yes, how could I have been so stupid and intolerant. Invite them here. Let them meet the Shaykh and the Imam so we can all discuss God, dogs and fucking in public.

TAWFIQ: Puppy—

KAMAL: Would this be tolerant enough for you?

TAWFIQ: He's . . . Hamza's—

KAMAL: *La'a.* Don't say it.

TAWFIQ: Yes, he is.

KAMAL: *Harram*—don't drag them into this. Even they would be offended.

TAWFIQ: But that's—that's what he is, he's—

KAMAL: My son is not that! *(To Mona)* And if you say, "So what," I swear to God—

MONA *(Forceful, stopping what she's doing)*: Swear to God what?

TAWFIQ: What were the cops doing prowling around there anyway, like they don't have more important things to do. That's what ticks me off. Get pissed off with them.

KAMAL: It's their job! It's against the law!

TAWFIQ: Then it should be struck off the books. It's nobody's affair.

KAMAL: There is another book and another law, and these you can not strike out. We apologize we are so ignorant for believing these things.

TAWFIQ: Exactly, that's why he couldn't bring him home.

KAMAL: It's not about where they could do this, it's filthy business wherever they do it!

TAWFIQ: Says who?

KAMAL: Every faith on the planet. Are they all wrong? Was every faith inspired by ignorance that they should come to the same conclusion?

TAWFIQ: Yes, they all came to be at a time when people were weirded out by sex—we've changed. And why on earth would God forbid consenting love between two people?

KAMAL: You call what happened "love"? That is love to you?

TAWFIQ: Why not, it might've been, it might've led to it.

KAMAL *(To Mona)*: Listen to your son talk. Two people in the bushes is love to him. This is what it means to live without God—these are the conclusions you come to.

TAWFIQ: I'd rather live without God and have some compassion than have God and use him to punish anything I don't like.

KAMAL *(Close to Tawfiq)*: You don't think I have compassion for my son? *(Even more intense)* You don't think I care for my son? That I would give up my life for him in a second?

TAWFIQ: I'm just saying we shouldn't—

KAMAL: *"Compassion"?*

MONA *(Trying to defuse the situation)*: Tawfiq. Go and get the rest of the furniture.

KAMAL: Today I went and got my son out of jail and your solution is: "So what?"

TAWFIQ: Was he supposed to bring him home and introduce him?

KAMAL *(Cutting him off firmly)*: I don't want to hear another word.

(Slight beat.)

Your thinking offers nothing but chaos to do anything you want. And no family could survive for a day with your ideas. There is a reason this book and our beliefs have lasted through wars, famine and even America. And yes, it will outlast even you, too.

TAWFIQ: And you wonder why I became an atheist.

(Hamza enters. Everyone stops to look at him. Hamza hesitates a beat.)

HAMZA: I . . . I promise you . . . what happened . . . it will never happen again. I don't know what . . . I wasn't . . . It was never supposed to happen. I wasn't even supposed to be there, I was heading somewhere else. I wanted to—I was going to surprise you with this song. I wanted to practice. I don't know how I . . . I was just going to practice. I found this quiet place, he . . . showed up. And . . . talked about the oud and knew about it, and I listened. I was coming home, I told him I had to get home, but he—he wanted me to continue. So I played. I played another song. Whatever you think, I'm not—it's not. It's not me. Please don't think that. I'm not . . .

TAWFIQ: Hamza.

HAMZA: The thought disgusts me. That you would think that of me.

TAWFIQ: You don't have to do this.

HAMZA: It disgusts me. And nothing happened, whatever the police said. I would never do that to you or myself.

TAWFIQ *(Approaching him)*: Don't do this.

HAMZA *(Stepping away)*: Leave me alone.

TAWFIQ: Don't make it worse.

HAMZA: Leave me alone! *(To Kamal and Mona)* It will be all right . . . I will make it up to you . . . I promise you.

(Hamza stands there for an awkward beat, then exits. The others stand there for a moment, then:)

TAWFIQ: Well that was healthy. Hamza is well on his way to becoming a healthy, functioning member of this society. A few more twists like that and he'll be just screwed up enough to fit right in.

(Tawfiq leaves through the same exit as Hamza did. Silence. Even after the shuffling, the furniture still looks scattered, disordered.)

KAMAL *(With some exhaustion)*: You don't say anything.

(Beat.)

Why don't you say anything?

(Slight beat.)

MONA: What do you want me to say? . . . You were doing well enough without me.

KAMAL *(Quietly)*: One of these days we have to talk about how I have to do all the dirty work, say what needs to be said . . . and you get to sit there like a saint. And I get to be the bad guy.

MONA: Nobody's calling you that.

KAMAL: One of my sons thinks that.

MONA: He's protective of Hamza.

KAMAL: And I'm not?

(Slight beat.)

Did we upset anyone? . . . Make someone jealous? That they would give us the evil eye? Really. What did we do wrong? To have the world turn upside down on us? . . . Mona, say something. And please don't say they're growing up.

MONA: I just hope he used a condom.

(This is too much for him. Perhaps he stands.)

KAMAL: Thank you, Mona. I knew you would say the one thing that would help us see things clearly.

MONA: We'd better pray he used one. Gay, not gay, we have to make sure.

KAMAL: Thank God the engagement's off. Thank God. Things work out after all. Imagine. "Excuse the mess, we were up all night and morning trying to get our son out of jail for doing something very bad in public and now we're having a discussion about what he should put on his privates."

MONA: What are you protective of? Your son, or your reputation?

KAMAL: I'm protecting him from himself.—To stop him going down a road he doesn't have to go down and make his life a hundred times more difficult.

MONA: Maybe it was a one-time thing. —It's possible. You lose your head. We all do it one time or another. He had the bad luck to get caught, or the good luck. Now he's embarrassed, he's very ashamed, and he won't ever do it again . . . That is also possible.

(Slight beat.)

KAMAL: You think so? . . . You really think that?

(Slight beat.)

MONA: I don't know . . . I don't know anything anymore.

(Kamal picks up the oud. Inspects it. Turns it over. Then raises it above his head ready to smash it against a piece of furniture.)

No!

(The doorbell rings. Kamal freezes. Slight beat.)

KAMAL *(Lowers the oud)*: Who's that?

(Slight beat.)

MONA: I called everyone to cancel.
KAMAL: Did Huwaida forget her key?
MONA: It might be the Jehovah's witnesses. I saw them around yesterday.
KAMAL: Wonderful. Tell them to come in. Tell them we're ready to convert.
MONA: Who else could it be?
KAMAL: Tawfiq should open the door. They'll regret ever having come to this house.

(The doorbell rings again. Neither of them move.)

MONA: We're acting like we're hiding out. See who it is.

(Kamal starts for the exit, hands Mona the oud and leaves. Mona's manner suggests something we hadn't seen when the others were around: a certain heaviness and a burden from what has occurred. She sits down. From offstage we hear the voice of Aziz, Murad's father.)

AZIZ *(Offstage)*: Salaam Alaykum. Ahlan, ahlan.

(We hear the sound of the door closing, and then kissing on the cheeks.)

At last, I get to visit you.
KAMAL *(Offstage)*: Aziz. This is—*fadal.* Come in.

(At the sound of Aziz's name, Mona is suddenly alert. She stands, and looks around at the mess.)

We were just coming to see you.

(Aziz and Kamal enter. Aziz walks with a cane. He carries a wrapped gift of food.)

AZIZ: I said I had to come and say hello. And good-bye. *(To Mona)* Hello.

(Mona goes up to him.)

MONA: Aziz. Welcome. I'm sorry we didn't come earlier.

(Mona and Aziz kiss on the cheeks.)

We were planning to.

AZIZ: No problem.

(He hands her the present.)

MONA: Thank you.

KAMAL: We were just talking about taking you to the airport.

MONA: This is a mess. I'm sorry.

KAMAL: Ten different things, of course, suddenly happen.

MONA: We were just trying to put all this back. Here. *(She directs him to a chair)* Sit here. How are you feeling? I'm sorry you have to go back so soon after you've gotten over your jet lag.

AZIZ: No matter. I like flying. It knocks me out, but I like it. I'm one of the few people who loves airplane food. I used to drive Hoda crazy asking her to lay out my food exactly like they do on planes. You know, so you discover your dessert in this corner, and your fruit salad in that, and the bread and cheese here. It always made me feel like I was going somewhere. I think it was one of the many things that drove her to her death.

MONA: You mustn't say that. It's not true.

AZIZ: I know. But I like to think I had a hand in all the important events in her life. I think she would like me to think so, too.

KAMAL: *Allah yarhamah.* I'm sorry she is not here.

MONA: She always spoke of you with nothing but compliments and love. Very rare so late in a marriage.

KAMAL: Is Murad coming?

AZIZ: Still sleeping. He stayed up late, thinking. He no longer wants to become a doctor, you know. I can't say I understand his reasoning.

KAMAL: I am sorry to hear that.

AZIZ: What can one say?

(A bedroom door slams offstage.)

MONA: Let me get you a cushion.

AZIZ: I am very comfortable.

MONA: So you can put your leg up. Kamal?

(She points to coffee table as she heads for the exit.)

Ana asaf gidan. Our house is not usually like this of course.

(Kamal drags the coffee table to where Aziz is sitting.)

AZIZ: Don't trouble yourself.
KAMAL: We wanted to clean everything out for the—the . . .
AZIZ: I'm sorry you went to this much trouble.
KAMAL: No, no; we needed a big cleaning anyway.
MONA: It's healthier for the carpets.

(Small, awkward beat.)

I'll get you a cushion. Excuse me.

(With one last look to Kamal, she exits.)

AZIZ: It's me who should apologize for spending all my time here
in bed.
KAMAL: Now that you're well, why not stay a few more days?
AZIZ: You have been kind enough as it is.
KAMAL: Stay. We'll take you around. Show you some of the places you
should see.
AZIZ: *Ma'lish.* Another visit. The sooner we get back, the sooner Murad
starts to think about what he wants to do.

(Slight beat.)

KAMAL: Honestly, Aziz . . . perhaps it is best the engagement is off. For
Murad's sake.
AZIZ: I don't think so. Huwaida would have been very good for him.
KAMAL: It's not Huwaida. Touch wood, out of all my children, she is
the sanest. Until her decision anyway. It is this country. It will
turn strange switches on and off in people's heads and make
them act in ways you don't understand.
AZIZ: You mean Huwaida changing her mind?
KAMAL: For instance. If she was in Cairo, the better choices would be
more obvious. She wouldn't have to wonder. Here, they are so
desperate to sell you anything, they will make madness seem like
a good choice if it can make a dollar.
AZIZ: This is everywhere.
KAMAL: Because this insane place is everywhere and the thinking that
goes with it. It is frightening to think I don't have to miss an
American TV show when I travel to Cairo because it will be playing there. No one around the world can get away from it.

AZIZ: You are right. Though I confess to being a big fan of *The Bold and the Beautiful.*

KAMAL: Aziz, no; believe me. It is much better for Murad that this is off. You have no idea what disasters can fall on your head here.

AZIZ: What is it, Kamal? You speak as if something else is the matter.

KAMAL: No, I'm just speaking. —I sometimes wonder why we came here.

AZIZ: But you have done well for yourself?

KAMAL: How? Moneywise? What does that matter if you lose everything else?

AZIZ: Why do you say that? —Like what?

KAMAL: No, it's—never mind. I do not want to burden you with my problems.

AZIZ: Tell me.

KAMAL *(Hesitates, then speaks):* For instance . . . One of my sons . . .

AZIZ: *Khar?* May he be well.

KAMAL: Yesterday he decides God is a joke. Complete nonsense.

AZIZ: Who?

KAMAL: Tawfiq. Suddenly he informs me. My son has evicted God. Imagine.

AZIZ: Really?

KAMAL: Just like that.

AZIZ: And what was his reasoning?

KAMAL: He didn't say. He didn't leave it open to discussion. It was, in fact, like he was serving an eviction notice. No room for anything. God is no longer in his life.

AZIZ: This is very interesting. I would like to speak to him.

KAMAL: I would not inflict him on you. You are still recovering. Besides, he is too stubborn to have his mind changed just like that.

AZIZ: I would not try to change it. It is rare to meet a real atheist. I have met many godless men, men who say they believe in God but live lives that include everything but God; but an atheist, this is hard to find.

KAMAL: This is what I mean. Yes, it can happen anywhere, but here you are encouraged. I swear, Aziz, we are ready to pack up our bags and follow you to Cairo.

(Mona enters carrying a cushion.)

MONA: And why would we do that?

AZIZ: I do not see how this is so terrible. If reasoning is what led him to this conclusion, then reasoning can lead him out.

MONA: Who are you talking about?

(She puts the cushion on the coffee table. Aziz will stretch out his leg on it.)

AZIZ: *Shukran.*

KAMAL: Tawfiq.

MONA: Kamal. We don't need to bother Aziz with Tawfiq.

AZIZ: What bother? This is intriguing. Every family should have an atheist. It keeps God's voice fresh and the faithful on their toes.

KAMAL: Aziz, please; you of all people. When it is happening to someone else's family it is intriguing, when it is yours, it is like an open wound with salt pouring in.

MONA: So why mention it? Can I get you something to eat? A lemonade?

KAMAL: I was telling him how lucky it is the engagement is off.

AZIZ: I am back on the fast, thank you.

MONA *(To Kamal)*: And why would that be? I'm sure we don't want Aziz to leave with the wrong impression.

KAMAL: I was using our son as an example of how this place can rob you in more ways than it can give, and why Murad would be better off finding a wife in Egypt.

MONA: I would not be so quick to use our children as examples. *(To Aziz)* And I'm sure such things have not stopped happening to families in Egypt. Are you sure I can't get you anything?

KAMAL: No, Aziz, go home and warn anyone who thinks of coming here to appreciate what they have; it's much better than anything they think this place can offer. You have permission to use us as an example.

AZIZ: I always admired the courage you had in coming here.

MONA *(Interrupting, to Aziz)*: Do you think it is God-fearing of someone to be blind to the gifts God gives and to keep moaning when all around you is evidence of the good things you have?

KAMAL: You speak to me of blindness? You who ignore your children's problems and not take responsibility?

MONA: *Me* be responsible?

KAMAL *(Overlapping)*: Excuse everything they do so they grow up thinking one behavior's as good as another.

MONA: And where are you, outside watching?

KAMAL: You make it so every time I speak to them I have to scream because you are cutting the legs off of everything I say.

MONA: No, sorry, do not use me as an excuse for your screaming, you enjoy it too much.

KAMAL *(To Aziz)*: This is what I'm talking about.

MONA: There is nothing the matter with our family!

KAMAL: No, nothing at all, except we're losing our religion and our souls and to you that's a detail!

MONA: Maybe it's not God he's stopped believing in. Maybe it's you. Have you ever thought of that? Everything you stand for, and do to keep this family together when everything you do ends up strangling us a little bit more each day making it so none of us can breathe.

AZIZ: My friends. My friends. Whatever is the problem, we will solve it. Please. It hurts me to hear you say these things.

(The front door slams shut. They all turn to the living room entrance. Huwaida enters still dressed in her just-shy-of-being-guady outfit, with full makeup, red lipstick and all. In this company, the effect appears even more garish. Huwaida freezes. Kamal and Mona stare at her.)

HUWAIDA *(To Aziz)*: Uncle . . .

AZIZ: Hello, my dear.

HUWAIDA: I . . . didn't know you were . . .

AZIZ: I had to come and say goodbye. And see your face. I haven't seen you all week.

HUWAIDA: Is . . . Murad here?

AZIZ: No. He's resting. Packing . . . You look . . . very beautiful.

HUWAIDA: No. No. This is. No, nobody was supposed to—I didn't realize anybody would be here. This is not what I—this isn't what I usually wear.

AZIZ: It's okay if it is.

HUWAIDA: No it's not. This was for a school . . . thing. I feel like a complete idiot wearing this.

MONA: What are you doing?

HUWAIDA: Is Hamza home?

MONA: *What are you doing?*

HUWAIDA: Is he okay?

MONA: Answer me!

HUWAIDA: It was for a meeting with a professor. She was criticizing me for wearing the hijab and I wanted to show her how ridiculous the alternative was.

KAMAL *(Quietly)*: You succeeded. I hope she gives you an "A."

HUWAIDA: Nobody was supposed to see this.

MONA: Nobody where, on the street?

HUWAIDA: I just got so irritated with this teacher.

MONA: What were you thinking? Go in and change at once.

HUWAIDA: That's what I came home to do. Is Hamza—?

MONA: Go in and change!

KAMAL *(Referring to Huwaida)*: Exhibit one.

(Tawfiq enters, stopping near the entrance. He's about to address his parents when he sees Aziz.)

TAWFIQ: Oh. Hi.

AZIZ: *Ahlan wasahlan.* How are you?

TAWFIQ: I'm . . . good. *(To his mother)* Could you . . .

MONA: Thank you. Stay and talk with *Am* Aziz. And you, get out of that now. *(To Aziz)* I'm sorry, I have to leave you for a moment.

(Tawfiq looks at his sister's outfit.)

AZIZ: Is everything all right?

MONA: Yes. It's Hamza. He's not feeling well.

AZIZ: It is not serious I hope.

KAMAL *(With some irony)*: No. Not serious at all.

HUWAIDA *(To her mother)*: I'll come with you.

MONA: Change.

(They both exit.)

KAMAL *(To Aziz)*: You wanted to talk to him. Here he is. Exhibit two. And perhaps if exhibit three comes down, you will go home happy. Happy you live somewhere else . . . Perhaps I will go bring him down myself.

(Kamal looks offstage, then exits. Slight beat.)

AZIZ: *Masha'allah.* Since I last saw you, how you've grown. And grown some more.

TAWFIQ: Between twelve and twenty—that's when it usually happens.

(Aziz goes up to Tawfiq and takes him by the arm.)

AZIZ: Quick. Before something else happens and you are called away. Let us talk. I want to know all about it. Tell me everything.

TAWFIQ: About what?

AZIZ: For a few minutes, I would be delighted to get in your mind and see the world as you see it. That would be a present to me.

TAWFIQ: What are you talking about?

AZIZ: Your father told me. About you and God.

TAWFIQ: Oh. That.

AZIZ: Is it true? Come, sit. Or stand if you prefer. Whatever you need to think clearly.

TAWFIQ: Is what true?

AZIZ: Are you an atheist?

TAWFIQ *(Wary at this sudden interest, hesitating)*: Er . . . sure. I'm not a big one for labels, but I guess that's the word.

AZIZ: Excellent. That is what I want to know about. Tell me. Now that you don't believe in God . . . how does the world appear to you?

TAWFIQ: How does? . . . What, you mean . . . not believing in God? . . . Do I see the world differently?

AZIZ: Yes. Very good. Do you?

TAWFIQ: Um. Why? This is so hard to imagine? I'm not exactly freak boy here. It's called waking up.

AZIZ: Excuse me for my excitement in wanting to know, but I wish to know what *I* cannot imagine. It is my failure, truly, and so my curiosity. I want to know what you have woken up to.

TAWFIQ: I've—just woken up.

AZIZ: To what? You were in this cloud of believing, yes? And then suddenly it clears, and you see what?

TAWFIQ: It's not like I'm seeing anything new. I've just stopped wasting my time in believing in something I *don't* see. And that frees me up to think about what I do. *This* life and not some next that might or might not exist. And to care about that. Instead of all this God-talk which is like Santa Claus to me.

AZIZ: Good, good; continue.

TAWFIQ: That's it. *(Shrugs)*

AZIZ: No. There must be more. What else?

TAWFIQ: That's just it. There's nothing complicated about it. You just— wake up. And that's liberating. It frees you up. I feel like I've been handed the deeds to my own life and that I now own it for the rest of my time here. I don't have to make like—mortgage payments to some unseen whoever whose existence has not been proved to me. Why hand your life over in that way? That's so crippling to me.

AZIZ: And so, what is it that gives you hope—strength? It is God for others . . .

TAWFIQ: Me. Relying on me.

AZIZ: Just you? A religion of one?

TAWFIQ: And each other. That's the point, relying on each other.

AZIZ: But then, if there's no God, some would say, why do anything? Why not do as you please? Be cruel when you want and kill when you feel like it.

TAWFIQ: People do that with God in their mouths all the time.

AZIZ: Yes, sure, these people speak his name, but in their hearts he is not there. They have collapsed into the worst parts of themselves. And that is us, not the religion. We fail the religion.

TAWFIQ: Which religion? They can't all be right.

AZIZ: Why not. Do we not speak different languages? One is not superior to the other.

TAWFIQ: That's just it, you may say that, but in your heart everyone goes around thinking their religion is just a little bit better than the next. And that little thought becomes the poison that ruins anything good about the religion.

AZIZ: But you can't judge God by the people who claim to speak on His behalf. We are not perfect enough to speak of something that is.

TAWFIQ: But then why speak of Him at all? If God is a language no one can speak properly, then why bother? Why not just shut up about it. Just—once and for all—*shut up.*

(Slight beat.)

AZIZ: And yet people can not. We can not seem to shut up about God—anywhere. Is that not a puzzle in itself? . . . We chatter on about Him like fools. Like the weak people we are, going on about someone we can not finally prove. I can not prove anything to you about Him. The evidence I would show you that He exists would be the same evidence you would show me to prove that He doesn't exist. And your argument should win the day. It should, really. We don't hear His booming voice. He does not appear to us. He does not make State-of-the-World addresses like the president here. Maybe God is something that happened to people long ago because they didn't have television. Something to amuse themselves in the desert, and God is a pretty good story, so why not. And yet . . . people still do not let go. Why? We should have to come to the conclusion by now that He does not exist. But so many continue with this fairy tale not because as you say we are weak, but because finally—we have to admit . . . we don't know. And perhaps as important as any faith is the equal need to surrender to the fact that—we don't know. And can never know enough; and not all the hard facts and knowledge of science could ever satisfy the longing of wondering if this is all there is. And to live that with all the faith and passion we have. And if not believing gives you that same excitement, then, maybe, you and I can end up believing in the same thing. That we don't know enough to ever close our eyes to anything. Especially to the fact of us being alive, right now, here, talking—as witnesses to that. Whether you call that miracle "biology"—or "God." And maybe in that way, we both move forward as . . . believers . . . Yes?

(Slight beat.)

TAWFIQ: That seems like a stretch to me.
AZIZ: Well of course it's a stretch. I've traveled two continents and an ocean to get here. Traveling a few more feet to you shouldn't be that difficult.

(The doorbell rings.)

Come here and kiss me and show me you know how to end a good discussion.

(Aziz takes a step towards him.)

I like you.

(He kisses Tawfiq on the cheeks.)

You grew up just as I hoped you might: You grew up to surprise me. But be patient with your parents, they worry.
TAWFIQ *(Referring to doorbell)*: I'd better get that.
AZIZ: They want to know you're okay and not changing into something very strange.
TAWFIQ: I might.
AZIZ: Okay, but do it in stages.

(Mona enters.)

MONA *(To Tawfiq)*: Aren't you getting that?
TAWFIQ *(To Aziz)*: Excuse me.

(Tawfiq exits to open the front door.)

MONA *(To Aziz)*: Where's Kamal?
AZIZ: I don't know; he went through there. How is Hamza?
MONA: He's fine.
AZIZ: Would you like Murad to take a look at him? I can tell him to come over?

(Murad and Tawfiq enter.)

You enter just when you are needed. Go and see what is the matter with Hamza.

MONA: Murad. *Ahlan.* How lovely to see you. Come in. *(She has gone up to him to kiss him on the cheeks)* Now that you're both here, you'll stay for *iftar.*

AZIZ: We do not want to trouble you.

MONA: What trouble. We prepared for an engagement; the least we can offer is dinner.

AZIZ *(To Murad)*: Go and take a look at Hamza.

MONA: No, really, he is just tired from school work. He'll be fine. Now tell me you'll both stay for *iftar.* *(Referring to the furniture)* We'll have all this put back in a second.

AZIZ: It is up to Murad.

(Murad is about to answer when Huwaida enters still dressed in her outfit. Some of the makeup has been removed, but enough remains. Perhaps she holds the cotton pad she was using to wipe it off. Slight beat.)

HUWAIDA: Hi.

MURAD: Hello.

(Slight beat.)

MONA *(To Murad)*: For your information, what she's wearing was for a school project: The psychological effects of dressing badly to see if you can age your parents more quickly. It has worked. *(To Huwaida)* Please go back and come out properly.

HUWAIDA *(Perhaps still looking at Murad)*: I will.

MONA: Do it now, please.

MURAD: Yes. Thank you for the invitation.

MONA: You'll stay for dinner then?

(Murad doesn't respond. Murad and Huwaida continue to stare at each other.)

AZIZ *(To Mona)*: Mona, on my way in I noticed the lovely garden you have talked of many times. I saw plants I didn't recognize—would you show them to me?

MONA *(Sensing the need to exit)*: Of course.—This is a good day to be outside. —Tawfiq?

TAWFIQ: What? . . . Oh . . . Sure.

MONA *(As she leads Aziz)*: Then afterwards we will put all this back so we can eat properly. *(To Huwaida)* Okay?

(Slight beat.)

I really wish you would change.

(Mona and Aziz exit. Tawfiq lingers by the door, looking back at his sister and Murad.)

HUWAIDA *(To Tawfiq, defiantly)*: What?
TAWFIQ *(Slight beat)*: Whatever.

(He exits. Beat.)

HUWAIDA: I always seem to be wearing something not quite right around you. Why is that?
MURAD: I have shown up when you don't expect me?
HUWAIDA: You have a bad habit of doing that.
MURAD: I'd ask if you wanted me to leave again, but I am worried you would say "yes."
HUWAIDA *(Referring to her clothes)*: If this doesn't scare you away . . .
MURAD: It was for a school project?
HUWAIDA: What if I told you it wasn't? . . . That this was how I wish to dress from now on. That I'd suddenly discovered a new me and she wanted to dress just like this.
MURAD: I would diplomatically suggest the new you speak with a fashion consultant.
HUWAIDA: Really. And what if I decided I wanted to wear this from now on? And let us say, for argument, we were married. What would you do?
MURAD: But you do not seem happy in it.
HUWAIDA: What if I decided I was?
MURAD: I would be . . . interested to know . . . how you came to this decision . . . And I would—start turning down the lights in the house, and become interested in shopping for women's clothes.
HUWAIDA: Never mind.
MURAD: Maybe this should be my new career. Helping women dress.
HUWAIDA: We can change the subject now. This *was* for an experiment, as a matter of fact. I am very inclined to experiments. And I reserve the right to make them. The expression "going out on a limb" is dear to me.

MURAD: I enjoy going out on a limb, too. Perhaps it is the same limb.

(Slight beat.)

HUWAIDA: Would you—help me put up the table?
MURAD: Yes, of course.

(Over the next exchanges, they assemble the table in a corner of a room and place the chairs around it. Also, the remaining pieces of furniture are put in their place so that by the end of their scene, the living room/dining room looks almost orderly again.)

Your art class went well? —I hope I didn't make you miss too much.
HUWAIDA: No, I got there. We were drawing still lifes. Only the still life was alive, and very nude, which they didn't tell me beforehand. I think they thought they were going to have a laugh at my expense. "Let's see how the hijab-wearing Muslim deals with a male nude. Ha, ha, aren't we cool." God, people can be so right-eous. Using me to feel good about themselves. "Look how modern we are." No, you idiots, you're as stuck in your own crap as everyone else is . . . Sorry. It just ticks me off.
MURAD: Most of my still lifes were dead.

(This stops Huwaida for a moment.)

Cadavers. For purposes of study.
HUWAIDA: Oh. Right. That can't have been fun.
MURAD: No, it was not.
HUWAIDA: Now that would freak me out. Alive and naked is one thing. —Is that why you . . . didn't want to become a doctor?
MURAD: A part of it . . . Also, our teachers. The example they set. I found the more I learned the less I remembered why I was doing this. I worried by the end I would care more about how much I would make, eventually, than about the patients.
HUWAIDA: But isn't that the case with most disciplines? For a while you get caught up in the details and forget the bigger picture. And don't you have to do that, sort of, if you want to get good.
MURAD: Perhaps . . . I'm not sure I have explained it properly . . . I felt it more important to protect the reasons for wanting to be a doctor, than to lose those reasons and become one. It sounds selfish, I know . . . I just felt the way we were being taught was wrong.

HUWAIDA: Then maybe you should learn all that you have to, get some experience, then go back and teach it the way you think it should be taught.

MURAD: Yes. That is also possible.

HUWAIDA: Being an idealist isn't bad. It's good. You just have to follow through, right? . . . I think you'd make a great doctor.

(Slight beat.)

MURAD: It is possible.

(Slight beat.)

HUWAIDA: Let me take that.

(She takes whatever piece of furniture he was holding and puts it in its place.)

There . . . Halfway liveable again. It was driving us all nuts. *(She surveys the tidied room)* Thanks.

MURAD: Not a problem.

(Slight beat.)

HUWAIDA: Murad . . . Were you upset that I'd cancelled? Or secretly relieved?

(Murad looks at her.)

I just felt . . .

(Slight beat.)

Perhaps you were also . . . I'm glad you came, though.

MURAD: Why?

HUWAIDA: I'm just glad you did . . . It was rude of me to suddenly change my mind like that.

MURAD: You have that right.

HUWAIDA: And you? —Did you come back to say good-bye? . . . Or did you hope I'd change my mind?

MURAD: I came back to see if I had changed *my* mind.

HUWAIDA: Have you?

MURAD: No. I have not.

(Slight beat.)

That, and also, I had a—a very strange dream.

HUWAIDA: Really? I've been having a few of those. What was yours about?

MURAD: Oh—it is . . . it is complicated. —Perhaps I will tell you another time.

HUWAIDA: I'd like that. Dreams can be so weird, can't they.

(Slight beat.)

I think I'll go change out of my experiment.

MURAD: It was a very interesting experiment.

HUWAIDA: More may follow.

MURAD: I do not doubt it.

(They look at each other, smile.)

HUWAIDA: I won't be a moment.

(She turns to exit, at the door she turns back to him.)

Oh. By the way. Can I draw you sometime?

MURAD: With or without clothes?

HUWAIDA: I think your face will be naked enough for me.

MURAD: Good. Because I catch cold easily.

(She smiles. Exits. Murad stands there for a moment before he turns to survey the room. Perhaps he adjusts an object, or piece of furniture. Then H.D. strides on carrying flowers. She is dressed as in his dream, wearing the hijab. She goes up to a vase and arranges the flowers. She turns to Murad, who is watching her, flabbergasted. She smiles. He continues to stare at her, dumbfounded. We hear Aziz's voice.)

AZIZ *(Offstage)*: It is amazing. It should be in a magazine. I don't believe Kamal did all this.

(At the sound of the voices, H.D. leaves through the kitchen exit.)

MONA *(Offstage)*: Yes, I swear. This is where he goes when he can't talk to anybody. He plants something. Or digs.

(Mona and Aziz enter. Mona carries a bunch of flowers.)

Ah, at last.

(She sees the tidied room.)

Thank you. Did Huwaida make you do all this?

MURAD *(Still digesting H.D.'s appearance)*: We did it together.

MONA: Murad, what she was wearing? Please, don't think she has lost her mind.

MURAD: I don't think she is the one losing her mind.

(Mona has gone up to the vase to put her flowers in and sees the other flowers.)

MONA: I didn't notice you had brought flowers. How beautiful. Thank you.

MURAD: I—don't—remember bringing them myself.

MONA: They are lovely.

(She places her flowers next to them. Tawfiq enters and is about to exit again to see Hamza.)

(To Tawfiq) Help me in the kitchen. I want to start bringing the stuff out.

TAWFIQ: I wanted to check on—

MONA: Leave it. Help me inside. *(To Aziz and Murad)* Now that we have a living room, relax. We'll bring out the CD player and play some music.

(She takes him by the arm and leads him out. Aziz goes up to his son and looks at him.)

AZIZ: We are staying?

MURAD *(Shrugs)*: I don't know.

AZIZ: You know. Your eyes say you know, and your heart is dancing like it already hears the wedding music.

MURAD: It's not up to me.

AZIZ: Yes it is. I saw her. She knows, too.

MURAD: Puppy . . . We'll see. —Let's just see.

AZIZ: We shall . . . *Inshallah.*

(Mona enters carrying a tablecloth, and behind her Tawfiq carries plates and cutlery. They proceed to set the table. Murad goes up to help them.)

MONA: Kamal's checking on the food. All the dishes to remind you of home—or remind us, anyway.

(Huwaida enters dressed in something more moderate.)

Now that's more like it. That way we can all digest our food.

HUWAIDA: That look happens to be in for some people.

MONA: Some looks are worth ignoring. Now please go into the kitchen and get the napkins. Thank you.

(Huwaida starts heading for the kitchen and almost bumps into Kamal.)

HUWAIDA *(To her father)*: Hi. —We're laying out the table.

(Kamal doesn't answer, she exits.)

AZIZ *(To Kamal)*: A fantastic garden. I'm impressed. Where did you learn this? This is like a professional. You should have a side business, landscaping. Carpets and landscaping. You take care of the inside and the outside.

KAMAL *(Half paying attention)*: Yes. Hello, Murad. Welcome.

MURAD: Hello, Uncle.

(Murad goes up to him and Kamal kisses him on the cheeks. Kamal's manner has changed: more somber, less energetic than we've seen him.)

AZIZ: I am not flattering you. This is a skill. And the colors.

KAMAL *(To Murad)*: It is good to see you.

MURAD: It's good to see you, too.

KAMAL *(To Mona)*: Where is Hamza?

MONA: He is still resting.

KAMAL: Ask him to come down please.

MONA: It is better if he rests.

KAMAL: Ask him to come down.

MONA: Kamal—he's tired.

KAMAL: Are you embarrassed that he should be here? . . . I will get him myself.

TAWFIQ: I'll get him.

(Tawfiq exits. Beat. There is a clear change of mood in the room.)

KAMAL *(To Aziz)*: I'm sorry. You came at a bad time.
AZIZ: Not at all. We are happy to be with you. It has been a long while since we have all sat down for *iftar* together.

(Huwaida enters with a tray of glasses and napkins, which she will put on the table. Murad goes up to help her. Slight beat.)

KAMAL: Murad. Sit down. You shouldn't be helping.
MURAD: It's all right. I want to.

(Hamza enters followed by Tawfiq. Hamza stops near the doorway, Tawfiq goes around him and helps with whatever remains to be done at the table.)

TAWFIQ: He was—coming down anyway.
AZIZ: *Assalam Alaykum, ahlan beek,* come here. I'm sorry to hear you're not well.

(Hamza goes over to Aziz, who kisses him.)

You and me. We must recover together and give each other strength. You are looking well, though. I don't see any fever.
MONA: He's taken on too much this semester. And with this changing weather.
KAMAL: That is not the reason.
MONA: Not the only reason, but it doesn't help.
KAMAL: It has nothing to do with that.

(Slight beat. Awkwardness.)

MURAD *(To Hamza)*: Hello.
HAMZA: *Salaam.*

(Slight beat.)

MONA: We can start putting out the food. —It's a while yet, but why not start.
KAMAL: No. —It can wait. If you don't mind. I'd rather we not do that now. Everyone, please, sit down. We still have time. Sit . . . please sit.

(Kamal, Hamza and Mona remain standing.)

Yesterday, Aziz . . . my son . . . was . . . he was practicing a song. He has taken up the oud, you know.

AZIZ: No. Wonderful. *Gidak* would be very proud. This is the instrument he loved.

KAMAL: Yes, he did. And yes, he would be proud . . . I never could play it . . . And sometimes the sounds my son makes tells me he, too, has trouble playing it . . . But it doesn't matter . . . When you're in love with something, the faults, the errors, what do they matter. They get you a little closer to what you want, and the sounds you know are there. And so—you keep going. —You find out all the music you shouldn't make—on your way to finding the music you should . . . It would be nice if Hamza would play for us what he has been practicing. —I would like that.

(Hamza stands there, not moving. Kamal goes, picks up the oud and walks over to Hamza.)

(Gently) If you don't mind.

(Hamza takes the oud.)

AZIZ: You mustn't be shy. You're playing in front of friends and family.

TAWFIQ: That's usually the worst crowd to play for.

MONA: Tawfiq.

TAWFIQ: Well it is.

(Slight beat.)

HAMZA: It's still very rough.

KAMAL: It doesn't matter.

(Kamal goes to stand by Mona. Hamza either sits or stands as he positions himself and the oud.)

HAMZA: I'm not sure you'll like it.

KAMAL: We'd like to listen anyway.

(Perhaps Kamal takes Mona's hand. Slight beat.)

HAMZA: All right . . . All right.

(Hamza looks to his mother and father. Looks to his instrument. He takes a breath. Light change. Everyone freezes. H.D. enters carrying a dish which she places on the table. She approaches the audience.)

H.D.: The thing I like most about Ramadan? . . . It's not the eating at the end of the day, which, let me tell you, can really hit the spot, of course. And it's certainly not the fasting. Sure, you can get a high after the first few days when your body stops crying out for the basics and you begin to settle down for the long haul. That's all good. But . . . what really makes Ramadan special for me . . . is the time just before we eat. When the whole family and the friends you've invited gather around the table and there's this wonderful anticipation of something delicious about to happen. Of relief and bounty, and of something shared. And it's that. That's the thing. What makes it extra special. The sense in the room that you've all been through something together. Most times of the year, you come to the table all in your own little worlds but at Ramadan—you come to the table experiencing a shared world. And that simple thing, all by itself is amazing. —Oh, sure, the family dramas don't stop. People can be just as petty and silly and quarrels will happen because we are who we are, damn it. But if you quiet down and pay attention, you may get a glimpse of being part of a bigger, better drama than your own; and the people you're with are the only ones who will help you play it out; in a way that'll make your part in it shine, along with all the others, and that you're *with* these people; with them in a way that sometimes escapes you the rest of the year . . . And so you sit down. You pass the food. And just before that first glass of water is drunk, all these good feelings come to a head. So that the first thing that passes your lips is tasted by something deeper inside. And maybe, somewhere, God enjoys that as much as we do. Maybe even applauds this struggle we have taken on. And somewhere, in our hearts . . . perhaps we do, too.

(Slight beat. Blackout.)

END OF PLAY

Glossary

Ahlan beek	"Hello" (one of several expressions used to welcome someone).
Ahlan wasahlan	"Hello" (another expression of welcome).
Al-Azhar	Oldest university in the world devoted to the study of Islam, built in 975 A.D. in Cairo.
Allah yarhamuh	"God rest his soul."
Am	"Uncle" (a term of respect, not necessarily referring to a blood relative).
Ana asaf gidan	"I am very sorry."
Assalam Alaykum	A Muslim greeting meaning: "Peace be upon you."
Ats	Lentil soup.
Ba-ba	"Papa" or "dad."
Fadal	"Welcome."
Gidak	"Grandfather."
Habibti	"Dear."
Hamdu'lillah	"Thank God."
Iftar	The evening meal that breaks the day's fast during the month-long fast (Ramadan), which Muslims practice every year.
Inshallah	"God willing."
Khar	In conversation this means: "I hope everything is well."
Ma'lish	"It doesn't matter."
Masha'allah	"As God has willed."
Masjid	"Mosque."
Shaykh	Muslim clergy.
Shukran	"Thank you."

YUSSEF EL GUINDI's most recent productions include: *Jihad Jones and the Kalashnikov Babes*, produced at Golden Thread Productions in San Francisco, at InterAct Theatre Company in Philadelphia and at Kitchen Dog Theater in Dallas, as part of the National New Play Network; *Our Enemies: Lively Scenes of Love and Combat*, produced by Silk Road Theatre Project in Chicago, where it was Jeff Nominated, and was among the six finalists for the 2009 American Theatre Critics Association's Steinberg/New Play Award. The American Theatre Critics Association has also given it the 2009 M. Elizabeth Osborn New Play Award.

Back of the Throat, winner of the 2004 Northwest Playwright Competition held by Theater Schmeater, won *LA Weekly*'s Excellence in Playwriting Award for 2006. It was nominated for the 2006 American Theatre Critics Association's Steinberg/New Play Award, and was voted Best New Play of 2005 by the *Seattle Times*. It was first staged by San Francisco's Thick Description and Golden Thread Productions, then later presented in various theatres around the country including the Flea Theater in New York. *Ten Acrobats in an Amazing Leap of Faith*, was staged by Silk Road Theatre Project and won the After Dark Award for Best New Play in Chicago in 2006. His two related one-acts, *Acts of Desire*, were staged by the Fountain Theatre in Los Angeles. *Back of the Throat*, and the two related one-acts, now titled *Such a Beautiful Voice is Sayeda's* and *Karima's City*, have been published by Dramatists Play Service. The latter one-acts have also been included in *The Best American Short Plays: 2004–2005*, published by Applause Books. Yussef holds an MFA from Carnegie Mellon University and was playwright-in-residence at Duke University.

Between Our Lips

Nathalie Handal

Author's Statement

My plays are born out of wander and wonder. My life has been one of wandering
through a constellation of diverse spaces
and spheres, as my family comes from one
of the most troubled regions in the world—
the Middle East. I was raised and have lived
in some of the most impoverished countries in Latin America and the Caribbean
and in some of the richest countries, such
as France and United States. Traveling
evoked my need to understand people out-
side of how they define themselves socially or how others define
them; to explore how the chaos inside manifests itself when it's alone
versus when it's in a crowded room; to search for who we are, how we
communicate our terror and reverie, and how the divine shimmering
inside of us enables us to be conscious of life around us.

I try to present characters that the audience would not otherwise
think exist, and these characters often have unresting lives and are
unrested souls. I am interested in exploring worlds and characters
people can relate to but think they can't. I try to find connections
where there do not seem to be any. When people recognize themselves or their lives in contexts that surprise them, that to me is the
beginning of a dialogue. I believe that communication can bring us
back to our humanity.

In my plays, I try to offer—whether through cries and whispers,
ruminations and revelations, questions and secrets, irony and laughter—
the journey into the characters' deep song, into the stories they reveal
and conceal. We do not pay enough attention to what is not exposed,
and perhaps it is in the silent beats that we discover the entire rhyme.

The stage is a world where we invite the audience to come to, to
stay for a moment, to return to or not. Theatre reflects the whirling of
the soul and, in so doing, spins our hearts and minds.

Production History

Between Our Lips received workshops and development assistance from Nibras, the Arab-American theatre collective, in New York City in 2005.

Between Our Lips was first performed at the Blue Heron Theatre, presented by Nibras (Najla Said, Artistic Director; Elias El-Hage, Managing Director) in New York City in September 2005. It was directed by Lameece Issaq. The production stage manager was Maha Chehlaoui. The cast was as follows:

HOMER MUSTAFA	Piter Marek
AYAT ABU RISHA	Rana Kazkaz

Between Our Lips was part of the The Public Theater's evening of readings, "New Work Now!," which was produced and organized by New York Theatre Workshop and Nibras in New York City in 2006. It was directed by Shoshana Gold. The dramaturg was Nancy Vitale. The production assistant was Lyndsey Goode. The cast was as follows:

HOMER MUSTAFA	Ramsey Faragallah
AYAT ABU RISHA	Lameece Issaq

Characters

HOMER MUSTAFA, Palestinian-American journalist
AYAT ABU RISHA, Palestinian photographer

Setting

A holding cell with a table and two chairs.

Note

A glossary of select terms appears at the end of the play.

There is only one thing that has power completely and that is love, because when a man loves he seeks no power, therefore he has power.

—Alan Paton, Cry, The Beloved Country

.

The stage is dark. Nina Simone's rendition of "I Wish I Knew How It Would Feel to Be Free" is playing. Lights up on a holding cell with a table and two chairs. Ayat stands facing the audience. The song fades. Homer enters, carrying his bag.

HOMER: Hello.

AYAT: *Ahlan. Tfadal.*

HOMER: Thank you for agreeing to see me.

AYAT: Your piece on Hebron's ancient Mamluk houses destroyed to build a road for settlers . . . is very powerful . . . I trust you will write a fair article.

(Homer sits, puts his leather, businesslike bag on the table.)

HOMER: Thank you . . . I've been given fifteen minutes to interview you. I assume you know who I am writing for . . .

AYAT: The *Times* . . .

HOMER: Exactly . . . I would like to offer my condolences . . . I . . .

AYAT: *Shukran* . . . So, what have you heard about the incident? What do you know?

HOMER: That you are under arrest . . .

AYAT: . . . about to be sentenced, probably for life . . .

HOMER: Many people say you were not well represented.

AYAT *(Ironic laugh)*: What difference does it make now . . .

HOMER: That you're incapable of . . .

AYAT: Killing.

HOMER: Can you start with the morning in question.

AYAT: Yes. Sameh . . .

HOMER: Your husband . . .

AYAT *(Nodding affirmatively)*: . . . We usually went to Rafah on Wednesdays.

HOMER: I understand you worked together in the refugee camps?

AYAT: Yes. We worked mainly with the children . . . The children loved him. He would do anything for them.

HOMER: What did you do there?

AYAT: We taught them photography . . .

HOMER: I have some of your books. Chilling images.

(Ayat nods in acceptance, then starts pacing back and forth.)

AYAT: That day, I went to the school ahead of him. The class started . . .

HOMER: How many children in the class?

AYAT: Seventeen.

HOMER: Go on.

AYAT: He didn't show up. It was strange.

(Homer says nothing.)

Then I realized one of the girls, Iman, was also missing.

HOMER: Tell me about her.

AYAT: What an inquisitive girl she was! Long hair, black eyes that would smile when she spoke. Sameh and I were very fond of her.

HOMER: Were you concerned that she was absent?

AYAT: I definitely felt something was wrong . . .

HOMER: So what did you do?

AYAT: I asked if anyone knew where she was. No one did. *(She recognizes Homer's bag)* You still have that?

(Homer does not answer.)

It's been a long time . . .

HOMER: Ten years . . . So what did you do next?

AYAT: I called her parents.

HOMER: And if what I read is correct, no one answered?

(She nods. The bag falls off the table, onto the floor, a book falls out of the bag. Ayat spots it and picks it up.)

AYAT: Where did you get this?

HOMER: Your house.

AYAT: What?

HOMER: Your family gave me permission to enter your home . . . I am sorry. I was going to ask . . . I just couldn't believe you kept it.

AYAT: *The Odyssey*. You bought it at that little store in the old city. Published 1917 . . . and what a year that was . . .

HOMER: Balfour Declaration . . .

AYAT *(Reading her old inscription)*: "To Ayat from Homer." You can have it.

HOMER: What happened after you called Iman's parents?

AYAT: Almost immediately after that, I heard screaming.

HOMER: What did you do?

AYAT: I ran outside like everyone else.

HOMER: What did you see?

AYAT: I heard you came to Palestine over the years but you never called Sameh and I. Why?

HOMER: And why are you still listening to Nina Simone.

(Ayat motions in surprise.)

. . . The albums were on your bedroom floor.

AYAT: Your favorite lady. I grew to love her, but I wish you could have sang Oum Khultoum instead.

HOMER: It's Nina's voice that kept you company all these years.

(Pause.)

What happened next?

AYAT: I heard gunfire. I saw blood.

HOMER: Bullets are tricky, you never see them fly or land.

AYAT: Death has a particular silence, it scrolls inside of you and when you are not watching . . . startles you . . . like love. Tell me. What does she look like?

HOMER: My daughter . . . Haya, she looks like me . . .

AYAT: I mean your wife . . .

HOMER: She is unlike anyone I know . . . So, Iman, the little girl, found herself in the military zone?

AYAT: She did.

HOMER: And Sameh ran after her?

AYAT: Yes.

HOMER *(Pulls out a picture from his jacket)*: Remember . . . *(Shows her the picture)* . . . the three of us on Mount Carmel . . . I can't believe he's dead . . . Do you miss him?

AYAT: Do you?

HOMER: I have been writing him a letter for ten years. He always told me, "You are the only Palestinian I know called Homer."

AYAT: But always said it was a name meant for you. The son of a literary man who loved the classics . . .

AYAT AND HOMER *(Simultaneously)*: "It all goes back to the Greeks, everything goes back to the Greeks."

HOMER: Yes, my father said that all the time.

AYAT *(Smiles)*: And you, Homer . . . also became a man who chose words, who chose journeying . . .

(Brief pause.)

Sameh loved you.

HOMER: He was like a brother to me—

AYAT: It tortured him that you didn't stay in touch.

(Pause.)

We couldn't wait to see our Palestinian friend from New York each year . . .

HOMER: Eighteen summers together . . . we were close . . . maybe too close.

AYAT: Is there such a thing?

(Pause.)

Your wife, what's her name?

HOMER: Why?

AYAT: I want her name . . .

HOMER: I'm married to a woman I don't know. Our only bridge is our daughter. We stay together because we have nowhere else to go.

AYAT: Even love is occupied . . .

HOMER: Why did you marry Sameh?

AYAT: You left.

HOMER: "Left"?

AYAT: *You* left me, went back to New York.

HOMER: I left only after I saw you with him . . .

AYAT: What?

HOMER: I never saw him happier. I couldn't take that away from him.

AYAT: We grew to resent each other.

HOMER: Why didn't you come that afternoon?

AYAT: I was there.

HOMER: I waited all afternoon. All evening. And the following morning. You weren't there.

AYAT: I got your note, it read, "Meet me at Yaffa Gate."

HOMER: I never sent you a note.

AYAT: I don't understand.

HOMER: I never sent you a note. I was waiting for you under that orange tree near Abu Moussa's house . . . I told your sister Salwa to tell you.

AYAT: Salwa didn't . . .

(Pause, Ayat reflects.)

Oh God, it was Sameh?

HOMER: Sameh?

AYAT: I went to Yaffa Gate looking for you and saw Sameh. He told me his heart was beating because I was there. I didn't know what he meant but I was angry at you so I agreed to . . .

HOMER: Marry him?

AYAT: Go for a walk with him . . . That same week I heard you went to back to the U.S.

HOMER: I came the next day to ask why you didn't come, that's when I saw Sameh holding you.

AYAT: So what did you want to tell me that day?

(He moves close to her and they kiss passionately.)

HOMER: I am going to get you out of here.

AYAT: Out?

HOMER *(With enthusiasm)*: I'll get you better representation.

AYAT: How?

HOMER: Trust me.

(They kiss.)

AYAT: Homer, I belong here.

HOMER: I am not leaving without you this time.

(Loud knock.)

We have to act now . . .
AYAT: Homer, listen to me.

(Ayat goes close to Homer and makes him sit, gives him his pen and motions for him to write. He listens and starts to write. At times while Ayat is speaking he stops, but she motions for him to continue.)

I can still hear the screams . . . I ran outside. Ran towards the crowd. It was her. Iman, thirteen. She was thirteen. Sixteen bullets. Sixteen. Three in her head. One in the right side, beside her ear. One went from the back of her neck to the chin. Damaged the area under her mouth. The rest all over her body—chest, hands, arms, legs. She was thirteen. Sixteen bullets. At close range . . . The commander then put his weapon on automatic and emptied it into her corpse . . .
HOMER: Where was Sameh?
AYAT: She was in her school uniform. Her school bag on her shoulder. Who knows why she wandered into the forbidden zone . . . By the time she got to the hospital, she had no more blood in her body.
HOMER: And Sameh?
AYAT: I did not see him anywhere. I started running. Calling out his name. I heard someone saying, *"Hon. Hon."* . . . I knew it was him.
HOMER: What happened?
AYAT: When Sameh saw Iman entering the forbidden zone, he ran after her, calling out her name, "Iman Iman Iman," but she didn't hear.
HOMER: They thought this was some kind of planned attack . . .
AYAT: All I know is a soldier identified a small figure one hundred yards from the fortified tower as "a little girl . . . running defensively . . . scared to death."
HOMER: And they still started shooting . . .
AYAT: At her and then at Sameh.
HOMER: What happened then?
AYAT: Homer . . . I did not help him.
HOMER: You did.

(Homer stands up.)

AYAT: No . . .

HOMER: I'm sure you did everything you could.

AYAT: He stopped me.

HOMER: From what?

AYAT: One bullet hit him, he could have survived. *But* he told me he wanted to choose his death. That he would rather die in my . . . arms than go to an Israeli prison. He knew he would be jailed for supposedly harassing that soldier or preparing an assumed attack . . . and if they didn't jail him they would kill him.

HOMER: What are you saying? He was shot.

AYAT: I did not help him. I could have saved him.

HOMER: *Khalas.* Please.

(They face each other.)

You did nothing. You'll be freed.

AYAT: What is freedom?

HOMER: Freedom is when we catch life between our lips . . .

(A knock on the door. The lights fade.)

END OF PLAY

Glossary

Ahlan. Tfadal   "Welcome. Please step in."

Balfour Declaration   "In November 1917, Arthur James Balfour, British secretary of state for foreign affairs, sends a secret letter to Baron Lionel Walter de Rothschild, a British Zionist, seeking Jewish support in the war. The Balfour Declaration promises a national home for Jews in Palestine and protection of the civil and religious rights of 'non-Jewish' inhabitants." (From, Jayyusi, Salma Khadra, ed., *Anthology of Modern Palestinian Literature*, New York: Columbia University Press, 1992, p. xxvi.) The Palestinians rejected the Balfour Declaration, and as Jewish immigration to Palestine increased, strife arose.

Haya   "Life" (also spelled *hayat*).

Khalas   "Stop talking" or "enough."

Mamluk   The Mamluk dynasty extended from 1250–1517. Mamluk buildings are distinctive for the lightness of their design. Arched entrances, red, white and black striped masonry, geometric arabesques and decorative use of Kufic lettering contribute to their beauty.

Oum Khultoum   A very famous Egyptian singer whose funeral attracted four million mourners. Called the "Star of the East," she has a museum dedicated to her in Cairo, and still sells more than a million recordings yearly throughout the Middle East (also spelled *Umm Kulthoum*).

Rafah   The largest Palestinian town in the Gaza strip. It is located on the borders between Gaza and Egypt.

Shukran	"Thank you."
Yaffa Gate	The only gate on the western side of the Old City, built by Sulayman in 1538. It is called "Yaffa Gate" because it leads toward Yaffa, an important seaport town.

NATHALIE HANDAL has been involved as a writer, director or producer for more than twenty theatrical and film productions worldwide. Recent credits include: *Hakawatiyeh* (writer, The John F. Kennedy Center for the Performing Arts, Washington, D.C.); *The Stonecutters* (playwright, Loews Theatre, New York City); *La Cosa Dei Sogni* (playwright, The Public Theater, New York City); *Between Our Lips* (playwright, Blue Heron Theatre; The Public Theater's "New Work Now!" festival); *The Details of Silence* (playwright, Symphony Space, New York City; Claudia Cassidy Theatre, Chicago); *Hi Joan!* (director, TBG Arts Center, New York City; Hudson Mainstage Theatre, Los Angeles); *Grenade* (director, Upstairs at the Laugh Factory, New York City) and *Before We Start* (director; Kraine Theatre, New York City). She has worked in local New York television as the co-host of a literary show, is a member of Nibras, co-founder of PTheatre in Motion, and Associate Artist and Development Executive for the production company the Kazbah Project.

Handal finished her MFA in Creative Writing at Bennington College and her MPhil in English and Drama at University of London. She also studied theatre and drama in France, Russia and Latin America.

She is the author of the poetry collections *The Neverfield* (1999), *The Lives of Rain* (shortlisted for The Agnes Lynch Starrett Poetry Prize/The Pitt Poetry Series, 2005), *Love and Strange Horses* (University of Pittsburgh Press, due out 2010), and the poetry recordings *Traveling Rooms* (1999) and *Spell* (2006). She is the editor of *The Poetry of Arab Women: A Contemporary Anthology* (Academy of American Poets bestseller and winner of the PEN Oakland/Josephine Miles Award) and co-editor of *Language for a New Century: Contemporary Poetry from the Middle East, Asia & Beyond* (W. W. Norton, 2008). Her work has been translated into more than fifteen languages, and she has been featured on NPR, KPFK and PBS Radio and Television. She was named an honored finalist for the 2009 Gift of Freedom Award.

Currently, she is part of the production team for the feature film *Gibran*. She is in residence at New York Theatre Workshop, working on her new play *The Oklahoma Quartet*.

Heather Raffo's

9 Parts of Desire

Author's Statement

This play was inspired by a life-changing trip I made to Iraq in 1993. It was only a few years after the first Gulf War ended, and I was longing to see my family. To my childhood memory Baghdad was the magical place I had been as a little girl and where I'd slept on the roof of my grandmother's house under the stars. But since the gut-wrenching war, Baghdad was simply where more than fifty of my immediate relatives still lived.

It would be my first time back to Iraq as an adult. The only way into Iraq at this time was by bus across the desert, a seventeen-hour trip in total from Amman, Jordan. When I reached the Iraqi border, everyone from my bus got into the line for "Middle Easterners" except me. To them I was classified as "other" so I had to go down a long hallway into a back room. There was a man behind a desk, he opened my passport, looked at me, then back down at the passport. He got up, walked all the way across the room and shook my hand. He said, "Welcome to your father's country. We hope you take back a good impression of the Iraqi people. Know our people are not our government. Please be at home here and when you return tell your people about us."

Seven hours later I was in Baghdad hugging all fifty members of my father's extended family. They called me their daughter. They fought over who would cook me dinner and whose house I would visit first. I was like an orphan finding her family on that trip, soaking up every story about their lives and how my father grew up. I saw buildings my grandfather and great-grandfather had carved from marble; I saw the house my father grew up in as a child; and I saw the obvious destruction of the country. Across the street from my uncle's house was a pile of rubble: a neighbor's house, casualty of a stray bomb. I visited the Amiriyya bomb shelter where many Iraqi civilians lost their lives when the shelter became a target in the 1991 war. I went to the Saddam Art Center, the modern art museum of Baghdad, and saw rooms and rooms of billboard-sized portraits of Saddam Hussein. Then I wandered into a back room and there was a haunting painting of a nude woman clinging to a barren tree. Her head was hanging, bowed, and there was a golden light behind her, like a sun. I stood motionless in front of the painting. The painting was titled *Savagery*.

This painting would prove to be an inspiration to me for many years to follow. When I first thought of writing about Iraq I began by researching the painting. The artist had been killed by an American air raid in June 1993, a few months before I saw the painting hanging in the Saddam Art Center. It was a national tragedy, a beloved female artist and curator of the museum, killed by an American bomb. I knew I would never meet her, but I wanted to talk to other Iraqi artists who were her contemporaries. One by one I was introduced to Iraqi women who had lived through more than I could imagine. Along the way *9 Parts of Desire* would come to include a multitude of women's stories. They shared so deeply of themselves and seemed to tell me almost anything, but only after I shared as much of myself with them. My process was not one of formal interviews, but rather a process of spending time together living, eating, communicating compassion- ately and loving on such a level that when I parted from their homes it was clear to all that we were now family. When an Iraqi woman trusts you it is because she has come to love you and that has been the process of finding and forming these stories.

With rare exception, these stories are not told verbatim. Most are composites and, although based in fact, I consider all the women in my play to be dramatized characters in a poetic story. I liken it to songwriting—I listened deeply to what each woman said, what she wanted to say but couldn't, and what she never knew how to say. Then I wrote her song.

Production History

Heather Raffo's *9 Parts of Desire* was originally produced by Erich Jungwirth, Voice Chair Productions; Richard Jordan, Richard Jordan Productions, Ltd. It had its world premiere at the Traverse Theatre in Edinburgh in 2003 and later moved to the Bush Theatre in London. Heather Raffo performed the play, which was directed by Eva Breneman. Set and costume design were by Amanda Ford. Lighting design was by Tyler Micoleau.

9 Parts of Desire had its New York premiere at Manhattan Ensemble Theater (Dave Fishelson, Artistic Director) in 2004. Heather Raffo performed the play, which was directed by Joanna Settle. Set design was by Antje Ellermann. Lighting design was by Peter West. Original music and sound design were by Obadiah Eaves. Costume design was by Mattie Ullrich. The production stage manager was Lisa Gavaletz.

Special thanks to Geraldine Brooks for the inspiration of her book Nine Parts of Desire.

Characters

MULLAYA
LAYAL
AMAL
HUDA
THE DOCTOR
IRAQI GIRL
UMM GHADA
THE AMERICAN
NANNA
UNCLE (voice-over)

Note

Throughout the play the woman uses an *abaya*, a traditional black robelike garment, to move from character to character. Some wear the *abaya* traditionally; others use it as a prop.

A double em dash (———) indicates a moment when the ideas driving the language come so close to the surface that the character finds herself in a moment of powerful lucidity.

A glossary of select terms appears at the end of the play.

The first sound we hear is the dawn call to prayer. In Muslim countries the call to prayer is heard five times a day: at dawn, at midday, in the afternoon, at sunset and, finally, when the sky becomes dark and daytime is over. The call to prayer is heard five times in the course of this play.

The Mullaya walks on stage carrying a great bundle on her head. She empties her load of shoes into the river. Traditionally a Mullaya is a woman in Arab culture hired to lead call-and-response with women mourning at funerals. She is considered very good if she can bring the women to a crying frenzy with her improvised, heartbreaking verses about the dead. Mythic, celebratory and inviting, this Mullaya's mourning is part of her ritual ablutions.

MULLAYA:
> Early in the morning
> early in the morning
> I come to throw dead shoes into the river
>
> without this river there would be no here
> there would be no beginning
> it is why I come
>
> Take off your slippers
> take off your sandals

take off your boots
appease the hungry
so I can sleep beneath the stars without fear
of being consumed
or

the river again will flood
the river again will be dammed
the river again will be diverted
today the river must eat.

When the grandson of Genghis Khan
burned all the books in Baghdad
the river ran black with ink.
What color is this river now?
It runs the color of old shoes
the color of distances
the color of soles torn and worn
this river is the color of worn soles.

This land between two rivers
I only see the one—
where is the other river
more circular and slow?
Why only this one straight and fast?
Where is the other?
And the other land?
Where is anything they said there would be?
We were promised so much
the garden of—

Let me tell you I have walked across it
Qurna, Eridu, Ur
the Garden of Eden was here
its roots and its rivers
and before this garden
the chaos and the fighting
loud and angry children—
the dark sea lies beneath my country still
as it has always done
sweet and bitter water, children of Nammu.

But our marshlands now are different
they've been diverted, damned and dried
I have walked from there to here
from the flood
to the highway of death
collecting, carrying
you can read the story
here it is, read it all here
on my sole.

My feet hurt
I have holes in my shoes
I have holes now even in my feet
there are holes everywhere
even in this story.

I don't want new shoes!
I would rather swim than walk—
bring me back the water I was created in
the water in which I woke each morning
and went to bed each night
the water in which I swam to school
and milked the buffalo
and listened to the loud voices of frogs
bring me back the marshes and the fishes
reed man, reed woman
I would rather swim than walk—
and now the river has developed an appetite for us
its current runs back
beneath Iraq
to where Apsu and Tiamat are cradling still
underneath my country
there is no paradise of martyrs
only water
a great dark sea
of desire
and I will feed it
my worn sole.

(*Layal, an artist, wears the* abaya *loosely hanging off.her shoulders like a dressing gown or painting smock. She is sexy and elegant, a resilient and fragile woman. She is a daredevil with a killer smile.*)

LAYAL:

Leave Iraq? *(She giggles oddly as she tries to imagine it)*
Well, I could move I suppose—

My sister wants me to come to London
she has a house and an art studio there now
I could go I have the money.

I don't know
maybe I feel guilty
all of us here
it's a shame if all the artists leave, too—
who will be left to inspire the people if all the
artists and intellectuals run?
Most of them already have,
my sister included.

I don't judge
I mean for most
they feel they cannot express themselves
because always it is life and death—
even I should have been dead twice before I tell you
but I'm not
death is only teasing me. *(She laughs)*
Maybe that's it, maybe I stay because
I feel lucky, I am charmed, what can touch me?

Besides, what's to paint outside Iraq?
Maybe I am not so good artist outside Iraq?

Here my work is well known
hardly anyone will paint nudes anyway
but this is us
our bodies—isn't it?
Deserted
in a void
and we are looking for something always
I think it's light.

Always I fight to keep
transparency
because once it goes muddy I can't get it back.

It's not oil, with oil you just paint over what you've done
with oil, light is the last thing you add
but with watercolor, white
is the space you leave empty from the beginning.

I think I help people maybe
to be transcending
but secretly.
Always I paint them as me
or as a tree sometimes like I was telling you.
I do not ever want to expose exactly another woman's body
so I paint my body
but her body, herself inside me.
So it is not me alone
it is all of us
but I am the body that takes the experience.
Your experience, yourself, I will take it
only you and I will know who it is
and the others let them say
oh Layal, again she is obsessed with her body. *(She laughs again)*

I did a painting once of a woman
eaten by Saddam's son
that's how I describe it.
A beautiful young student from University of Baghdad.
Uday, he asked her out, she couldn't refuse,
he took her and beat her brutally, like is his way—
she went back to campus and
her roommate saw the bruises and things and asked her,
"What happened?"
And she so stupid, innocent girl told her the truth.
Why she talks such things?
Iraqis they know not to open their mouth
not even for the dentist.
Of course, Uday, he took her back
with his friends, they
stripped her
covered her in honey
and watched his Dobermans eat her.

See in my painting she is the branch's blossom
leaning over the barking dogs

they cannot reach
no matter how hungry they are
not unless they learn to climb her
but they are dogs, they never will.

You see, nobody knows the painting is her
but I believe somewhere she sees.

That is me, *(Laughing)* my philosophy!
These stories are living inside of me
each woman I meet her or I hear about her
and I cannot separate myself from them
I am so compassionate to them, so attached—*la, la,* it's the opposite
maybe I am separate, so separate from the women here
I am always trying to be part of them.
I feel I could have been anybody if I looked different—

Some other artists more senior than myself
would have hoped to be curator of Saddam Art Center
these jobs they are hard to come by and
it takes a lot to get them.
Always they make a rumor of me
I got this position because I was having an affair
at that time they said
with Saddam's cousin—
they can believe what they like
I don't care what people say.
Anyway he's dead now of course
this cousin
a mysterious plane crash
you see?

If—
If I'd had an affair with him
how would that have made my life any easier?
Isn't everything in this country a matter of survival?
I don't care if you are with the government
or a prisoner of it.
Even loving
just the simple act of loving
can make you suffer so deeply.

So if I am now in a position of grace, favor, rumor
so be it
I don't care
I am still trying
to be revealing something
in my trees, my nudes, my portraits of Saddam—

I fear it here
and I love it here
I cannot stop what I am here
I am obsessed by it
by these things that we all are but we are not saying.
"Either I shall die"—how does it go?
Oh my favorite, Shaharazad! *(An aching giggle)* "Either I shall die
or I shall live a ransom for all the virgin daughters of Muslims
and the cause of their deliverance from his hands to life!"

Well, I am not a person of great sacrifice
I have sacrificed in my life, sure,
but nothing like what I see around me.
Anyway that is life. You cannot compare only be compassionate.
I try to have understanding of all sides, and I have compassion
just not enough.

I'm a good artist.

I'm an okay mother.

I'm a miserable wife.

I've loved yes, many
but
not enough.

But I am good at being naked
that's what I do, in secret.

*(Bright, festive and robust, Amal is a woman of thirty-eight who looks
so intently at whomever she is talking to you would swear her eyes
never blinked. She asks many questions; she really thinks there is an
answer out there for her. Amal wears the* abaya *fastened behind her
head and flowing voluptuously about her body.)*

AMAL:
I see with my heart
not with my eyes.
I am Bedouin
I cannot tell you if a man is fat or if a man is handsome
only I can tell you if I love this man or not.
I think you see with your heart like a Bedouin.

I do, I very much feel this void
I have no peace
always I am looking for peace.
Do you know peace?
I think only mens have real peace
womans she cannot have peace
what you think?

My mother, when I come home, she is so happy to see me
she sing to me
she sing, "Amal my beautiful girl
Amal whose hair is black like night
Amal whose eyes are black like deep coal
Amal my daughter whose body is strong for her love"—
and my voice, I have to sing to my mother, "I am home again!"
But never I think I am different
we in our village we believe our mothers.
I have *tis`ah*—nine brothers and five sisters
and nobody make me feel fat.
But I learn now I am big.
So don't you think I am fat?
La, la, I am very big
but I am diet now and my childrens, too
both my childrens they are diet.
Aa, aa I have two childrens
fourteen and eight.

My husband, first husband, he was Saudi,
he is now in London
on this big road they call it
where all the big plastic surgeons are.

Aa, aa, I was there with him
I like London very much

I study there
I like to
walk with my friends in this Portobello market and—

I left him.
I was feeding my daughter, Tala, at the time
and driving my son, Omar, to school
I forgot some papers for Omar
so I drove back home to get them
and I saw my husband in bed with my very close friend
and really I am shock
because he is Bedouin,
but Saudi Bedouin.
And even he would say to me when I talked
during our relations
he'd say, "Don't say these things they are dirty things."
I wanted to enjoy myself with him
but he—
and then he goes and—

So
I didn't say anything.
I told a friend
go into my house
and get my passport and the childrens passport
and I left.
I never told him why I left.

I came back to Iraq
but I didn't like to live in our town
it's too small, I don't feel free even,
always my brothers looking out for me I feel too much closed
and so I come—
not here, *la*, I—

I went to Israel first.

You see, our very close tribesman came to visit
because my father he is the sheik.
This tribesman, he is of the same Bedouin tribe as me
but born Israeli—
and always when I was a girl I thinking

oh to marry one from my tribe
we have the same accent, same eyes, same nature, very big heart!
This tribesman he never feel the woman his enemy
he feel sorry for her and feel only to keep her happy
and the woman she feels him very man—
we are very special together
so I marry him, my second marriage,
and I went to his village in Israel.

He promise me
we would move and go to Europe somewheres or Canada
but then we never move
his wife didn't want
aa, his other wife, number one, she makes him stay.
He would have taken both of us
it could have been good
but she was crazy
really she was, I think they fight a lot.
Number one, she would leave him to go to her father's house
for six months at a time and I taking care of her eight childs.
I mother one of her childs
I fed her son—oh Qur'an, you must know it—
if you feed for more than seven days, full feeding,
that child is like your child
and this child must never marry with your child
because now they are brother and sister in the milk
so it is *haram*, sin,
because they have your blood inside them both.
But wife, number one, she was very skinny, not well
she would go away for such a long times—
we couldn't live together like this
he is very jealousy man, very Bedouin
and I am looking for this freedom
and he says, "No, we are not going to Canada."
So I care very much for him, but again
I left.

I come back to Iraq with my children
but to Baghdad to be in city.
I come here, and my family don't like
they don't support me but—

I got some money.
I got some money from a friend of
my first ex-husband, this friend, his name's Sa`ad.
And we start to talk on the phone, this friend, Sa`ad,
he is in London, and me here. We talk for one year.
I talk to him honest, I am very honest person
I told him exactly I am thirty-eight, and this is how I look.
I hide nothing from him
I told him everything in my heart
everything I hope and
I felt peace.
It is beautiful to talk so much
because he
he tells me from inside himself too
very deep, very sincere
for one year.
I felt safe the first time in my life
I felt myself with this man and
I love him! *(She laughs)*

We talk and we say we will get married, third marriage, oh!
He says let us meet in Dubai
because the war it was then and if he comes back home to Iraq
they may keep him.

So I left my job, I left everything.
I telephone to his family congratulations
he telephone to my family
and we go to meet in this hotel in Dubai
we go to dinner
he says after dinner,
"I am going I will call you later,"
and I waiting in my hotel room so happy to see this man I love.
I telephone hims at two A.M. and he says, "No, not now
I am drunk"—
I say, "Let us talk I want to talk
we spent one year on the phone talking everything
finally we see each other
my heart is so full to share"—
He says, "No Amal,
no," he says, "it is over
do not talk to me anymore."

I am crying really I don't understand him say this thing
but him say,
"You are too pure for me
what you do with a man like me? I am twenty year older than you
soon I will be very olds man and you have to take care of me
you are too good, too innocent for me."
I don't understand hims say this thing because I love him,
and him says, "No,
no," he say,
"you are not the Amal I love."

What does this mean?
I am not the Amal he love?

How he say this?
Why can this be?

I am shamed to my family
they think he slept with me that night
we meet in Dubai
and change his mind.

I don't have peace.

Always I am asking myself what he think of me?
What he seed in me that change him?
I see now I am fat.
Now I look for the first time to dress myself more pretty
I am doing my hair this way,
but I don't see hims fat, I don't see hims old
I see hims with my heart not with my eyes
and never have I love a man this much.
Even I love him.
Even.

My ex-husband, first one,
got us passports to bring the children to London
so they will see their father on the weekends
and have their schooling there
la, la, I think I told you this already.
But always I am thinking
I will have my freedom there
but not my peace.

Maybe freedom is the better than peace?

——

I have never talked this before
nobody here knows this thing about me
I keep it in my heart only
oh, I talk a lot!

I wish to be like this *(She laughs)*

I want to be like you
this is the most free moment of my life
really I mean this
oh really I love you, like a sister I love you
the most free moment of my life.
Don't leave, stay with me
oh I need to talk every day this way.
Is this American way?
Tell me what you think
what should I do?
I want to memorize what you say,
so I can be this way
freedom again.

But what do think he means, I am not the Amal he love?

(A whiskey drinker and fifty years a smoker, Huda is an Iraqi exile in her seventies, now living in London. She has a keen sense of humor.)

HUDA:
Well, exile in London for the intellectuals
is mostly scotch, of course, politics and poetry
it used to be Gauloises, too, but I have given up smoking, well—
Anyway, I tell you our dilemma
some in the opposition praised America one hundred percent
they knew they were the only power
and the whole policy of the world was in their hands.
Personally, I had my doubts about American policy,
I felt they're making their own map of the Middle East,
still I preferred this chaos to the regime
because Saddam was the worst enemy to the people
than anybody else.

One summer, he beheaded seventy women for being prostitutes,
but he made them prostitutes.
Saddam's stooges, they'd kidnap a woman
just going from her car to her house,
and take her as a slave, sex slave,
or house slave when they were in their hideouts,
and when they'd finish with her
he would go to her family saying, "She is a prostitute,"
and he'd behead her and put her head in the street.
There was no law if you are a prostitute, you are beheaded.

And where are these killers now?
For three decades Saddam created monsters.
No one is born knowing how to behead—they learned torture
he took ordinary men, they were forced to watch videos
to cut off a hand, a tongue.
These men cannot now be liberated
for them there is no peace
they cannot stop killing.

Maybe it's the only way
but
still I am
for this war.
I protested all my life, I was always political
even I was bourgeois—
in '58 anybody who was intelligent was Communist.
When I lived in Beirut during their war I protested, too,
everywhere I go there is a war. *(She laughs and hacks)*

I walked for peace in Vietnam,
I walked for Chile,
but this war it was personal, this war was against all my beliefs
and yet I wanted it.
Because Saddam
Saddam was the greater enemy than, I mean,
imperialism—

*(Nauseated, The Doctor throws up. She washes her hands, then dries
them on the* abaya. *Throughout, she is desperate to keep her hands
clean. Exhausted, she clings to the forensic.)*

THE DOCTOR:

I'm sorry, it's probably just the smell of the sewage backing up in the ward. I feel fine, fine, lets go on, it's just, it's so hot and the smell of it makes me—

(She yells offstage) Would somebody come clean this shit up before I slip in it!

Damn it! I lost her. The baby should be dead, not her. God she had enough, she had three girls at home, but she insisted, hoping for a boy. What am I supposed to tell her husband? Here, it's your first born son, I'm sorry he has two heads?

More than ultrasound, incubators, Panadol, anything, I need some—who can I ask? Look, just this month, I'll tell you, I've started counting: six babies no head, four abnormally large heads, now today another one with two heads. Such high levels of genetic damage does not occur naturally. These things you see them in textbooks.

And the cancers, *la*, I've never seen them before in Iraq, girls of seven, eight years old with breast cancer. I told this girl, ten years old, she came in, she thought her breasts were developing but it was only on one side. It was the cancer. I told her it's okay, you can be like me, see how strong I am, I had breast cancer. She said, "I want to see it," so I showed her my scar, she hugged me. She thought she was developing. But it's toddlers even with breast cancer, more than one cancer in the same patient, whole families each one suffering from cancer.

And what can stop it? I mean the children, they play at the sites even when they're fenced off, they take the bullets to school to show their classmates what they collected from America. One came in wearing a bullet around his neck, a bullet tipped in depleted uranium around his neck.

Especially here in Basra, it's in the Shatt al-Arab, so it's in all the water, it's in the food, but if it's airborne like they say— haven't you noticed something? It could be depleted uranium, or chemicals that were released from the bombings during the Gulf War, but I can see something changed the environment—giant squash, huge tomatoes. They say the radiation in plants now is at eighty-four times the safety limit. But who can clean it? Ever? We will have this depleted uranium for what, four thousand years? How many generations is that growing up handicapped? I am afraid to see them when they're grown.

It's better maybe, death.

My husband says death is worse, *il-mawt yihrig il-glub*, death burns the heart. But I don't believe—

Most of our men are already deformed from the wars. My husband he sits at home without his legs. He can't make money sitting at home, what's left of the man, I can't even look at him now, he's my death sentence. I don't care, honestly I don't care what I say. I'm a little ashamed of myself but it sickens me. We won't survive it, I won't, I'm a doctor, if I can't do anything. I trained in England, we all trained in the West, I could have gone anywhere, I came back, you know what I'm talking about, we had the best hospitals in the Middle East, everyone was coming to us, and what are we now? We're the experiment.

Look at us
Look at us
Wayn Allah, wayn Allah?

(She is nauseated again.)

No I'm fine, I'm fine
I'm pregnant.

(The Iraqi Girl plays with the abaya, *wrapping it about her head like long luxurious hair and other times bundling it up to be her baby doll. However, we first catch her dancing with great abandon in her living room to a band like 'N Sync on her new satellite TV. The electricity suddenly goes off. She yells out something like: "Momma, the electricity is out! Momma, put the generator on! Momma, my video! 'N Sync!")*

IRAQI GIRL:

I hate my momma!
Baba, my father, he said I am smart
but Momma says I am stupid.

I have not been to school
since America came
"You are stupid," she say, "you don't need to go to school."
But I think she didn't like the soldiers cames to our school
they looked like 'N Sync, mostly Justin Timberlake,
and they made all the girls to laughing really hard
and since that day she won't let me go to school
because I waved to them.

So I never leave the house.
Even though I can speaks English better than anyone.
My grandparents were scared because they don't speaks English
and soldiers came knocking on their door speaking English
it was the night
but they didn't understand
so they ran to hide under their beds
and a tank—I think it was an Abrahams—
they ran the Abrahams into the house
and it took down half the house.
They were eighty years old my grandparents
but they didn't speaks English.

So even we are afraid to sleeps on the roof.
In the summer I used to
put my bed on the roof under the stars
and Baba, my father, he used to told me
all the stories of the stars began from Babylon—
It's just down the road past Saddam City—
no,
Sadr City.

We have so much problems on TVs.
On TVs I see suicide bombings,
not just for Baghdad but all over Iraq and I felt bad,
but my cousin Karem, he says, "No
these are not Iraqis.
Iraqis don't know how to kill themselves."

I think something must be a secret
because
now we can't go anywheres without
my uncle, Ammu Abdul,
he comes here with his sons, mostly Karem and Khalid,
because we have no men.
But even they haven't taken me to the swimming pool
for two summers now.
Maybe it's dry up?
My friend Lulu, she thinks the Americans are using it.

We don't go anywhere—
really!!!

Momma she doesn't even go to work anymore
she was "let off."
She never leaves the house
except to go to the market
with my uncle
and before she goes she covers her hair
she is afraid of getting stolen by gangs
now they steal women for money
or to sell them.
I try to tell Momma she won't get stolen
her hair is not that nice
they only steal people whose families have money.
But she says,
"Don't tempt your fates,
now they steal little girls to take them out of the country!"
Today I thought
maybe I should get stolens
so I could leave my country.

On TVs, on *Oprah*, I saw people
they have so many hard lives, at first we feel bad for them
but always by some miracles their things get better!
Today even they showed
Papa Saddam on TVs
and they look through his hair to make fun of him,
"Do you have lice in your hair?" That is always how we tease
in the school when we want to be the most cruel
to the poorest kids.
Do you have lice?
I don't know if he had lice
but to see it like that he looked like an old man
like a baby.
I felt sorry for him
but I didn't cry.
Momma, she cried.
She said, "Saddam stole my sons,
he stole my sons"—
I had three brothers who were bigger
I didn't really know them, they were martyrs,
she always says, "Saddam stole my sons"—
so maybe she cries to see him on TVs
thinking, Now he won't give their bones back?

Because she says,
"What now?"
"What now?"
"What now?"
She is very—

I am not stupid.
I count bombs even
I count between the
hissing when it is high
until the sound becomes low
then two seconds—and it explodes!
If I hear the hissing I know it's in our neighborhood
like in a few blocks
then I hear glass breaking for four seconds
after the hit.
I can tell if it is RPGs or American,
tank or armor vehicle,
Kalashnikov or M16
and I have bullets from both—
but I gave one to Karem, he made a key chain from the M16 bullet
because they are longer and, he says "more elegant."
We don't have a machine gun anymore.
Everybody on our street has maybe a pistol or machine gun
in case for troubles. Now we have a pistol. But only one.
Momma taught me how to use it.

I know I am not stupid.
I found my father's notebooks upstairs
hiding under the floor
he had some math books there and some notebooks
I took this one—
I look to it to keep my head busy
even though the maths are for people bigger than me.
And I can understand some of the maths.
But today
I read in his notebook
that "Sammura,"
that is me, it's dated 5 October 2002—
"Sammura my beloved was at school
and they asked her,
'Have you ever visited Babylon?'

And Sammura, she told them, 'Of course I've been,
even at night because
my father says Saddam put his name on the bricks of Babylon
but he cannot put his name on the stars over Iraq.'
They will arrest me now for this and I am sure to die.
I should have taught her how to lie."

———

I remember some mens came to our house
to take my father—they said
my *baba* is so smart about the stars over Babylon
our president, he needs him.
I have not seen him since I was seven.
Momma thought after the war with America
he might come home
but nobody seen him
and we haven't moved.
I still want to study because if he does come home
I have to be smarter than when he left.

Actually
I cried today, too,
when I saw Papa Saddam on TVs
because he stole my father so
I thought he was bigger than anyone
but he didn't even fight to death.
I felt ashames, because why I am afraid from him all my life?
Momma she is right
I am stupid.

(Umm Ghada lets the abaya *fall to the stage floor; the* abaya *becomes
a black hole at the center of a bomb shelter. She is a woman of great
stillness and pride, peaceful and dispassionate.)*

UMM GHADA:
I named my daughter Ghada.
Ghada means tomorrow.
So I am Umm Ghada, Mother of Ghada.
It is a sign of joy and respect to call a parent by their *kunya*.

In Baghdad, I am famous now as Umm Ghada
because I do live here in yellow trailer

outside Amiriyya bomb shelter
since the bombing
13 February 1991.

Yes I was inside
with nine from my family
talking, laughing
then such a pounding, shaking
everything is fire.
I couldn't find my children
I couldn't find my way out
but somehow I did.

In the whole day later
I am searching, searching charred bodies
bodies they were fused together
the only body I did recognize
is my daughter Ghada
so I did take her name *(With so much pride)*
I am Umm Ghada, Mother of Ghada.

I am hard to understand
why I survive
and my children dead.
I asked to Allah, "Why?
Why you make me alive?"
That night all people died
four hundred three people
and there's nothing we can do. They are dead.

This trailer is my witness stand
All photos on this wall—and here—are me
with emissaries from the world
who come to Amiriyya shelter to look
what really happen here
not what they read in papers
or see in the CNN.
Here is guest book they all sign,
your name will be witness, too.
La, I must show it to you first. *Ta`alu.*

(She enters the shelter. It is the first time we see her subtle limp.)

This is Amiriyya bomb shelter.
Here they write names
in chalk over the smoked figures.
Here, on the ceiling, you can see
charred handprints and footprints
from people who lay in the top bunks.
And here a silhouette of a woman
vaporized from heat.
This huge room became an oven,
and they pressed to the walls to escape from the flames.

In the basement, too
bombs burst the pipes
hot water came up to five feet
and boiled the people.

La, la, I do not want to show you there
it is too much—
the walls are stuck with hairs and skin.

Come, I will take you to the roof
you can see how the hole was made.

*(As she walks toward the hole in the roof we hear the midday call to
prayer off in the distance. She pauses briefly.)*

Two bombs from U.S. airplane
come to this point of the roof.
The first bomb is drilling bomb
drilled this hole
second one
come inside exactly same spot
and exploded in fires.

The U.S. said they thought this is
communication center for military.
Myself,
I think they were testing bomb.
these bomb had never been use before, but it is special
two-bomb design for breaking only a bomb shelter.
It is very purpose.
It is very purpose.

Now look around this hole
wild greens they are growing
life did choose to root
here in this grave of Iraqi people.

All my family is here, Ghada is here
so I am Umm Ghada, Mother of Tomorrow.
My full name is dead with them.

Come.
Now you sign the witness book.

(Layal picks up a paintbrush.)

LAYAL:

We have a story:
There is a restaurant with a sign,
"Come in, eat all you want,
free of charge
your grandson will pay the bill."
So a young man, a teenager,
he goes in
happy for the free meal,
he eats, and eats, and eats
when he is done eating all he wants
the waiter brings him a bill.
The young man says to the waiter,
"No, your sign says free of charge,
my grandson will pay the bill."
The waiter says, "Yes, indeed, sir,
but this—
this is your grandfather's bill." *(She laughs)*

My grandfather's bill!

You know my house was hit, from Bush's war, *aa, aa,*
I wasn't there, *il-hamdu lillah,*
but we lost everything, my paintings for the new exhibition
my family's things, everything.
That's why I'm living here, at my sister's house.
It was only eight houses from here—
this neighborhood they bomb, Mansur, can you believe it?

So how smart is this bomb
if it bomb a painter? *(She laughs)*
Maybe they think I am dangerous?

Maybe I am, I am attached like I will die if I leave.

I think you're dangerous.
Americans they are not so attached this way
they feel so free, even to be alone.
I am afraid to be alone
I don't want freedom—to be alone?
I don't care for it, I like protection
all I want is to feel it, love—

I am crazy for it,
I am hungry every morning like I have never eaten before,
and there is never enough to feed me
so when I find more
I risk everything for it
oblivion even, I don't care
I submit completely.
And still I am empty
I never feel worth
because I shouldn't be so hungry
because others are not so hungry
or they can control it—but I cannot control myself
I cannot keep my mind from flesh.

I tell you, even when I fell in love
not with my husband
after I was married
really I fell in love
it humiliated me
to finally see
how much of myself I could never be
and I hated it
not to be full
not to feel whole
it's the worst feeling this occupation
to inhabit your body but not to be able to live in it.

So I had an affair! *(She laughs)*
I let myself love him—

we were just a boy and a girl in art school
painting, drawing, very expressive
you can't imagine the freedoms
we had teachers from all over the world coming to Baghdad
I was very messy
and when my husband found out
he shot me.

I thought I was dead.

And even in the emergency room I was saying,
"No it was me
with the gun, it was me, it was an accident."
We never spoke about it
but he never stopped me from having an affair again!

I think
most women they must be so hungry
because they love with such a sacrifice
an aching
but I tell you,
when you're this way
so attached
always loving like you will die without something—
you love like an Iraqi woman! *(Laughing)* Shaharazad!
Oh Americans, they have this passion to save everything
because they have such a big footprint, they feel guilty.
They are a very handsome teenager
so tall and strong
passionate, selfish, charming
but they don't think.

You have
our war now
inside you, like a burden, like an orphan
with freedom, intelligence, all opportunity and choice
yet we tether you to something so old you cannot see it—
we have you chained
to the desert
to your blood
you carry it in you—it's lifetimes
and you fight your war to unchain yourself

you come back
you feel at home here
maybe different
maybe more than in your country—
but you hate us, too
because you cannot breathe
because we are not free—
you are not free, you love too much.
It's the same, all, anywhere you live
if you love like an Iraqi woman
if you love like you cannot breathe.

(Huddled, The American hasn't left her studio in New York City for days. She is glued to the TV.)

THE AMERICAN:

Now they're digging through mass graves with their bare hands
and one guy on TV I saw him
he found a pack of cigarettes
he said my brother smoked
this kind of cigarette
so this is my brother's body
and he took the bones with him
so he could bury them
what he thought
was his brother.

I've never seen men cry like that.

I watch my dad
try not to cry
because when he's watching TV
and it's green
nighttime footage of
bombs
he can recognize the street
and the neighborhoods
where all his family
lives
still.

I watch TV
looking for

faces
of our family
so all I do is cry.
But my dad he can't
so
he ends up choking and
making himself
sick.
I mean
he's lived here in the U.S.
for forty years
he plays golf
five times a week.
He's just sad
but contained
because you
can't
you just can't
watch it
on TV.
I'm on my knees usually
in the middle of my apartment
with my mom
on the phone
I'm watching
I'm holding a rosary
watching
CNN
I want to pray
but I don't have
words
so I say their names
out loud
Sati`
Zuhayr
Huda
Zuhira
Behnam
Rabab
over and over trying
to see them
alive

because we don't know
anything
we can't
call
we can't get through on the phones
still
and
now
now people are burying their dead in their backyard
in their garden
the football field
it's every day
a police station
my uncle Sati` lives in Baghdad next to a police station
uncle Zuhayr lives next to the airport
Ama Huda, next to the Palestine Hotel
Ama Zuhira, in Karada, Mount Lebanon
my cousin Maysoon she used to work for the UN
but the whole face got blown off, I'm reading on the bus—

They never forget ever.
They carry everything with them.
I mean everything they are, they're so attached like
great-grandparents, parents, children
it lives in them, walks with them
they can't let go
of anything
they hold it all inside them.
So when they cry
it's lifetimes
I've never seen anything like it.

HUDA:
I can't move
I am here in London now
this is where my husband died, in this house
and I didn't change a thing from that time
I kept the house the same,
his picture, everything.
I was invited to go back,
so many people I was working with have returned but
I have moved five times in my life—always fleeing

Baghdad, Lebanon, Istanbul, Baghdad again, anyway.
America offered me lots of money to go back
but I don't believe in this, some Iraqis
they are just selling themselves.

I said let the young ones living there
have a chance with the policies
but they are shell-shocked, all these girls
they're going backwards
they abandon their education and now, since the occupation,
now they are wearing the veils.
Their grandmothers are more liberated than them.

I am in a period of disheartenment everywhere.
Maybe I should be there.
I don't know what to do with myself now, I have doubts
yeah, well, about my whole life.
I don't feel I have achieved what I wanted, my potential.
The worst thing I fear most is this civil war.
Iraqis don't want to be cut up, to be separated.
Ya`ni, we had fine interrelations
my family married with the Shi`a, my husband was a Kurd
there was no segregation sort of thing, these people
they have been living together in this area for thousands of years.
If we want to sculpt a nation
we cannot hack away at it
without a plan for the human being.
Each moment is vital—

Iraqis still don't believe America is really there to help them.
I wanted, we all wanted Saddam to go during the Gulf War
that was our moment—the people made this big rebellion
sixteen of the eighteen provinces fell
and they were sure America would help them
then America turned its back. America made a no-fly zone
but when they saw Saddam going with his helicopters
to execute his own people
they allowed him to fly. It was a blood bath,
Saddam killed tens of thousands, trucks full,
and buried them just in mass graves.
If we had let the people get rid of him themselves
they would not now be so humiliated.

Then the worst thirteen years' suffering—
This what do you call it? *Hisar?* Embargo?
And it made Saddam stronger
and the country more backwards and religious,
and funny enough, Saddam he was never religious,
but when the middle class
were selling their books on the street in order to eat
they felt the whole world had abandoned them.
And this isolation mentality cannot now be changed suddenly
this thirteen years' embargo
just gave the fundamentalists their legitimacy.

And now they're controlling the country
and Saddam is the martyr?

No.
Even dead he is a savage.

I don't believe anymore in revolution, *ya`ni*
development must grow carefully, gradually, not suddenly
it has to grow more deep-rooted.
Even though I can say
we all can say,
Congratulations
the regime is gone.
Saddam is gone.

*(Nanna is an old, old woman, scrappy and shrewd; she has seen it all.
She is selling anything she can on the street corner. She wears the
abaya traditionally over her head so only her face and hands remain
showing. The afternoon call to prayer sounds in the distance.)*

NANNA:
    Hallo hallo
    you like to buy?
    These things very nice
    very old
    from good family.
    We have old—
    no
    not that old.
    Not ancient.

Shhh
not loud English—
you want
my head on
the side of the road?

I have for you
but
shhh.

You
should
fear
now
everyone
is Saddam—

looking—
what you are
your accent
your name
what you sell
where you get it
from who
what neighborhood
what your first name
you must be Shi`a
you must be Sunni
middle class— *(She makes a motion indicating having her throat slit)*

I tell you
everything I have
here's
stolen.
My name
my accent—
my own mother
wouldn't recognize me.
(Laughing) I'm not thief!
Chal chal alayya!
It's freedom to have!

Hallo hallo
you like to buy?
Very nice
from good family— *(She fails to make a sale)*

I have too much existence
I have lived through twenty-three revolutions
my life has been spared
if my life has been spared
to whom do I owe my debt?
I have so much to repay.
To whom do I owe my debt?

I give you
old
history old
shhh
from the beginning,
I saw from the beginning
the looting
peoples
bringing petrol,
and
burning
all
National Archives,
Qur'anic Library
all—
I saw a map
they knew what to take
they were told what to take
I followed
and nobody stopped me
then they burned them gone.
Our history is finished.
Sunni, Shi`a, Kurd,
Christian even, Jew—
if they take what we share
it is easier
to finish.

When I was young in the school
they had us to draw
our family tree—
my mother had a new dress
it's with ruffle and flowers
that I loved
and she wear it in the house
I think every day for many weeks.
So I draw my mother like a big flower
with ruffles.
My teacher say no
it is wrong before Allah
drawing her hair and her body showing—
I am disrespecting.
So I look to the other children and
they drawing only the fathers and grandfathers
because of the name line.

So I just erased her, my mother
it was only pencil.

THE AMERICAN:
Here
there's space
we throw our arms wide
amber alerts and
seven men get trapped underground
and we stop everything
we fly in engineers
to save
everything
we make a movie
we go on *Oprah*, we talk about it
like we are moving on
or maybe
we can't move on
but just one trauma we say:
Okay.
This can change you,
possibly
your psychology, for the rest of your life.

Okay.
But there's no one saying—

when their parents get
blown apart
in front of their eyes
or their sons
are kidnapped
trying to go to work
or hacked
to death
and there's a head in my *ammu*'s front yard—
or they survive
everything
over and over and over again for as many years as I've been alive
my cousins
who are, who could have been
the same as me
told me they wouldn't
get married
because if they
some day
saw a chance
to get out
they had to take it
and not look back.
They never stop looking back.
The three that escaped
they had to watch it on TV
the second war
they said maybe it's worse seeing it on TV
sick, they can't protect the family.
But my dad said
maybe it's better
for the future
but if we lose
just one
one
it won't be
worth it.

Behnam
Rabab
Ammar
Bashshar
Nassar
Luma

——

I should get out
get something to
eat.
I'm fat.
I should just go to the gym and run.
God I'm so stressed out
maybe
I should take a yoga class instead?

Anyway I can watch it at the gym.
People work out
to the war
on three channels.
They drink beer at the bar to the war.
I mean, I'm blond
I hear everything people say.
I can't stop
I wake up and fall asleep with the TV on
holding a rosary
watching—
I know
I should just
turn it off
but I won't
I hate it when people say
I don't watch
it
anymore
it depresses me
yeah
it depresses me
I can't
breathe—

I'm sick
my stomach
I can't get out of my—
it's a beautiful warm day
and I'm a cave.
I can't walk down the street
and see people smiling—
dragging bodies through the street
for the rest of my life
Iraqis are animals cheering, dragging bodies through the street.
But my family can't even leave their house
and I can't call
still
and we're
smiling
pointing
at
a man
naked
with a sandbag on his head
raped
with a chemical light, told to masturbate.
I cannot carry it
and they're
thumbs up
smiling
don't tell me
they didn't know
their job
not with smiling
every photo
they were
smiling.

How can I ever
go home again
and sit
in my *amma*'s kitchen
and say
I'm sorry
I'm sorry
I'm—

we just keep going
subway
rush rush
Christmas shopping
and
the war, it's all so heartbreaking don't you think?
I don't even know
hundreds of thousands?
How many Iraqis?
And
a woman actually turned to me
and said that
she said,
"The war, it's all so heartbreaking."
She was getting a pedicure.
I was getting a fucking pedicure.
I walk
I can't walk
down
the street
I want
New York to stop.
Why don't we count the number of Iraqi dead?

Why?

LAYAL:

Why are you here?

Don't look at me like that
always this pressure on me
I can't bear it—your look.

You tell me about freedom, about choice and possibilities,
then you look at me like a whore for choosing
to paint myself naked
and you look at me like a whore for choosing
to paint portraits of Saddam
and now you look at me like a whore for thinking, just thinking
to do this mosaic for the floor of the Rashid Hotel?
But what are you creating with your freedom?
I am more free than you.

You beg me to leave
to get out while I can, I am getting too involved
insisting I get out for my safety.

Why? What is safe? There is no safe.

I wish I were afraid
I am beyond afraid—
I am just running, running
straight into it
always like this I am running
since the day my husband shot me
because I should have been dead
but I wasn't—
So what am I?
Why am I alive?
To be made love to—passed around from one man to another
his cousin, his brother, the ministers of—
and now—

I am aware that I must die.
I am complicit. Where else can I go with my hate.
Who will protect me but the regime?
Always I run to them, I come crying, begging, take care of me
they need me to do it, oh they love me to run to them crying—
If I am not afraid then there is no feeling.

Your eyes say to me that I am a whore
their eyes say I am the most beautiful woman in Baghdad
I am their fountain
I have been raped and raped and raped and raped
and I want more
they see me, they recognize me for what I am
that is freedom
they will never kill me—

HUDA:
     —we just woke up
we heard a shot and gunfire and things and
we thought it would pass and something would happen
nothing—
we gathered all the friends, in the street you know

to see what's going to happen
and we never went back to our house—
this was the coup, 1963—it was a Friday.
They came with their Kalashnikovs and their boots and so on
going house by house arresting people.
I was held, eh, two and a half months,
my husband, four and a half months,
we were pro-Abd al-Karim Qasim, we were the leftist.
One hundred eighty thousand people
were just arrested from Baghdad and all the elite you know,
the artists and architects—everybody, intellectuals—
we were Communist then but not violent
the Ba`thist only took us because we disagreed.

The prison status was terrible
we stayed lying on the floor
only lying like sardines. We were naked.
I remember one woman she got her period.
You know what they do when a woman gets her period?
They hang her upside down naked
her blood runs on her, for her whole cycle like that, upside down.
Anyway. That was that.

The fearsome thing was that every night at sort of two o'clock
we heard the gates and chains opening
and they'd call a list of women and they'd take them and
they wouldn't come back.
We could hear things, all night, always rape,
or rape with electronic instruments.
But their way, I promise you, their way
was to torture the people close to you
that is how they'd do it.
One woman I was with
they brought her baby, three-months-old baby, outside the cell
they put this woman's baby in a bag with starving cats
they tape-recorded the sound of this and of her rape
and they played it
for her husband in his cell.
That is how they do it.

So how these people could have liberated themselves?

Anyway, nightmare.

When we got out of jail we made passports, fake passports,
and we fled across the desert with our wet clothes on our back.
I did washing
but we didn't wait to dry them. *(She laughs and hacks)*

Myself, too, it takes a lifetime to be liberated.

Okay, are you hungry? I'm having another whiskey. *(She pours
    herself another drink)*

You think the people don't want liberation?
Every day they risk their lives just to go to work
to school
the children even
they leave the house and don't know if they'll come back—
my brother patrols his street at night, at sixty-seven
he cannot get a visa to get out
and yet anyone can get in.
For every martyr who comes in
there are two hundred more
waiting in line
desperate to risk everything
to take his place.
How many Iraqis have died?
Protect them, empower them.
Otherwise to live like this it is not liberation it is masochism.

*(A loud bombing raid; everything is shaking. Layal is screaming into
the phone:)*

LAYAL:
When is this going to stop?

I don't care what time it is
Why don't you do something about it?
I hear the sounds—something—like it's in my house
and I can't make it through another one.

La, targets!
How they blow up a house in this neighborhood?

This is a rich neighborhood
and they say it is an accident?
No, it is on purpose or stupidity!
How they do it?
Why my house?
I feel like an animal every time I hear that sound.
I am tired, I want my house back—

No, I am sorry.

No, eh—
of course it's late, your wife, she's next to you
I'm just, I am angry and I don't know where to be in this.

No, my husband he sleeps upstairs
he can sleep through anything.

Don't ask me now again.
I told you I don't know how to do mosaic—
I am a painter, why he wants me?
I don't know how.

La, don't tell him I don't want to do it—just tell him
I am not so good at it
I have no knowledge for mosaic.
Okay, I think about it
I'm just angry now and
why can't you do something?

Oh
not tonight I mean—

No of course, I think of you
I'm
I'll come tomorrow
Okay.
At your office
Okay.
Fine. Fine. Fine. *(She hangs up the phone)*

Shahryar!

I said yes to the mosaic.

(A man's voice on a telephone answering machine cuts in. He is loud and urgent. It is The American's uncle calling her from Baghdad.
  First phone call:)

UNCLE:
  (Voice-over:)
  Hallo Hallo Hallo
  I am your uncle calling from Baghdad.
  We have tried to phone you since Tuesday.
  We are very sorry—

THE AMERICAN:
  It's just his beautiful broken English
  he calls me his heart's
  daughter
  my uncle Behnam
  trying
  to reach me
  for three days
  they saw the dust and the papers blowing
  everything they saw New York on TV.
  He called to say
  he was sorry
  can you believe that?
  Sorry for my great city
  hopes this never happens again—
  all the family
  worried sick about me.
  And
  my mom's family in Michigan
  they all called my parents in Michigan to see if I was okay
  I know they love me but
  they didn't call me personally
  and my Iraqi family are calling from halfway around the world
  calling New York
  they didn't stop until
  they heard my voice.

  Our last conversation
  was before the bombs started in Baghdad

I finally got through to my aunt
and I'm screaming into the phone,
"I'm calling from New York—"

(Second phone call:)

UNCLE:

(Voice-over:)
Hallo Hallo Hallo
we have tried to phone you since Tuesday
we are very sorry to hear this terrible things happen.
Our family worry about you—

(Layal rushes to the phone to answer it.)

LAYAL:

Hallo! Hallo! Sabah? *Habibti!* My daughter!
Shlonich?
Aa, aa, fine, fine we are okay, okay,
how are you?

Aa, aa, I know our phones they don't work for sure. *(She laughs)*

I'm calling for three week but we couldn't get through
oh *habibti*, my daughter, I kiss you, I hold you, oh, I miss you
I miss you, *habibti*
I miss you—

La—don't come home
not this summer.
Stay
take some summer classes or,
why not go to your aunt's house in London? *Aa?*

La, la—
It's, getting sort of
well it's getting very hot already and, eh
the air condition is broken
we are old-fashioned now, even me, who can believe it?

Sabah, it is too hot for you to come home!

(The line is cut off.)

Sabah? Hallo?
Hallo?
Sabah?
Sabah?

(Devastated, Layal drops the phone.
  Third phone call:)

UNCLE:
(Voice-over:)
Hallo Hallo
We are very sorry to hear this terrible things happen.
Our family worry about you.
We hope you are always well
and wish you all the happiness.
Again we are deeply deeply sorry
and hope this will never happen again.
We love you very much.
All the family does love you.
We are waiting for you to visit us.
You must come and visit us.
It is very hard for us to come to you
but you must come here
and visit us.
And you must bring your father
and you must bring your mother
and you must bring your brother.
We are waiting for you—
we miss you very much, all the family,
your uncles and aunts with their children
and we love you—
we are waiting for you.

THE AMERICAN:
"I'm calling from New York!" I'm screaming into the phone,
our last call before the bombs started and
my *amma* Ramza finally picks up the phone
the first thing she says to me
clear as English is,
"Go to church and pray,"

her only other English is I love you
I love you
habibti, habibti
I love you
I love you
I love you
I love you
I love you
I love you
I love you
I love you
I love you
Behnam
Rabab
Ammar
Bashshar
Nassar
Luma
Fadhila
Mazin
Zena
Nadia
Zuhayr
Mufida
Karem
Rashid
Muther
Zuhira
Jaber
Geanne
Siba
Reem
Rand
Ramza
Zaki
Aubai
Rawah
Raid
Mary
Jacob
Muna
Huda

Nabil
Myriam
Salma
Adnan
Fadiya
Layth
Maysoon
Yousif
Zayd
Sa`ad
Salaam
Basil
Sati`
Aamira
Milad
Masarra
I love you
I love you
I love you
I love you
I love you
I love you
I love you
I love you
I love you
I love you
I love you
I love you
I love you
I love you
I love you
I love you
I love you
I love you
I love you
I love you I love you
on and on like that
five minutes, ten minutes
until they cut the phones off.

And—

LAYAL:

I will never leave
not for freedom you do not even have
call me what you like, look at me how you will
I tell you
so many women have done the same as me
everywhere they have to do the same.
If I did the same in your England or America
wouldn't they call me a whore there, too?
Your Western culture, sister, will not free me
from being called a whore
not my sex
women are not free
go home
you are cold, you are a cave
go back to your safety.

I will do whatever he asks of me.
But this
I do this for me, this is for me—

(Suddenly genuinely amused.)

I will make the mosaic of Bush's face
on the floor of the Rashid hotel
and I will write in English for all the world to read,
"Bush Is Criminal."
Why not? What's the worst?
Everyone walking into the hotel
will walk across his face.
And I will walk across his face.

(Layal begins to destroy her art studio. She smashes pottery and any-thing she can find as she looks to make the pieces for the mosaic.)

And two hundred more
waiting in line
risking everything to take my place
without my legs
buried in the backyard
they're making their own map of
me anyway—sure after every

bomb
first bomb drilling bomb
all I want is to feel it—love
we were just a boy and a girl
bodies were fused together—
second bomb come inside exactly same spot
here—he made them prostitutes
eight houses from here
don't come home
I am not the Layal he loved
third bomb—boil the people
I don't want freedom
Mullaya why are you here?
so old you cannot see it
yaboo yaboo
I'm fine I'm fine I'm *(Layal begins to beat her face and chest)*
La ilaha illa Allah (The sunset call to prayer is heard)
La ilaha illa Allah
La ilaha illa Allah

I'm dead.

(The Mullaya continues Layal's pace and fractured language without pause. However, what was for Layal explosive and destructive, is for the Mullaya effortless.)

MULLAYA:

A silhouette of a woman
vaporized from heat
in a void
deserted
fighting to keep transparency
my body but her body
herself inside me
why do you look at us as we have two hearts?
we have only one heart
you know us better
and all what is left of us
Baba oh *Baba*
I have too much existence
I have lived through seven thousand revolutions

to the well one day you'll return
thirsty, assured it will be there
but you'll not find—spring, nor river
so beware of throwing a stone
into the well
paint with real restraint
always fight to keep transparency
because once you go past
between the shore and the river
it goes muddy, it's muddy forever
the marshes are witness
if you drink water out of the well
it's the space, you leave it empty from the beginning

look
around this whole
I'm afraid to see them
when they're grown
wild greens they are growing
life did choose to root
here in this grave
all my family is here
same accent
same eyes
same nature
very big heart
we couldn't live together like this?
always it is life and death
and life and death—

(She steps into the river, raising water to her face. As she continues she becomes fully immersed.)

carry it with you
so when they cry
so old you cannot see it
try to reach me
for three days
hear my voice
upside-down
broken English
collecting

carrying
house by house
I can't move
I can't breathe
I cannot choose to leave
throw our arms wide
sing to my mother
I am home again
oblivion even
I don't care
I submit completely

late in the evening
late in the evening
I come to collect worn souls from the river
because
I love you
I love you
I love you
I love you
I fear it here
I love it here
I cannot stop what I am here
either I shall die
or I shall live a ransom for all the daughters
of savagery.
She called it "savagery"
when you love like you cannot breathe.

(We hear the final call to prayer. Darkness, it is the end of the day's cycle. Nanna continues to gather the few props, which is indeed everything she now owns, to sell on the street corner.)

NANNA:
Hallo Hallo
Hallo
you like to buy?
these things very nice, very old,
from good family
we have books
carpet
shoes.

Hallo Hallo
you like this painting?

(Nanna reaches for Layal's painting.)

It is very worth
she call it *Savagery*
famous artist
her name
Layal—

You recognize? *Aa,*
I was her neighbor
I knew her good
bomb fell her house
la, la, again, another bomb, her sister house,
she dead
her husband dead
her daughter blind.
Aa, aa, very sad—
so it is more worth
more worth!

She is martyr, all of us
all, the president he used to love her, he praise her
he put her painting in
Baghdad museum of arts.
It was full only his portrait
room and room of him
and I did saw it
he put her body, her trees
next to his face.
You must buy, buy
you must buy.

I tell you
this her last painting alive
all the rest
they are burned dead in the museum
I run
I took it.
Our history is finish

so it is more worth
more worth.

I give you secret
some trees are womans
this one, little one, is me
I let her paint me
aa, she see me
shhh
don't say
my husband he thinks it's just a tree.

I have to sell it
I have to eat
two dollar?

(Nanna's hand is outstretched and open.)

Two dollar?

END OF PLAY

Glossary

Aa	"Yes."
Abaya	A garmet worn in some areas of the Persian Gulf. It is worn by both men and women. Men wear it hanging from the shoulder; women wear it hanging off the top of the head. In Iraq it is usually a square, long-sleeved, floor-length, loose, black garment worn over the clothing.
Amma	"Aunt."
Ammu	"Uncle."
Apsu and Tiamat	In the epic of creation *Enuma Elish* (ca. 2000 B.C.), Apsu and Tiamat are the water god and goddess who become the father and mother of all creation.
Chal chal alayya	A verb meaning "to engulf."
Habibti	"Darling," "sweetheart."
Il-hamdu lillah	"Thanks be to God."
Kunya	An honorific term used to refer to parents in relation to their first-born son.
La	"No."
La ilaha illa allah	"There is no God but God." This is the first half of the Muslim profession of faith and is spoken the moment a person hears about or witnesses a sad or calamitous event.
Nammu	The first deity recorded in Sumerian mythology (ca. 4000 B.C.); she is the mother of all creation who gave birth to heaven and earth; she is represented by the sea.

Qurna, Eridu, Ur	Various ancient cities and villages, all located within the current boundaries of Iraq, which are thought to be the original site of the Garden of Eden.
Sabah	A girl's name meaning "morning."
Shaharazad	The Persian name of the main narrator and heroine in *One Thousand and One Nights*; she saves herself and the women of her country from death at the hands of King Shahryar by weaving a compelling story each night over the course of one thousand and one nights.
Shahryar	The name of the king in *One Thousand and One Nights*; each night he marries a virgin and then kills her the next morning so that she can never betray him.
Shatt al-Arab	The point of confluence of the Euphrates and Tigris rivers in the town of Qurna in southern Iraq.
Shlonich	"How are you?"
Ta`alu	"Follow me."
Tis`ah	"Nine."
Wayn Allah	"Where is God?"
Yaboo	A cry of disaster or tragedy.
Ya`ni	"I mean."

As the playwright and actor of *9 Parts of Desire*, **HEATHER RAFFO** received a Susan Smith Blackburn Prize Special Commendation, the Marian Seldes-Garson Kanin Fellowship and a 2005 Lucille Lortel Award for Outstanding Solo Show as well as a Helen Hayes nomination, Outer Critics Circle nomination and a Drama League nomination for distinguished performance.

9 Parts of Desire had its first production in August 2003 at the Traverse Theatre (Edinburgh) followed by the Bush Theatre in London's Off-West End. It was selected both as "First Choice/The Best Shows in London" by the *Times* and as one of the "Five Best Plays" in London by the *Independent*. *9 Parts of Desire* was next developed as part of the Immigrant Voices Project in 2004 at Queens Theatre in the Park. The Public Theater selected it as part of their "New Work Now!" festival. In October 2004 it had its New York premiere at the Manhattan Ensemble Theater where it ran for nine sold-out months and was a critics' pick for more than twenty-four weeks in a row. In 2005 the play began touring the U.S. with productions at the Geffen Playhouse Berkeley Repertory Theatre, Seattle Repertory Theatre, Arena Stage, Guthrie Theater, Actors Theatre of Louisville, Wilma Theater, Geva Theatre, Lyric Stage Company of Boston and Next Theatre Company at the Chicago Museum of Contemporary Art, as well as many others. It was recorded for viewing at the New York Public Library for the Performing Arts and is currently being translated for international productions in France, Brazil, Greece and Sweden. Original publications are by Northwestern University Press and Dramatists Play Service.

This is Raffo's first work as a playwright. She trained as an actress and has spent the last eight years performing Off-Broadway, Off-West End, on national tours, in regional theatre and in film. Raffo received her BA in English from the University of Michigan, and her MFA in acting performance from the University of San Diego at the Old Globe Theater. She has also studied at the Royal Academy of Dramatic Art in London. Born in Michigan, Raffo now lives in New York. Her father is originally from Iraq and her mother is American.

Desert Sunrise

A Tragedy with ^Some^ Hope

Misha Shulman

Author's Statement

It's a real place, the South Hebron Hills. The stories these characters tell are true. Some of the lines are quotes from various people who make up this place, this conflict. The fiction comes in with the story line of the play, the characters, the specific set of circumstances that force two Palestinians and an Israeli to spend a night together in the desert.

The encounter between an Israeli, with the full set of cultural programming built in, and a Palestinian, with his own cultural baggage, is taken from my own political process. During the years that led up to the writing process of *Desert Sunrise*, I went into the West Bank several times with an organization called Ta'ayush, which is one of the hundreds of joint Israeli-Palestinian partnerships working together toward peace. After growing up in Israel, knowing virtually no Palestinians, I met the hard-edged, wonderful people of the South Hebron Hills. The daily oppression they live with cut through any of the reasons, excuses, explanations that the Israeli system may have for the treatment of the Palestinian population and the support of the settlement movement in the West Bank.

It's a place where things are just what they are. From the rocks and the donkeys to the terror inflicted upon these decidedly nonviolent families. When you get shot at for trying to harvest wheat from your field, when your children get beaten up by settlers on their way to school every day, when you get arrested for drawing water from your ancestral well, then you know the meaning of the word "terror."

What I've learned in my process is that it is possible to strip yourself—even for a moment—of the slogans, the history, the countless forms of emotional self-defense you were taught. Then you can allow yourself to experience reality in a more straightforward manifestation, person to person. It's scary and challenging, and in many ways more depressing than the reality we choose to experience day by day. But it also allows you to make peace with your enemies, if that really is what you want.

This play was inspired by my father's book *Dark Hope: Working for Peace in Israel and Palestine* (University of Chicago Press, 2007), by Barbara Victor's *Army of Roses: Inside the World of Palestinian Women Suicide Bombers* (Rodale Books, 2003) and by Aeschylus' *Agamemnon*.

Desert Sunrise was first produced at Theater for the New City (Crystal Field, Executive Director) in September 2005. Due to critical success and popular demand, it was revived in April 2006. *Desert Sunrise* was directed by the playwright, Misha Shulman. Set design was by Celia Owens. Lighting design was by Itai Erdal. Original music was by Yoel Ben-Simhon. Choreography was by Bhavani Lee. The production stage manager was Melissa Robinson. The cast for the 2005 production was as follows:

ISMAIL	Haythem Noor
TSAHI	Aubrey Levy
LAYLA	Alice Borman
SOLDIER 1	Yifat Sharabi
SOLDIER 2	Morteza Tavakoli
CHORUS/MUSICIAN	Yoel Ben-Simhon
DANCER	Bhavani Lee

For the 2006 production, the cast and crew were the same except that Jared Miller played Tsahi and Dalia Carella choreographed and played the Dancer.

Desert Sunrise was produced at Northwestern University in Chicago as part of the Difficult Dialogues program in April 2007. It was directed by Misha Shulman. Set design was by Celia Owens. The cast was as follows:

ISMAIL	Haythem Noor
TSAHI	Jared Miller
LAYLA	Alice Shulman
SOLDIER 1	Yifat Sharabi

| SOLDIER 2 | Roy Aialon |
| DANCER | Dalia Carella |

Desert Sunrise was produced at the Lillian Theatre in Los Angeles in July 2008. It was directed by Ellen Shipley. Set design was by Elephant Stageworks Designs. Lighting design was by Matt Richter. Costume design was by Ronda Dynice Brooks. Choreography was by Jenna. The rehearsal stage manager was Charlie Pacello. The cast was as follows:

ISMAIL	Dominic Rains
TSAHI	Oren Dayan
LAYLA	Miriam Isa
SOLDIER 1	Yael Berkovich
SOLDIER 2	Yoni Tabac
CHORUS	Shahab Abbas
DANCER	Jenna

Characters

ISMAIL, a young Arab Palestinian shepherd

TSAHI (from the Hebrew name Yitzhak, Isaac), a young Israeli soldier
off duty

LAYLA, a young Arab woman. Layla has dark features, dark hair and
dark penetrating eyes. She wears a hijab over her head but not over
her face. She can be dressed in simple clothes, perhaps green. Layla
has moments in which she is extremely present, full of powerful emo-
tion. On the other hand she also has moments in which she seems to
be somewhere else, not on earth. She drifts from one state of mind to
the next quite gracefully yet, at times, abruptly. At some moments she
is completely at peace, while at others she is in complete inner tor-
ment. Layla's character is influenced by the Trojan character
Cassandra. Some of her lines are adapted from Cassandra's lines in
Agamemnon

TWO ISRAELI DEFENSE FORCES (IDF) SOLDIERS

CHORUS/MUSICIAN AND DANCER

Note

While the action that takes place in the play is fictional, the facts and
stories mentioned by the characters are all based on true events. For
information about the cave dwellers, please reference www.taayush.org.

The play takes place in the South Hebron Hills in a shallow wadi
from which, at daylight, the Dead Sea is visible in the distance to the
east. The stage is wide, perhaps surrounding the audience from three
sides. To the left of the stage there is a Musician, who acts as Chorus,
accompanying much of the play. In the New York City and Chicago
productions, the Musician played the oud, guitar and Arab drum, and
performed vocals. The Musician speaks the Chorus lines while playing
various instruments, and simultaneously the Dancer accompanies

with movement behind the scrim. It is also possible to produce the play without a live musician or dancer. In this case, pre-recorded music would accompany the actor playing the Chorus.

The stage is divided into two parts by a long scrim. The action takes place in front of the scrim; behind it dances occur that accompany the choral odes and a few select moments during the dialogue.

For my father.

Acknowledgments

Special thanks to Crystal Field, Muke Rutenberg, Ellen Shipley, Ellen Gould, Morteza Tarakoli and the wonderful casts and crews in New York, Chicago and Los Angeles.

ACT ONE

Dusk. The sun has already set. Music: an earthy, simple, distinctly Arab melody played on the oud. The Dead Sea in the distance is disappearing into darkness. Ismail is sitting on a small dirty carpet near a big rock, playing a drum.

CHORUS:
>Dusk falls on the empty desert.
>I stare at the darkness and dream of a light.
>A mountain glows, then another, and more,
>All the way to the city of light—
>"Peace! After so many years. Peace!"
>Not here,
>It's my ancient companion, terror, smiling at me
>With his foxlike grin from behind
>Every rock on the earth,
>>Every star in the sky.
>Fear. Only fear.
>Like a block of cement in my lung.
>Will this old hunk of land ever change?

ISMAIL *(Hears a noise, stops playing his drum, excitedly yells out)*: Layla!

(Hears no response and continues to play. Tsahi enters pointing his gun at Ismail.)

TSAHI: *Ata! (You!)*
ISMAIL *(Stops playing and again yells out)*: Layla?
TSAHI: *Ata! (You!)*

(Ismail realizes what's going on, puts drum down.)

Yadayim Lemala! (Hands in the air!)

(Ismail puts hands up in the air.)

Yesh lecha neshek? (Are you armed?)

(Ismail doesn't understand.)

Don't play dumb. I know you all understand Hebrew. Are you armed?

(Ismail puts staff down. Tsahi walks over and searches Ismail, then hangs rifle around his neck.)

Eyfo hakvish le Yerushalayim? (Hebrew for "Where's the road to Jerusalem?")

(Ismail is silent.)

You won't call it *Yerushalayim.* Okay—which way is Al Kuds?
ISMAIL: *Inta mashi allal Kuds? (You're walking to Jerusalem?)*
TSAHI: I'm what?
ISMAIL: *Mashi? (Making walking gesture)*
TSAHI *(Mimicking his walking gesture)*: *Mashi* to the road, then. *(Makes a hitchhiking gesture)*
ISMAIL: Hitchhiking.
TSAHI: *Aywa.*

(Ismail laughs.)

Why are you laughing?
ISMAIL: Do you know how to get to the road?
TSAHI: No, that's why I asked you.
ISMAIL: You didn't ask me.

TSAHI *(In Hebrew)*: Be'Ivrit.

ISMAIL: *Ana lo medaber Ivrit. (I don't speak Hebrew.)*

TSAHI: You know how to say: "I don't speak Hebrew," *in Hebrew*?!

ISMAIL: You know this desert?

TSAHI: No.

ISMAIL: It's very difficult for you to find.

TSAHI: You explain it to me.

ISMAIL: Now with your wall there's only one place, and you won't find it in the dark.

TSAHI *(Thinks for a moment)*: So you take me.

ISMAIL: *Ana? (Me?)*

TSAHI: *Aywa, inta* take me to the road.

ISMAIL: *La.* No. *La la la.*

TSAHI: *Ken. Aywa. Yalla bo. (Yes. Yes. Let's go.)*

ISMAIL: I can't take you there.

TSAHI: *Lesh? (Why?)*

ISMAIL: Why? *Il Jesh. (The army.)*

TSAHI: *Il Jesh? (The army?)*

ISMAIL: The army. *Mamnu.* It's not allowed. They will put me in prison.

TSAHI: You're with me. I'll take care of you.

ISMAIL: They'll put you in prison, too.

TSAHI: Me? I'm a soldier, I *am* the Jesh.

ISMAIL: Are you?

TSAHI: Yes.

ISMAIL: Why aren't you in uniform?

TSAHI: I'm on leave for the weekend.

ISMAIL: If the soldiers see us they'll say you were selling me guns.

TSAHI: Take me to the road.

ISMAIL: *La!*

(Ismail thinks he hears someone. He looks around.)

TSAHI: What are you doing here?

ISMAIL: Nothing.

TSAHI: You probably *are* buying guns.

ISMAIL: I don't care about your guns.

TSAHI: You're not allowed to be here.

ISMAIL: This is my land, my home, I can go wherever I want.

TSAHI: Not to the road.

ISMAIL: Yes, if I wanted to, to the road, too. You don't know anything.
Irja al beitak taba keh bil busa al baher. (Go back to your rich house near the ocean.)

TSAHI: I don't have a rich house, and I don't live near the ocean.

ISMAIL: You probably have more money in your pocket than I'll see all month.

TSAHI *(Takes out a coin)*: Ten shekels, that's all I've got. I'll give it to you if you take me to the road.

ISMAIL: I don't need your dirty money.

TSAHI: You probably make more money than me.

(Ismail looks around again.)

Who are you waiting for?

ISMAIL: No one.

TSAHI: Well I'll just wait here until your terrorist friend shows up, and then both of you can walk me to the road.

ISMAIL: Then you'll really be in trouble. Walking with two Arabs in the middle of the night. They'll put you in for life.

TSAHI: So there is someone coming. Who is it?

ISMAIL: None of your business.

TSAHI: Is it a *Hammasnik*?

ISMAIL: *La.*

TSAHI: Is it . . . a *Hammasnikit*? *(A female Hamas agent)*

ISMAIL: *Khalas!*

TSAHI: Ah, I get it. It isn't a terrorist is it? It's a lady.

ISMAIL: *Ruh min hun! (Go away!)*

TSAHI: I'm right, aren't I? Uh-oh, that's much more dangerous than a terrorist. A woman!

ISMAIL: Go find the road.

TSAHI: Tell me how to find it.

ISMAIL *(Trying to get rid of him)*: You go that way until you reach the third hill, walk around it, no the second hill, then walk around it, when you reach a patch of plants turn left up the wadi, then walk straight until you get to the wall. Then walk down until you find it.

TSAHI: That's too complicated.

(Ismail starts pouring water into a kettle that contains tea leaves.)

I don't even have any water.

(Pause. Ismail takes a sip of water.)

Look, if you don't take me there, I'll have to stay here with you.

ISMAIL: You can't.

TSAHI: I haven't drunk anything in hours. I'm too thirsty. I won't make it.

ISMAIL: Get out of here.

TSAHI: I'm telling you I'm thirsty. I could die. Doesn't that mean anything to you?

ISMAIL *(Smiles)*: Imagine this. You are in the desert, thirsty. You walk to a well you know from childhood. You find it full of dirt and big rocks, and you can't get to the water. Next to the well passes a pipe full of fresh water. You can hear it flowing, feel it right next to you, but you are forbidden to touch it. It is Jewish water.

TSAHI: How did those rocks get in the well?

ISMAIL: The mysterious workings of God and his messengers in olive green.

(Pause.)

TSAHI: Will you let me have some tea? Please.

(Upset, but appreciating the request and the way it was made, Ismail finally, reluctantly, pours both of them some tea.

A long silence. Then oud music: a non-rhythmic improvisation that sits heavy and low at first and then breaks into high-pitched, gentle notes. Tsahi looks around for a place to sit. He walks toward Ismail's small carpet. Ismail stares at him. Tsahi gets the message and sits down on the sand further stage left.)

So who's this woman of yours?

ISMAIL: She's . . . my life.

TSAHI: *Helwa, (Arabic for "beautiful")* your wife?

ISMAIL: Not my wife yet. My life and, yes, she is beautiful.

(Pause.)

What are you doing here?

TSAHI *(Bitterly)*: I came to see a woman.

ISMAIL: Where?

TSAHI *(Looks around, trying to figure out which way he came from, then gives up)*: A settlement around here, Susya.

ISMAIL: You love a girl from Susya?

TSAHI: Not anymore. *Khalas* love. Finished.

ISMAIL: Never trust a woman from Susya.

TSAHI: Never trust a woman anywhere. *Nekuda. (Period.)* You want to know what I'm doing here? I had the weekend off from my unit, so I came all the way from Bet Shemesh to see her. I even brought her flowers, *(To himself)* Hamor! *(Donkey!)* I get here and she says let's go for a walk. *Sababa.* We walk out of Susya into the hills, and I try to take her hand. She doesn't let me, *sharmuta. (bitch)* What's wrong, I ask, and she starts saying she doesn't want to see me anymore. Why? The bitch was cheating on me! She was with some guy from Kiryat Arba.

ISMAIL: What did you do?

TSAHI: She was with this guy for the past five months. Can you believe that?

ISMAIL: Did you kill her?

TSAHI: I should have.

ISMAIL: You didn't?

TSAHI: You *are* a terrorist, aren't you? No I didn't kill her.

ISMAIL: Good.

TSAHI: What do you mean "good"?

ISMAIL: What did you do?

TSAHI: I was so upset I couldn't even talk to her. I just walked away. For months she would look me in the eye and tell me she loves me, do you understand? *Bat zona kazot, walla. (Fucking bitch, really.)* I should have killed her.

ISMAIL: So you've been walking through the desert all day with no water?

TSAHI: *Bat zona . . . (Bitch . . .)* Then it started getting dark and I didn't know where I was. Still don't. I could be in Saudi Arabia for all I know.

ISMAIL: You're in Palestine.

TSAHI: Not yet. It's more like the Wild West.

ISMAIL: That's right, Cowboy, except here the Indians will win. We'll kick you out like your girlfriend did.

TSAHI: I'll kick you in the face, Little Indian Girl. You terrorists use womanly tactics, don't you? Your bombs are like a deep scratch in the skin of a man.

ISMAIL: And then you beat us down. Give us what we deserve, right? Make us believe it's our own fault.

TSAHI: If I had slapped that girl, whose fault would it have been?

ISMAIL: Why was she cheating on you in the first place? You must have been slapping her . . .

TSAHI *(Threateningly)*: *Tizaher. (Watch it.)* I don't slap women. Even when they deserve it.

ISMAIL: But Palestinians you do.

TSAHI: I haven't slapped you yet.

ISMAIL: Even though I deserve it. Who's the woman here?

TSAHI: I have the gun. You made the tea.

ISMAIL: You just got dumped, I'm waiting for my woman.

TSAHI: She's late, isn't she? She's probably in another wadi with your brother.

ISMAIL: *Deir balak. (Watch it.)* I'm not afraid to slap anyone.

TSAHI: Take my advice, don't trust her.

ISMAIL: Advice from an Israeli with a gun. I'd trust any woman before I'd trust you.

TSAHI: I wouldn't trust a woman, and I don't trust you.

(Music: a rhythmic, energized and ominous tune that never releases its own tension.)

CHORUS:

> As the smoke of suspicion
> Swallows the sand
> Two long-winged prey-birds glide through the bright-lit night.
> One has a black tail, the other's is white.
> We gaze at the hawks
> And see in their claws
> A small squealing mammal, a pregnant she-fox.
> What will come of that moment, we wondered.
> We sing as we tremble,
> Everything will begin again.

TSAHI: So why are you meeting down here in the middle of the night?

ISMAIL: There's no place to be alone where I live.

TSAHI: Why not?

ISMAIL: Do you know what I live in? You say you're not rich, you don't live in a house by the ocean. Well, I don't live in a house at all. I live in a cave. One space for the whole family, and in the winter the animals, too.

TSAHI: Why do you live in a cave?

ISMAIL: My ancestors moved into these natural caves around here two hundred years ago to live a peaceful life. They had their sheep, their olive trees and their water wells.

TSAHI: So?

ISMAIL: Twenty years ago the army started trying to make us leave. They came and stuffed our wells, blew up our caves.

TSAHI: The army?!

ISMAIL: My family's already had to move to a new cave three times.

TSAHI: You guys *must* be terrorists if they did that to you.

ISMAIL: The people of Jbal El Khalil are shepherds and farmers, not terrorists. The army knows that.

TSAHI: The bomber in Be'er Sheva last month came from around here.

ISMAIL: He wasn't a cave dweller.

TSAHI: The army fights terrorism. If there were none, we wouldn't be
   here.

ISMAIL *(Laughs)*: You talk like a child.

TSAHI: You just told me that there are terrorists here.

ISMAIL: Here everyone is a terrorist.

TSAHI: A soldier is not a terrorist.

ISMAIL: You *are* a fool, aren't you?

TSAHI: I should just get rid of you right here, before you come to
   Jerusalem and blow up my family. *Ani ar'eh lecha (I'll show you)*
   who's the fucking fool. *(Points gun in his face)*

ISMAIL *(Not taken aback at all, puts his face in front of the gun)*: Who's the
   terrorist you fucking Israeli bastard?! Who's the fucking terrorist?!

TSAHI *(Brings rifle closer to Ismail's face)*: Fuck you.

ISMAIL *(Pushes the gun down and comes right in Tsahi's face. Pointing to a
   thick scar in his face)*: You see this? Do you see?! Two weeks ago
   I was herding the sheep near our olive grove. Suddenly the settlers
   came. Five of them, with guns. They shot at me and all of my sheep
   started running, but they wouldn't let me go after them. They
   needed to "explain something to me." The shortest one of them,
   a young guy with a hoarse voice pushed me to my knees. He said,
   "You are my donkey. You always were and always will be. For thirty-five years now we've known: the Jews are going to ride the
   Palestinians like donkeys into the twenty-first century." He beat
   me with the butt of his rifle, and told me they would kill me and
   my family if I came back there. To my own family's field! They
   said it's not my family's anymore, but belongs to the state of Israel.
   Now you understand why I have to meet my woman here in the
   middle of the night? Because this place is infested with terrorists.

TSAHI *(Affected, but not wanting to show it)*: Is that a true story?

ISMAIL: Want to hear some more?

TSAHI: No.

ISMAIL: When I walk out of my cave I step on the ruins of my father's
   home. When I walk to my family's well I get shot at . . .

TSAHI: I get it.

ISMAIL: When I cross the wadi to harvest my wheat I get arrested.

TSAHI: It must not be on your land then.

ISMAIL: My great-grandfather lived off of it!

TSAHI: Look, I'm sorry.

ISMAIL: You're sorry? Great, problem solved.

TSAHI: I'm a medic. I treat the wounded.

ISMAIL: Every time the soldiers came to demolish my home there was a medic there with them.

TSAHI: Shit happens to all of us. Do you think you're the only ones getting screwed?

ISMAIL: Don't compare my situation to yours.

TSAHI: If the army weren't around you'd be much worse.

ISMAIL: All the army does around here is to protect the settlers and their interests.

TSAHI: Like not being killed.

ISMAIL: Like forcing us to leave, just like your government wants. *(With no bitterness)* But I'll tell you this the only way they'll get us out of here is to carry our dead bodies away. You're just a toy in their game.

TSAHI: Don't talk to me about games, you little Palestinian pawn. You *are* your leaders' game. They want you and your family to be oppressed, hungry or dead so that the world will see you and not their fat Swiss bank accounts. Why do you think Hamas is in power now? Because they want you to be free and prosperous? Their fine suits are weaved out of your blood. They want it more than anyone.

ISMAIL: You want it more.

TSAHI: Do you think I even care about you and your blood? Do you think we sit in our "rich" houses dreaming of poor Ahmad's flowing blood?! Nobody gives a sheep's ass about your blood. Not Abbas, not Bush, not Sharon in his hospital bed, and not Arafat in his grave. Your blood is cheap to them all.

ISMAIL: My blood is the cheapest thing you can find around here. Nothing cheaper in the whole Middle East.

TSAHI: What about Iraqi blood?

ISMAIL *(Getting into the dark humor)*: Okay, the second cheapest. But your blood comes in third.

TSAHI: What's the exchange rate for blood in the Suk today?

ISMAIL: One kilo American blood is worth ten kilos Israeli. One kilo Israeli blood is worth twenty kilos Palestinian.

TSAHI: Wait, it depends what kind of Palestinian.

ISMAIL: You're right. One kilo Israeli blood sells for ten kilos Palestinian woman, five kilos Palestinian child. And for us cavemen— buy one get one free. I could kill you now, make some money.

TSAHI: You'd be a rich prisoner for the rest of your life. If I killed you at least I'd be free.

ISMAIL: I got it! Let's kill each other—then we'll be both free *and* rich!

TSAHI: That would work for me, but they'd probably still put your corpse in prison, just in case.

ISMAIL: Someone has to pay for *your* blood.

TSAHI: You see, mine's worth more than yours because my leaders at least care about my blood.

ISMAIL: It's simple. When Israel bleeds, it wipes its blood with me. *(No bitterness)* We're part of the same bloodstream you and me. It's hard to tell mine from yours.

TSAHI: If we weren't bleeding all the time you'd be much better off. Tell that to your people and things will start improving.

ISMAIL: I'd listen to a female sheep before I'd listen to you.

TSAHI: See that's your problem. You take advice from sheep. That would explain why you had a leader who looked like one for forty years.

ISMAIL: Who do you take advice from? Your rich uncle from Washington. That would explain why you had a fat elephant in power.

TSAHI: You know what a fat elephant uses when she has her period?

ISMAIL: What?

TSAHI: A sheep.

(They both laugh.
Music: an upbeat dabka, which is a traditional Arab dance. Ismail takes a smoking pipe out of his pocket and stuffs it.)

CHORUS:

> In the heart of a sandstorm
> I come face to face with my doubts.
> It's lies that they fed me to make me the tiger they need.
> Our dead are dead, their dead are, too.
> We are alive! Enough of these morbid tunes.
> Let's play a different song! Yalla!

TSAHI: *Shu hada? (What's that?)*

ISMAIL: *Ata lo yodea? (You don't know?) Hada hadiyat Al ard.* The gift of the earth. You know what it does? It makes you forget everything, so you can feel.

TSAHI: You call hashish the gift of the earth?

ISMAIL: Or the gift of forgetting. We need a lot of this.

TSAHI: Believe me we need it more. You have one hundred years to remember, we have three thousand. And we remember every day of it.

ISMAIL: Every bad day. *(He lights the pipe, he smokes)* Bidak? *(You want some?)*

TSAHI: I'm a soldier. I'm not allowed.

ISMAIL *(Laughing)*: Nobody is allowed. So what? *Yalla*, you need to forget your woman.

TSAHI: *Bat zona . . . yalla tavi. (That bitch . . . give it here.)*

(Ismail passes him the pipe. Tsahi looks at it, then smokes, coughs, smokes again and smiles, then hands the pipe back to Ismail.)

I haven't smoked this shit since high school.

ISMAIL: You smoked hashish?

TSAHI: Everyone smokes hashish in Israel.

ISMAIL: I thought you only drink alcohol.

TSAHI: That too. *Ten, ten od shahta. (Give me another drag.)*

ISMAIL: You like it, ah? *(Gives him the pipe; he smokes)*

TSAHI: Forgetting goes against everything I was brought up to believe in.

ISMAIL: Exactly. That's how it works.

TSAHI: But if you forget, what do you hang on to? There's nothing . . .

ISMAIL: There's plenty. Can't you feel your own balls?

TSAHI: What?!

ISMAIL: You got balls don't you? Use them.

TSAHI: I have other uses for my testicles.

ISMAIL: Do you think we're happy creatures?

TSAHI: Who?

ISMAIL: Us. Humans.

TSAHI: No.

ISMAIL: I spend a lot of time with my sheep.

TSAHI: I get it. So you use your balls with them. Better leave some for your woman.

ISMAIL: Sheep are easy to please. Give them food and water and they're happy. They experience the world directly. No bullshit. You understand?

TSAHI: Until one day they get slaughtered.

ISMAIL: They get slaughtered no matter how they live their lives.

TSAHI: I like this forgetting business. I can't remember anything. Where I am . . .

ISMAIL *(Laughing)*: You don't *know* where you are.

TSAHI: What day it is, what happened today, what happened yesterday, what happened a week, a month, a year ago. *(Laughing)* What happened on November fifth 1995, what happened between 1939 and 1945, what happened in fucking Egypt three thousand years ago! I can't remember any of it. I can't even remember my sister.

ISMAIL: Your sister?

TSAHI: Until I see my gun here. Then I remember it all. *(Looks up at Ismail)* Except your name. I can't remember your name.

ISMAIL: I haven't told you my name.

TSAHI: That would explain it. In the spirit of forgetting, my name is Tsahi.

ISMAIL: Ismail. Only in the spirit of forgetting.

TSAHI: In the spirit of forgetting, *ahalan ya, (hello)* Ismail.

ISMAIL: *Ahalan wasahlan. (Hello and welcome.)*

(They both laugh.)

Tsahi, what name is that?

TSAHI: From Yitzhak.

ISMAIL: Yitzhak like Ishak? So we are brothers then.

TSAHI *(As he sits down to examine Ismail's drum)*: Who says?

ISMAIL: The Qur'an.

TSAHI: You smoke too much. It's the Torah that says it.

ISMAIL: They both say it.

TSAHI: All right, in the spirit of forgetting, we are brothers. Who's the older one?

ISMAIL: I am. *(Takes the drum from Tsahi and starts drumming an Arab beat)*

TSAHI: But I win the rights of the first born from you because you're so stupid and hungry.

ISMAIL: *La, la.* That's your sons, Yaakov and Esav.

TSAHI: Right. You're the one that God said would be a wild ass or something.

ISMAIL: You want to get into animals? All right, in the Qur'an Jews are pigs, monkeys . . .

TSAHI: Come on, I remember one little detail and you bring all of Noah's ark out on me?

(They suddenly find themselves drumming together. They continue for eight bars.)

ISMAIL: How about we re-forget the names.

TSAHI: Which names?

ISMAIL: Exactly.

TSAHI: *Lo be'emet, (No, really,)* which names? What were we talking about?

ISMAIL: Your girlfriend.

TSAHI: That's right, the donkey!

ISMAIL: The donkey from Susya.

TSAHI: Where's your donkey?

ISMAIL: My hawk.

TSAHI: Do you all call your women hawks?

ISMAIL: Do you all call your women donkeys?

TSAHI: We should both call them bitches.

ISMAIL: You really loved this girl, didn't you?

TSAHI: We would see each other only every few weeks. You know what that's like?

ISMAIL: No.

TSAHI: It's like night and day. You only meet for a quick meeting before one of you has to disappear again. All you have is dusk and dawn. You don't really know each other. Then when you're apart you can create whatever picture you want of her. And you either love that picture or you hate it. It's up to you.

ISMAIL: You loved her.

TSAHI: I loved my own invention of what she is. And now I finally woke up. She's got nothing to do with the image I had of her. I was sleeping the whole time. I was a bat. Blind.

ISMAIL: And now she's a donkey.

TSAHI: Now she's night. I wish she were dead.

ISMAIL: No you don't.

TSAHI: I wish this night were over.

(Pause.)

ISMAIL: You know what I do when I'm out with the sheep and can't wait for the day to be over? I make up stories.

TSAHI: I don't want to make up a story.

ISMAIL: You're right. It's nighttime, we should make up a dream.

TSAHI: I don't want to make up a dream.

ISMAIL: You will once I start. It's another way to forget.

TSAHI: My dreams make me remember.

ISMAIL: That's because you're not the one inventing them.

TSAHI: Who is then?

ISMAIL: Your soul. But now you can dream a conscious dream. We'll call it an upside-down dream. What do you say? *(No response)* I'll start. In my dream I find a lion cub crying in the desert. I cautiously come up to him and he looks at me sweetly. I touch him and he cuddles into my arm. He licks my finger, but his sharp teeth accidentally scrape it, and my finger begins to bleed.

TSAHI: I took my hand away and the cub lay down on its back, like a dog.

ISMAIL: You *take* your hand away, and the cub *lies* down on its back.

TSAHI: What's the difference?

ISMAIL: I only make up stories in the present tense. Same goes for dreams. Nothing that *happened*, it's all happening now.

TSAHI: What about flashbacks, are those allowed?

ISMAIL: No, it's all taking place right now.

TSAHI: All right. So he lies down on his back and I see that it's not a he, but a she. My finger starts bleeding more heavily, but I don't have my medic's kit. So I look for water. I walk and walk, and the cub follows me, until I reach the sea.

ISMAIL: But when I get there the cub won't let me go near it. She bites into my leg and holds it tight in her mouth.

TSAHI: I look back at her and see that she is growing rapidly into a full-grown lioness. I need to get to the water . . .

ISMAIL: But I'm afraid to go near it, and I realize that the cub's teeth are sinking deeper and deeper into my leg, but the leg doesn't hurt at all.

TSAHI: My bleeding is getting worse. I have to wash my leg. I look at her and say, "I need the water, please let me go to it."

ISMAIL: And she replies in a catlike voice, "It's too salty. This sea is dead."

TSAHI: "I need salt to disinfect my wound," I say.

ISMAIL: But she squeals, "There is more salt in the desert earth than in the water."

TSAHI: "I don't *know* the desert."

ISMAIL: "I don't *know* the sea."

TSAHI: "I'm afraid of you."

ISMAIL: "I'm afraid of *you*."

TSAHI: I suddenly remember when I was eight and . . . .

ISMAIL: We said no memories!

TSAHI: But this is a good one.

ISMAIL: No!

TSAHI: This is my dream, too!

ISMAIL: No memories!

TSAHI: I suddenly remember when I was eight and I dreamed my sister was kidnapped by pirates. In the dream I realized I'm dreaming and I could help her. So I beat up all of the pirates and rescued her.

ISMAIL: What does this have to do with our dream?

TSAHI *(Back to making up the dream)*: I realize I'm dreaming and take control. I pull both of us into the water.

ISMAIL: You'll kill us both!

TSAHI: We get in . . . and float! Both of us. The lioness looks at me and smiles.

ISMAIL: I look down at my leg and see it's gone. All eaten up. I watch her swim out of the water and walk away. And I'm left in the sea, unable to bring myself to shore.

TSAHI: I think, an upside-down dream is salty.

ISMAIL: And wake up. That was very good.

TSAHI: The night's not over yet. My woman is still here. I can feel her. Go away, night!

ISMAIL *(Looks around for Layla)*: You know, it's funny you call her night.

TSAHI: *Lesh? (Why?)*

ISMAIL: That's my hawk's name, Layla.

TSAHI: *Walla? (Really?)*

ISMAIL: But she's not only night for me. I know her from the day she was born. I grew up with her, played with her, watched her become a woman.

TSAHI: Is she your sister or something?

ISMAIL: My cousin. I've been in love with her since the eighth grade.

TSAHI: Does she also live in a cave?

ISMAIL: No, she's a city girl, from Yata.

TSAHI: What's she like, this hawk of yours?

ISMAIL: She's proud and strong. And she talks like a poet sometimes.

TSAHI: Sounds dangerous.

ISMAIL: She's been fighting with her parents quite a bit this year.

TSAHI: Why?

ISMAIL: She wants to go to university, but they won't let her go.

TSAHI: What does she want to study?

ISMAIL: English literature. She was very good at it in high school.

TSAHI: That's what my sister studied.

ISMAIL: She is very brave. She is my night and my day.

TSAHI *(Sings)*: *At li layla, at li yom, at li layla.* *(Speaking)* You know Boaz Sharabi?

ISMAIL: No.

TSAHI *(Shocked)*: *Keef la? (How no?)* Boaz Sharabi! Anyways, he's got a song called "At Li Layla"— You're my night. And the chorus is, "At li layla, at li yom"—"You're my night, you're my day." *(Sings:)*

> *Rak otach ohav halalyla (It's only you I want tonight)*
> *Dimdumim umanginot. (Dusk, dawn and a melody.)*
> *Vehamatana sheli halayla (But my gift tonight)*
> *Bli otan ha'achzavot. (Comes without the same old disappointments.)*

(Ismail gets drum and joins in, which pleases Tsahi. Throughout the next verse Tsahi starts to dance a slow dance with his rifle as if with a woman.)

> *Ko zara at li velama (Why did you leave me and)*
> *Halacht li le'olam acher (Go to another world?)*
> *Lifamim ani hoshev (Sometimes I spend the whole night)*
> *Eich le'ehov otach halayla. (Thinking how to love you.)*
> *At li layla. At li yom. At li layla. (You're my night. You're my day.*
> *You're my night.)*

(Musician continues playing and singing.)

(Frustrated with having no one to dance with and feeling in a funny mood) Do you dance slow dances in your caves?

ISMAIL: Slow, fast, we dance all kinds of dance.

TSAHI: No, no, "slow dance," it's a kind of dance, like I was just dancing now.

ISMAIL: I saw it once in an American movie.

TSAHI: But you've never danced it?!

ISMAIL: *La. (No.)*

TSAHI: You should learn, it's fun. You can dance it with Layla.

ISMAIL: *La, shukran. (No, thanks.)*

TSAHI: Come on, try.

ISMAIL: Look, I don't dance. Not even the Dabka. My body's like wood. It doesn't move right.

TSAHI: Sure it does!

ISMAIL: Layla is the dancer. Her body curls like a panther. She's the best in the entire area. To Layla the body is holier than the Qur'an.

TSAHI: Well, don't you want to dance with her? It's just hugging and moving. You do hug Layla sometimes.

ISMAIL: *La.*

TSAHI: Never?

ISMAIL: After we marry.

TSAHI: You've never hugged her?

ISMAIL: Not yet.

TSAHI: What are you waiting for?

ISMAIL: I'll tell you a secret. I'm going to ask her to marry me tonight.

TSAHI: *Be'emet? (Really?)*

ISMAIL: *Wallahi. (I swear.)*

TSAHI: *Mabruk ya habibi. (Congratulations my friend.)* In the spirit of forgetting I will shake your hand. *(He does)* So now you can learn how to slow dance and dance with her tonight.

ISMAIL: We don't touch each other until the wedding.

TSAHI: You can have one little dance. Don't you want to feel her body against yours? It feels great. *(Pretends to be Ismail, dances with a pretend Layla)* Oh, Layla, you feel so good.

ISMAIL: *Khalas! (Enough!)*

TSAHI: Here, you take her. *(Hands pretend Layla to Ismail, who hesitates)* She's yours isn't she, this beautiful woman?

(Ismail takes her, awkwardly dances.)

Mumtaz! Excellent! Loosen up a bit, you're holding her too tight. Good. Now just take little steps sideways and back. No, no, not like that, and take your hands off her butt, they should be higher. You want the hands on the waist. *(Places his hands higher)* Good, keep going. Left and back, and right and back . . . Wait, no, you're not doing it right. All right, I guess we have no choice. Pretend I'm Layla.

ISMAIL: Get away from me!

TSAHI: Come on, it's the twenty-first century. What are you, some kind of caveman?

ISMAIL: Back off.

TSAHI: Don't you want to hug her for real tonight? You're the man. You have to know how to lead her. I'm sure Layla knows how to do it.

ISMAIL: *La!*

TSAHI: *Shuf, (Look,)* I don't want to do this either, but you have to learn, and this is the only way.

(Tsahi takes his rifle off and leans it against the rock. He grabs the pipe and matches from the ground.)

Here, we'll have another *shahta* and then we're doing it.

(They do. Tsahi offers himself to Ismail, who after a moment takes him in his arms.)

Good. Now move. Right and back, and left and back. Good. Keep your hands on my hips. Now turn me around, slowly. *Metzuyan! (Excellent!)* Now look me in the eye. And smile.

(They dance, getting into it with their stoned-ness, to the jolly music of the Musician. Layla enters. She watches for a moment, horrified, then picks up Tsahi's rifle and points it at the men.)

LAYLA: *Dashra! (Let him go!)*

(The men, startled, put their hands in the air.)

ACT TWO

Continued from the moment Act One ends.

ISMAIL: Layla!

LAYLA: *Ma t'harak. (Don't move.) (To Ismail) Inta Kwayes? (Are you okay?)*

ISMAIL: *Aywa. (Yes.)* Layla, *huti slah el-ard. (Layla, put the gun down.)*

LAYLA *(To Tsahi): Wakif walla batuhak, (Stop or I shoot you,)* sound familiar?

ISMAIL: Layla . . .

LAYLA: Where should I shoot him, Ismail? In the head like your uncle? In the stomach like my brother?

ISMAIL *(Comes toward her)*: Don't be crazy, Layla.

LAYLA *(Points gun at him)*: Ismail, stay away.

(Tsahi tries to move, she points the gun at him.)

I said don't move! *(To Ismail) Shu sawal-lak? (What was he doing to you?)*

ISMAIL: *Hu masa walishi . . . (Nothing, it's nothing. He . . .)*

LAYLA: *Hu salat alek I slah urasabak? (Did he point his gun at you and force you to do that?)*

ISMAIL: *La. (No.)*

LAYLA: *La? I lesh inta sawet? (No? So why did you do it?)*

ISMAIL: *Ana bus . . . (I just . . .)*

LAYLA: What were you doing with that Jewish son of a whore?

TSAHI: *Tizahari, isha. (Watch it, woman.)*

LAYLA: You are now at school. This is what it means to be Palestinian. Don't move. Don't think. And speak only when spoken to. Learn!

ISMAIL: Layla, *habibti*, it's okay, he . . .

LAYLA *(To Ismail)*: Who is he?

ISMAIL: He's okay, Layla, he got lost in the desert and is waiting for morning to go back to Jerusalem.

LAYLA: Ah?

ISMAIL: I tried to get rid of him but . . .

LAYLA: I saw how you tried to get rid of him.

TSAHI: He did try to get rid of me.

ISMAIL: See?

LAYLA: You're lying. Both of you. Ismail, why are you lying to me?

TSAHI: He's not lying.

LAYLA: No one's talking to you!

TSAHI: I asked him to take me to the road and he refused.

LAYLA: So you became his best friend.

ISMAIL: He had no water, so . . .

LAYLA: I know what's going on here. You've become an informer. He's a Shabak agent.

ISMAIL: Layla you're crazy. Who would I have to inform on?

LAYLA: Why are you asking me that?

ISMAIL: Because it's ridiculous. I don't know any Hamas people.

TSAHI: Now you're lying.

LAYLA: You see, he knows you do, because you've told him.

ISMAIL: He doesn't know anything.

TSAHI: What's there to know?

LAYLA: Nothing! There's nothing to know.

ISMAIL: Layla, calm down, please.

LAYLA: Calm down? I come all the way from Yata to see you, and when I get to the cave the whole village is . . .

ISMAIL: Is what?

LAYLA: . . . and I find you hugging an Israeli with a gun, and then you make up some stupid story about getting lost. Nobody walks around this desert but shepherds, you lying Israeli bastard!

TSAHI: Don't yell at me, you whore!

ISMAIL *(Grabs Tsahi by the neck as Layla stands farther back with the rifle pointed at him)*: Talk to her like that one more time and I'll break your neck.

TSAHI: Shut up.

ISMAIL: Insult my woman once more and I'll rip you apart like a tiger eats a sheep.

LAYLA: Ismail! Promise me that you are not a collaborator.

ISMAIL: Of course I'm not a collaborator. I promise. *(He lets go of Tsahi and moves toward Layla)* Layla, please give me the gun.

(Pause.)

Have I not always been on your side? I loved you and cared for you, out of the whole family it's always been me. Trust me, Layla, shooting him will only bring us grief.

LAYLA: I'll wait.

ISMAIL: What?

LAYLA: Do you trust him?

(Pause.)

ISMAIL: He won't hurt us.

(She holds the rifle in front of her for him to take.)

TSAHI: Give it to me.

(Layla drops the rifle on the ground. Both men yelp and jump to the ground in fear of a stray bullet. Then they realize the gun didn't go off and both men run to grab the gun. They battle over it for a moment.)

LAYLA: Hey!

(They look at her and see she's holding the cartridge in her hand.)

Your cartridge.

(Tsahi grabs the rifle.)

(To Ismail) What were you doing hugging him?

ISMAIL *(To Tsahi)*: Look, you little *hmar, (donkey)* you got me doing that stupid dance, you help me out now.

TSAHI: Fuck you.

LAYLA: What dance?

ISMAIL: It's an Israeli dance. What's it called?

(No response from Tsahi, who enjoys watching Ismail try to explain himself. He sits cleaning his rifle.)

We were talking about you.

LAYLA: What about me?

ISMAIL: He was talking about "layla"—night—and I said that's your name. And then he started singing a song. In Hebrew. *(Sings)* "*at li layla.*" He wanted to teach me how to dance like in that movie, so I could dance with you.

TSAHI: But he couldn't do it alone, so I had to step in, as you. And I told him that he has to pretend that I am you. And he was doing a very good job until you walked in and—

LAYLA *(To Ismail)*: You pretended he was me?

ISMAIL: Yes.

LAYLA: Do I look anything like him?

ISMAIL: No, but—

LAYLA: He's an ugly Israeli man.

TSAHI: Hey!

ISMAIL: I know he is, it was just for the dance.

TSAHI: I was teaching him how to slow dance.

ISMAIL: That's the name, it's called a slow dance.

LAYLA: And in this dance you hug and look each other in the eye.

TSAHI: And move from side to side, and sometimes around.

LAYLA: You did what you can't do with a woman, with him?

ISMAIL: Layla, I . . .

LAYLA: How could you? Do you forget so quickly? Two weeks ago you were beaten like an animal by them, and now you hug this soldier?!

ISMAIL: I wasn't hugging an Israeli. I was hugging a man.

LAYLA: He beats our men—your father, my father. He destroys our homes!

TSAHI: You're like a hungry baby crying to his father for milk. Your leaders send you out to die and then you come crying to me.

LAYLA: It is like a crocodile meeting a helpless child, powerless except for his screams. Does the crocodile understand a conversation that doesn't include a weapon?

TSAHI: Those who aim for helpless children are you.

ISMAIL: My younger sister is eight years old. She was beaten by settlers every day this week on her way to school.

LAYLA: They broke her bones.

ISMAIL: Who has killed more innocent children—you or us?

LAYLA: You deserve to die.

TSAHI: And what about Hamas, Ms. Night of Death, don't they deserve to die?

LAYLA: Only the lucky ones. The rest just keep suffering. Stuck to this earth like heavy beasts. They can never leave it. They can never fly away like a bird.

(The Dancer appears very large on the scrim dancing a majestic bird dance. The Musician drums an ominous beat.)

CHORUS:

> She's like a raging bird, possessed
> By her own demonic song. A strange,
> Wing-flapping devil.

TSAHI: You did say she was a hawk.

LAYLA *(Walks back to the scrim to touch the bird)*: I'm a hawk with no wings. Soon. Soon I will fly.

CHORUS:

> She is determined to seek out the blood.
> Wherever it lies on the trail to death—she will find it.

(While playing the drum, the Musician sings high-pitched, gentle notes.)

TSAHI: Where will you fly to?

LAYLA: High above the checkpoint, high above the soldiers, high above the lines, high above the road for the Jews and high above the road for the Arabs. I'll fly my broken wings. I'll fly like garbage.

TSAHI: Garbage?

ISMAIL: Layla, are you okay?

LAYLA: Do you remember it, Ismail? Do you remember the garbage flying high up in the air above the checkpoint?

ISMAIL: They were just a few plastic bags from the garbage dump.

LAYLA: They looked like strange, beautiful birds. Like me. Didn't they look like me Ismail?

ISMAIL: Layla, what's gotten into you? Of course it didn't look like you. You're beautiful. You're not garbage.

LAYLA: I want to fly like the garbage!

TSAHI: Let's all fly like garbage!

(The Musician stops drumming, but the soft singing remains.)

LAYLA: I was in the line at the checkpoint. The woman behind me, her baby was dying. Across the checkpoint was the ambulance. To save the baby. The soldiers wouldn't let her go ahead of me. Red, the baby's face, red. I begged them. I begged, and they laughed. The soldier, he said, "Kiss me on the lips and I'll let the baby through." Off, he ripped it, my hijab, hair everywhere, woman's hair, my hair. His lips were dry like the desert. His lips, cigarette breath, my lips wet, I'm wet. My eyes open, I see the sky, I see the garbage flying. Strange beautiful birds of the desert. Join them, join them, grow new wings and fly like a woman, fly. He lets baby go through, to ambulance, too late, death. Face white, death. Grow new wings and fly . . .

ISMAIL: Layla, enough.

LAYLA: Fly like a woman! Fly like garbage, right, Ismail? You were there. You saw him kiss me. You saw him rip off my hijab. Everyone saw! Everyone saw me.

ISMAIL: Layla, don't worry, I will help you.

LAYLA: Were you jealous? Is that why you danced with him? Maybe I should have kissed a female soldier, then at least you wouldn't bring shame on your family.

ISMAIL: *Khalas! (Enough!)*

LAYLA: Soldier! Kiss Ismail. Ismail wants to be kissed. For him it doesn't matter. Even if the whole world saw, he could still marry. Because he's a man. A man!

ISMAIL: Layla, you can marry, I . . .

LAYLA: I will never marry!

ISMAIL: Nonsense.

LAYLA: I was stained forever by the lips of an Israeli soldier. No Muslim man can ever erase my mark of shame.

TSAHI: Why don't you marry a Jew then?

LAYLA: I will have a wedding with eternity. I will be Allah's bride.

TSAHI: I hear he can be quite demanding, especially of women. You may want to reconsider.

ISMAIL: Layla, what are you saying?

TSAHI: She's saying that no man can help her. Only Allah.

LAYLA: He understands better than you.

ISMAIL: I will help you, Layla, I will.

LAYLA: You don't know who I am.

ISMAIL: Of course I do. I've known you since you were a little girl. I saw you growing up.

LAYLA: You saw me learning to be a slave. Just like my mother.

ISMAIL: Not a slave, a woman.

LAYLA: My mother has not made one decision her entire life. Everything was decided for her. She is worse than a slave, she is a shadow. She doesn't even exist.

ISMAIL: Layla, don't talk that way about your mother.

TSAHI: Why don't you beat her so she'll stop? You told me you're not afraid of slapping anyone.

ISMAIL: You stay out of this.

LAYLA: Ismail, do you remember the day your father got beat up in the soccer field, and we all watched. Then my father came and tried to stop the soldiers. So they beat him, too. That wasn't the only beating I witnessed that day. No, my father's not one to let beatings go unaccounted for. Thank Allah he had a slave shadow. Otherwise who would he beat?

ISMAIL: Do not disrespect your father.

LAYLA *(Puts her hand in the air signaling, "Stop. I've had enough.")*: I'm leaving. Good-bye, Ismail.

ISMAIL: Layla, wait.

LAYLA: Thank you, Ismail. *Ma'a Salame. (Peace be with you.)*

ISMAIL: Layla, please, your father loves you. It hurts me to hear you talk that way about him.

LAYLA: I always hoped *you* would grow up to be a man. You, too, are a child.

ISMAIL: Remember when we were kids and we would gallop like horses and jump off the big rock as if we were Ibn Waleed's stallions?

TSAHI: Neigh!

LAYLA: Ismail, you may have been a horse—I was flying! You kept trying to teach me those stupid horse sounds. You wouldn't accept that I was a bird.

ISMAIL: We're human, Layla. How can we fly?

TSAHI: Like this. *(He demonstrates)*

ISMAIL: Were you happy then, Layla, when we held hands and jumped?

LAYLA: Yes. We were children.

ISMAIL: I need to do something, Layla. Something very important, but I can't do it without you.

LAYLA: What is it?

ISMAIL: I will tell you.

LAYLA: *Mata? (When?)*

ISMAIL *(Signals waiting motion with his hand)*: Soon. *(He smiles)*

LAYLA: Sometimes you remind me of my father.

TSAHI: It's that beating quality of his.

ISMAIL *(To Tsahi)*: You want a taste of it?

TSAHI: Did your father beat you, too?

ISMAIL: It is the duty of a father to control his family.

LAYLA: Is it the duty of an Israeli to control his land?

ISMAIL: These are two different issues.

TSAHI: Are they?

LAYLA: Yes they are, you Israeli fool! You think you can go on killing and humiliating and then blame us and our society for your own deaths? For you, death is a punishment. For us, it is a reward.

TSAHI: You're a sick people.

LAYLA: Death is an act of charity here, a gift to a suffering people. A divine shout in the wilderness—we are not powerless! *(She picks up sand in her two hands)* I am a woman fighting for equality, a person standing up for freedom. *(She walks with the sand toward Tsahi and offers it to him)* Death, after all, is part of life. Who does not love life? Who?

(Tsahi moves out of the way, Layla lets sand fall onto the ground. A choral ode. The three move to different parts of the stage to be alone. Layla remains in the center, performing a simple action that subtly implies that she is the subject of the ode. Perhaps she plays with the sand.

The Chorus performs a tribal drumbeat, accompanied by a Berber dance of hands. On the scrim, we see enormous hands shaking to the primal beat.)

CHORUS:
> She waits . . .
> Terror wrapped in rage
> Faster and faster,
> Further and further
>> Into the future.
> The mother's womb—
>> Memory child avenging fury
>> Fury child avenging whom?

TSAHI: I hear you want to go to university.

LAYLA: I see you've told him all about me.

ISMAIL: I like talking about you.

TSAHI: Do many women from your village go?

LAYLA: You see, here I'm considered the rebel girl. Everyone knows I am difficult. I cry and I scream. And I have too much pride. Right, Ismail?

ISMAIL: You are proud. That is not a sin. But you disobey your father.

LAYLA: My father has one son and six daughters. Poor man. He thinks his injured pride will be healed when his son becomes a famous businessman.

TSAHI: So he wants to send him to university.

LAYLA: But not his daughter.

ISMAIL: He thinks there is nothing to be gained by reading American novels.

TSAHI: Sounds like my father.

LAYLA: My father fears me almost as much as you do.

ISMAIL: Your father is not afraid of you.

LAYLA: I have a power that neither of you have. A Muslim womb, the greatest fear of the "free world"!

TSAHI: I'm more scared of him than I am of you.

LAYLA: Life is a battle. That's all it is. So I will fight and fight and fight until I am dead. *(To Ismail)* I will fight you. *(To Tsahi)* And I will fight you, and I will fight your people. I never lose a struggle.

TSAHI: You bring misery on yourself. There's no joy in battle.

ISMAIL *(To Tsahi)*: So why do you do it?

LAYLA: Because there's satisfaction. The satisfaction of knowing that my fight has yielded fruit.

TSAHI: More misery?

LAYLA: Your people's project, the Zionist project has failed. Instead of safety it has given you constant bloodshed. Soon we will out-number you, and that will be the end of the Jewish state.

TSAHI: Is that how you measure success, by someone else's failure?

ISMAIL: At the moment that's all we have.

TSAHI: You derive pleasure from blood.

LAYLA *(With sick pleasure)*: Not pleasure. Satisfaction.

TSAHI: Maybe I should shoot you then?

LAYLA: You think *we're* sick? We learned to live for battle from the Americans. You know Hemingway, *The Old Man and the Sea*? I am the old man. He fights and fights with the big fish, almost dies. But he reaches the shore safely.

TSAHI: He doesn't win. He comes back without the fish.

LAYLA: He's a hero. When he reaches the shore he turns to look at the sea, and— *(She spits toward Tsahi's feet)*

ISMAIL: Layla!

LAYLA: Spits at it . . . and leaves.

(After a brief pause, Tsahi, very emotional, lunges at her. Ismail gets in the way and tries to stop him.)

TSAHI: *Ya bat zona ani yaharog otach! (You bitch, I'm going to kill you!)* You want me to kill you, is that what you want?

ISMAIL: Leave her alone!

TSAHI: You women wish for death like it's some kind of an orgasm. Fuck the world! Your father, your mother, your brother—fuck them all! *(He throws Ismail to the floor)*

LAYLA *(Mockingly)*: Fuck *you.*

TSAHI: You crazy bitch! *(He slaps her)*

(Ismail grabs Tsahi and throws him to the ground.)

ISMAIL: I warned you. *(He kicks him in the stomach)*

(Tsahi stays lying on the ground crying.)

Are you okay, Layla?

LAYLA: Why don't you go help your boyfriend?

ISMAIL: Layla, you're not acting like yourself tonight. What's gotten into you?

LAYLA: Layla.

(Silence.)

ISMAIL *(Looking at Tsahi, who has not moved)*: Are you okay? *(No response)* Hey, Israeli man, you okay? Ishak, Tsahi! Don't tell me one kick in the stomach knocked you out.

(Tsahi turns around, his eyes red with tears.)

TSAHI: Your woman, she reminds me of my sister.

LAYLA: Is she a spitter, too?

TSAHI: I saw her spit once. At my father's feet. That was the only time he ever slapped her. But it didn't help. She went and did just what he forbade her to do, and never came back.

LAYLA: Where was she going?

TSAHI: To a pub. In Ramallah. It was called Brivacy. With a B. It was like no pub in Jerusalem. A pub only for women. My father told her not to go. He didn't know where it was, he only knew what kind of pub it was, and that was enough. He told her that he raised her to be a woman, not a man. They yelled and screamed at each other. She was crying, my big sister. *Tsipi.* But through her tears I could see her black eyes blazing with fire, and she shot her words at him like bullets: "You love me only in your chains. You don't love *me.* You despise my nature." "I despise your choices," my father said. "That's right," she answered, "you like it when I have none to make." My mother tried to calm her down, but she just got more violent. "Don't talk to me, Mother, my freedom is your worst nightmare." I stood in the corner and through my little ten-year-old eyes I watched my family rip itself apart, and did nothing. A terrible fear came over me, as if death were outside our door, waiting. *(He walks toward Layla. He speaks to her without anger)* My father told her she is a disgrace to her family and a disgrace to women. That was when she spat at his feet, and stood there in front of him waiting to be slapped, like a lion cub waiting to be fed. *(Layla walks away from him)* After he slapped her, he told her to leave. She walked out, leaving the door open. *(Again, he moves toward Layla)* I ran to the door and called her name. She turned and looked at me, her dark green dress shining in the moonlight. "*Tsipi, Al telchi,*" I said. "Don't go." She walked towards me and, trying to smile through her tears, said, "It's time for me to go." *(Layla sits next to Ismail)* When she turned around and started walking I wanted to run after her. *(To Ismail)* But I was too afraid to leave the house.

(Pause.)

LAYLA: What happened to her?

TSAHI: We didn't hear from her for months. Finally the police contacted my parents. Her body was found in a wadi halfway between Jerusalem and Ramallah. She had been stabbed all over.

LAYLA: She was a *shahida*.

ISMAIL: What?

LAYLA: A martyr.

TSAHI: How dare you? *(He goes toward his rifle for comfort, then collapses, crying)*

ISMAIL: She didn't die for anyone. She died for death. And more death. She died for pain.

LAYLA: She died for her people. She died for women. She died for her god.

ISMAIL: She died because she was Israeli! That's it, Layla. Her death didn't help anyone, and her god doesn't give a damn whether she's dead or not. She died for me to get beat up and told I'm a donkey, and for you to get humiliated by a soldier. She died for the soldiers to keep killing and for the politicians to keep lying and for every one of us to be miserable. She is dead. And her family has been grieving ever since.

LAYLA: A rose, she's a rose.

ISMAIL: Layla *khalas*! She's not a rose, she's dead. Dead dead dead. No paradise. No virgins.

LAYLA: Women don't get virgins. They get a pure husband.

ISMAIL: Just death. Never-ending darkness. Like this night. That's all they . . .

LAYLA: Ismail!

ISMAIL: What?

LAYLA: Do you think she was brave?

ISMAIL: She stood up to her father.

LAYLA: Answer the question. *(Hopefully)* Please. Was she brave? *(Pause. No response. Bitterly)* She was braver than you.

ISMAIL: She's dead. I'm still alive.

(The Chorus sings an ancient Andalusian love song in Arabic—"Lama Bada"—as the Dancer dances with her veil.
Layla makes tea.)

LAYLA *(Looking at the kettle)*: L'alakat beyna nas zai kas el hadid, elela taba'atna bidirna. Ihna ma nikdarsesh nitcharar min el hadid, min kuthrat el kawanin. *(Human relationships are like a steel form into which we are poured by our family. We cannot liberate ourselves from the steel because there are so many rules.)*

(The Musician continues "Lama Bada.")

TSAHI: What was that?

LAYLA: Human relationships are like a steel form that our family pours us into. We cannot liberate ourselves from the steel because the rules are so strict. Tradition is so strict.

ISMAIL: There is freedom within those rules. There is life.

LAYLA *(Cynically)*: Life. What's that?

TSAHI: My father came from Iraq when he was a little boy. He saw the world changing. The steel melting, being molded, changing shape. That is life. He was afraid of it, so he accepted it too late. Life taught him how to cry.

LAYLA: Your sister taught him to cry.

ISMAIL: We like to say that Muslims are fearless. It is not true.

(Layla gets up and starts wandering, her walk expressing the trajectory of the moon.)

LAYLA: What will *I* teach my father?

TSAHI: Teach him who you are.

ISMAIL: Our nights have become dreamless.

(Ismail gets up and wanders his own night-sky trajectory.)

LAYLA: When I was very little I brought home an injured raven. He wrapped a cloth around its broken wing.

(Tsahi gets up and wanders his night-sky trajectory.)

TSAHI: This morning I was not alone. I had a girlfriend.

ISMAIL: I haven't remembered a dream in years. I used to dream every night.

LAYLA: Or was that a dream?

TSAHI: All day I've had her in my thoughts, my sister.

ISMAIL: Do you still dream?

LAYLA: I don't know. Do I?

TSAHI: I dreamed of her.

ISMAIL: At night.

LAYLA: All fragments.

TSAHI: Making love.

ISMAIL: Night pieces.

LAYLA: Random pictures.

TSAHI: By the sea.

ISMAIL: Dawn.

LAYLA: Steel.

TSAHI: Alone.

(As the Musician sings his Andalusian love song and the Dancer dances behind the scrim, the three characters stop and look at each other, realizing they've all been doing the same thing separately. When the song is over:)

Sometimes I wish she could have seen me in uniform, once.

LAYLA: Why?

ISMAIL: It's who he is today.

TSAHI: No. It's who I wanted to be.

LAYLA *(To Tsahi)*: Tell me the truth. How did you get here?

TSAHI: I came to see a woman. She dumped me. So I wandered around the desert thinking about my sister until it became dark.

(Ismail hands him tea.)

ISMAIL: Here, *ishrab (drink).*

TSAHI: *Shukran. (Thanks.)*

LAYLA: How do you know Arabic?

TSAHI: My grandmother, the Iraqi one, always spoke to me in Arabic. Do you understand Hebrew?

LAYLA: *Kzat. Achla, sababa, walla, habibi. (A bit. Cool, fun, really, my friend.)*

ISMAIL *(As he hands Layla tea)*: She understands the Arabic words the Israelis use in Hebrew.

TSAHI: The truth is all our best slang words are from Arabic.

ISMAIL: *Ganavim.*

LAYLA: What's *ganavim?*

TSAHI: Thieves. But we don't steal just anything, only the good stuff.

ISMAIL: Words and land.

TSAHI: You stole a song from me earlier.

ISMAIL: What did it mean?

TSAHI: "It's only you I want tonight. You are like a million songs. Why did you leave me and go to a different world? Sometimes I spend the whole night thinking how to love you. You are my night. You are my day." *(To Layla, sweetly)* "You are my night."

LAYLA: *Jamil jidan. (Beautiful.)* It reminds me of the love songs my mother used to sing to me when I was a child.

ISMAIL: You would always start dancing.

LAYLA: Until someone would tell me to stop.

TSAHI: Why stop dancing?

LAYLA: There were men around.

TSAHI: They didn't like it?

LAYLA: It's forbidden. *Haram.*

ISMAIL: I always loved your dancing.

LAYLA: No you didn't.

TSAHI: He was telling me all about it before. He said you're the best dancer in the region.

LAYLA: But all these years you would just sit silently when they would tell me to stop. Why didn't you ever tell me?

ISMAIL: I was saving it for tonight.

LAYLA *(Touched)*: *Shukran, (Thank you,)* Ismail.

TSAHI: Why don't you dance for us? Just one quick dance before the night is over.

(Layla is reluctant.)

ISMAIL: Please, Layla.

TSAHI: What do we have to do to get you to dance? We'll do anything. *(He belly dances)*

ISMAIL: Whatever you like.

LAYLA *(Softening)*: Don't do anything. Just watch my dance, and remember it.

(She dances a good-bye dance to all that is in her life, including the desert, Tsahi and, especially, Ismail. She dances her love, her fear, her passion, her despair. This short dance should mean very much to Layla but look like an Arab dance that breaks away from tradition toward its end. The dance ends with Layla twirling herself down to the ground. Tsahi claps when she's finished. Ismail is in a daze but eventually joins the clapping shortly after. The dance has shed Layla of her anger and leaves her nakedly innocent.)

TSAHI: Bravo!

ISMAIL: Thank you, Layla.

LAYLA: Ismail, I'm sorry I made you wait.

ISMAIL: That's okay. What kept you?

LAYLA: When I got to the caves from my town I heard some shots fired and everyone got scared. I had to hide in your parents' cave. Then it took a while for everyone to go to bed.

TSAHI *(Getting nervous)*: Who was shooting?

LAYLA: I don't know.

ISMAIL: Where in the village were the shots coming from? You must have heard that.

LAYLA: I don't remember.

ISMAIL: What do you mean you don't remember?

LAYLA: There are gunshots every day. I don't notice . . .

ISMAIL: There are never shots at night.

LAYLA: Ismail, leave me alone. I don't know anything.

TSAHI: Are you sure nobody followed you down here?

LAYLA: How would I know?

TSAHI *(To Ismail)*: Put the fire out.

(He does.)

ISMAIL: Did you hear any shouting?

LAYLA: There were some people shouting.

TSAHI: In Hebrew or Arabic?

LAYLA: It was far away. I couldn't tell.

ISMAIL: It must have been the settlers. Did you hear my father say anything about the settlers? He starts cursing when they're around.

LAYLA: Look I don't know, Ismail. I came down here to tell you something, and that's all that was on my mind.

ISMAIL: I understand. I also have something important to talk to you about. But he's right, they could have followed you down.

TSAHI: What makes you so sure these were Israeli gunshots?

ISMAIL: They kept the women in the caves. They only do that when there's danger.

TSAHI: Danger doesn't have to be Israelis.

ISMAIL: In my village it's only the Israelis who bring danger.

TSAHI: It could have been Hamas. They've started killing collaborators again lately.

ISMAIL: We don't have any collaborators in the village.

TSAHI: How do you think the army knew that bomber was from here? Because we have collaborators, informers. Now Hamas wants to get them.

ISMAIL: The settlers came just a few days ago to harass us with their rifles and they said they'd be back.

TSAHI: Bullshit.

ISMAIL: What the fuck do *you* know?

TSAHI: I know enough.

ISMAIL: I bet you do. I bet you know exactly what happened up in the village.

TSAHI: You think so?

ISMAIL: You're a goddamn soldier! How could I have even considered trusting you. Showing up out of nowhere asking me questions about who I'm meeting . . .

TSAHI: Oh, and I should believe that you've got nothing to do with this? What a coincidence that you should be meeting your death-poetry-spewing woman as chaos is breaking loose in the village.

ISMAIL: What are you suggesting?

TSAHI: That you're working with whoever is shooting up there.

ISMAIL: Tell me what the fuck you're doing here!

TSAHI: Fuck you!

LAYLA: Aieeeee!

(She goes away from them and sits by the rock. Both men stop and look at her. Silence. The men look at each other.)

ISMAIL: Can I trust you?

TSAHI: Yes. Can I trust you?

ISMAIL: Yes.

TSAHI: If you fuck me over I'll rip your balls out and feed them to your sheep.

ISMAIL: If you fuck me over I'll kill your whole family.

TSAIII: I need the cartridge.

ISMAIL: Layla.

(Layla stands in a position to be frisked. Ismail goes over to her and pulls the cartridge off of her hip. She remains in that position.)

TSAHI: What are we going to do?

ISMAIL: We should see if there's anyone around. I'll check this way you look that way.

(The men exit in different directions. The dawn begins to rise very slowly. Moments pass. Layla takes center stage, the Dancer d. Music: guitar and voice, a lyrical, sad and beautiful Sephardic-Jewish melody.)

LAYLA:

>Earth—Mother—rape of the earth—Allah!
>Where have you led me now?

CHORUS:

>You shriek like a nightingale,
>That dark bird that sees no daylight.

LAYLA:

>Me, a nightingale?
>I can only squeal her songs.
>>Allah gave her an easy life, wings to carry her away.
>>The explosion waits for me.

CHORUS:

>Your words are nails.
>>Your song is terror.
>>Your dance is a human beast.

LAYLA *(To the audience)*:

>>Here is the bride.
>>Is she fresh?
>>Is she loyal?
>Time for the truth—
>My body is not my own.

CHORUS:

>I hear your destiny—unbearable screeching,
>>Sobs that rip the ears.

LAYLA:

> Allah himself—
>> I can feel his caress.
> Scalding fingers full of pity.
> Now it is my turn to give.
>> My time to die.

CHORUS:

> Run! There is still time!

LAYLA:

> No time left, friends.
> All doors are bolted around me.

CHORUS:

> I haven't seen bravery until this moment.

LAYLA:

> Oh sun in the sky,
>> The last light to touch my skin,
> Grant me this:
> The men's blood shall be avenged, that much we know.
> But let the avenger remember
> The blood that streamed out of my chained body, too.
> Even a woman's blood must be paid for.

(Tsahi returns holding his rifle.)

TSAHI: What was that about?

LAYLA:

> A lion who lacks a lion's heart.

(Ismail enters.)

TSAHI: Your woman's talking funny again.
ISMAIL *(Goes over to her)*: Don't worry, *habibti*. Everything will be all right.
TSAHI: Did you see anybody?
ISMAIL: No. You?
TSAHI: Only a fox.
LAYLA: You are near-sighted. My eyes see deep into the darkness.
TSAHI: What does that mean?

ISMAIL: Did you see anybody?

LAYLA: I see my body falling. Don't you?

ISMAIL: What do you mean, Layla?

TSAHI: We don't have time for this.

LAYLA: I have no more time. Sand falling through my hands, disappearing into the desert earth.

TSAHI *(Ignoring her)*: Ismail, if they start shooting . . .

LAYLA *(To Ismail)*: Blood, Ismail, blood! The earth will turn orange like the sun.

ISMAIL: Layla, please, not now. *(To Tsahi)* Listen, if they start shooting . . .

LAYLA: I'm slipping through your hands.

ISMAIL: We're sick of your damn riddles, Layla! If you have something to say, tell it to me now. Otherwise be quiet.

LAYLA: I'm telling you, Ismail.

ISMAIL: What are you telling me?

LAYLA: Please help me before you understand.

TSAHI: This is ridiculous!

ISMAIL: What? Understand what?

(She gently takes his face in her hands.)

LAYLA: I want to live.

ISMAIL: Can't you see we're talking about something important?! *(He breaks away from her)*

TSAHI: Don't listen to her!

ISMAIL *(To Tsahi)*: If they shoot at us you yell back at them in Hebrew that you're Israeli.

LAYLA *(Simultaneously with Ismail, above, and Tsahi, below)*: Don't yell, Ismail. You will want to have whispered.

TSAHI: No way. You should yell first in Arabic.

LAYLA *(Hugs Ismail from behind)*: You yell at your guilt to abandon you.

ISMAIL: I'm telling you it's the settlers. If they hear Arabic they won't stop shooting.

LAYLA: Your shame will explode onto your heart.

TSAHI: If it's the settlers, Hebrew won't help. Arabic is the only language that can help us.

LAYLA *(She walks away from the men)*: No words will help. No language. Just listen.

ISMAIL: The only ones who would randomly shoot are the Israelis.

LAYLA: Just listen.

TSAHI: Bullshit.

LAYLA: Just silence.

TSAHI: I'm sure it's the Hamas. If they hear me . . . *(He accidentally fires his rifle)*

ISMAIL AND TSAHI: Fuck!

(Layla, startled, jumps up. More gunshots.)

TSAHI: *Al tiru! Ani Israeli!* (Don't shoot! I'm Israeli!)   ISMAIL: *Ma tidrabuna! Ihna Filastiniya!* (Don't shoot! We're Palestinian!)

(More gunshots. Tsahi shoots back.)

TSAHI *(To Ismail)*: Tell them we're Palestinian!

(More gunshots.)

ISMAIL: *Ma tidrabuna! Ihna Filastinia! (Don't shoot! We're Palestinian!)*

(More gunshots.)

ISMAIL: Tell them we're Israeli!

TSAHI: *Al tiru! Ani Israeli! (Silence) Al tiru! Ani hayal tsahal! (Don't shoot I'm an IDF soldier!)*

SOLDIER 1 *(Offstage)*: *Mi atem? (Who are you?)*

TSAHI: *Ani hayal. Hashavti she'atem mehablim. Al tiru! (I'm an IDF soldier. I thought you were terrorists. Don't shoot!)*

SOLDIER 1 *(Offstage)*: *Torid et haneshek vetasim oto al ha'adamah. (Put the rifle on the ground.)*

(Tsahi puts his rifle on the ground.)

(To Tsahi) Tagid lahem sheyarimu yadayim lemala. (Tell them to put their hands in the air.)

TSAHI: Put your hands up in the air.

(Ismail does.)

SOLDIER 1 *(Offstage)*: *Gam ata. (You, too.)*

(Tsahi puts hands in the air.)

Anachnu baim. (We're coming.)

(Two Soldiers enter. They frisk both men.)

SOLDIER 2: *Ra'item po bachura?* . . . *(Did you see a young woman here?)*

TSAHI: *Hem lo mevinim Ivrit. (They don't speak Hebrew.)*

SOLDIER 2: Did you see a young woman, about nineteen years old, black hair?

TSAHI: Ken, hi . . .

(Ismail turns around and finds Layla lying on the ground bleeding, unconscious.)

Elohim. (Oh God.)

ISMAIL: Layla! Layla! *La* Layla, *la! (To the Soldiers) Intum ataltuha! Intum ataltu* Layla! *(You killed her! You killed my Layla!)* You bastards! You shot her! *(He lunges at them. Tsahi stops him and holds him back, hugging him)*

SOLDIER 2 *(To Tsahi)*: You better calm your friend down.

SOLDIER 1 *(Goes over to Layla as Tsahi tries to calm Ismail)*: *Zot hi.* It's her. *(To Ismail, as Soldier 2 frisks Layla)* Your girlfriend was about to become a shahida, a martyr. She was working with the Al-Aqsa Martyrs Brigade, and was about to leave tomorrow for her final training before blowing herself up.

ISMAIL: No. It can't be true.

SOLDIER 2: Her contact was arrested earlier in the village, but she managed to hide.

LAYLA *(Wakes up)*: Ismail . . .

TSAHI: She's calling your name.

(Ismail starts running toward her, but Soldier 2 gets between Ismail and Layla, pointing his gun at Ismail.)

(To the Soldiers) Please.

(Soldier 2 looks to Soldier 1 for approval. She nods and Soldier 2 moves out of the way. Ismail runs and kneels at Layla's side.)

ISMAIL: It's not true, right, Layla, they're lying. Tell me you didn't want to die.

LAYLA: Forgive me, Ismail.

ISMAIL: *La* Layla, *la. (He holds her)* Marry me, Layla. We have a life to live together. Children, a future. You are my life, Layla, don't leave me. Please, *albi*, please . . .

(She loses consciousness.)

Layla! Layla! *La! (To the Soldiers)* Do something!

(Tsahi runs over to Layla. He tries to give her air. He checks her wrist. After some time:)

TSAHI: She's dead.

(Ismail falls on Layla's body, crying. Tsahi watches him for a moment, then begins to sing as Ismail picks Layla's body up to dance with her.)

> *Ko zara at li velama*
> *Halacht li le'olam acher.*
> *Lifamim ani hoshev ech le'ehov otach halayla*
> *At li layla. At li yom. At li Layla.*

SOLDIER 1: We're going to take both of you in to the base to ask you some questions.
TSAHI: What are you going to do with her body?
SOLDIER 1: We're taking it to be examined.
ISMAIL: Can I carry her up to the road?
SOLDIER 1 *(Slightly confused by the question)*: All right.

(Ismail tries to put Layla's body in a position to carry her off.)

TSAHI: Wait.

(He comes to help pick up Layla. The two men hold her at shoulder height and begin to walk off.
The Dancer enters the stage veiled to dance a final dance as the sun rises. The Dead Sea can be seen glittering behind the men in the distance. Musician sings the song "Zaman a-Salam" ("Time for Peace") as the two men, seen in silhouette, carry Layla's body finally off. The Musician enters the stage with his guitar and says:)

CHORUS:
> That is all,
> A woman has spoken her word.
> Now I ask only one thing of you—
> Accept the truth.

(Brief pause.)

Can you?

(Pause. He sings the "Zaman a-Salam" chorus as actors enter and stand with him.)

END OF PLAY

Currently a member of the Emerging Playwrights Program of New York's Theater for the New City (TNC), as well as Writer-in-Residence at Toronto's Crow's Theatre, MISHA SHULMAN recently completed his MFA in Playwriting at the City University of New York, under the tutelage of renowned playwright Mac Wellman. Misha was born and raised in Jerusalem, and served in the Israeli army as a Commander in charge of Education. Most recently his comedy *Apricots* played to sold-out houses in Toronto's Factory Theatre. In 2008 Misha directed DADAnewyork in his play *Brunch at the Luthers*, and Off-Broadway at Theater for the New City. Dealing with the Israeli/Palestinian conflict, Shulman's play, *Desert Sunrise* was produced at TNC in 2005 (directed by Shulman), and was revived twice due to critical success and popular demand. *Desert Sunrise* was subsequently produced in Chicago, as well as enjoying an extended run at the Lillian Theatre in Los Angeles. Misha is the founding director of the Boundless Theater, for whom he wrote and directed *The Vermillionaire* (Midway Rock Club, New York City, 2007) and directed *Stop! Border Ahead* (Alma Beach, Tel Aviv, 2007), *ANIMALS!* (Prism Theatre, New York City, 2005) and *Jonah—an Interactive Theatrical Dream* (Hunter College, New York City, 2004). As an actor Misha has worked extensively with the famed Living Theatre and with DADAnewyork. Shulman's earlier drama *The Fist* was produced at the Public Theatre of South Florida in 2003 and in New York City in 2004. It was chosen as "pick of the week" by nytheatre.com, and has since been presented at several venues around the U.S., as well as in Melbourne, Australia. For the Board of Jewish Education of Greater New York, Misha wrote and directed several plays, including *In the Stomach of a Whale* (2003) and *A Sephardic Masquerade* (2004–2006). Upcoming 2010 productions include *The Fake History of George the Last* (TNC, New York City) and *These Beaten Eyes* (Crow's Theatre, Toronto).

Browntown

Sam Younis

Author's Statement

I began writing *Browntown* in reaction to my audition experiences as an Arab-American actor. When I earned my MFA in Acting and started looking for work in New York, I encountered many perplexities, some disgruntling, others comical. Why am I routinely a candidate for terrorist roles? Why are these terrorists always named "Mohammed"? Why does that Indian guy keep getting the Arab terrorist parts over me? Why should that upset me? Am I a sellout?

Such questions have always been inevitable for "actors of color," especially in television and film. For Middle Eastern and South Asian performers in particular, the issue of stereotyping has become even more relevant in the wake of the 9/11 attacks. Since that catastrophic event, some American films and television shows have bravely and intelligently explored aspects of Middle Eastern identity never before addressed in the mainstream, while countless others have continued to put forward unexamined and harmful depictions of entire groups of people. Although the existence of negative stereotyping is age-old and practically indisputable (for those who doubt this, I refer you to Jack G. Shaheen's book *Reel Bad Arabs: How Hollywood Vilifies a People* (Olive Branch Press, 2001, 2009), it would be irresponsible to place blame entirely on the shoulders of any single party. The creation of a movie or television show is by nature collaborative, so all parties involved bear responsibility for the final product. Moreover, everyone is capable of gross ignorance and insensitivity, even those who most complain about being a victim of it. With this in mind, I encourage anyone who reads or performs *Browntown* to consider the pressures and complexities of television and film production before passing judgment on any of the characters in the play.

My sincere hope is that *Browntown* can provide a launching pad for dialogue, not only among minority actors, but also among all professionals in theatre, television and film. We live in an era in which cultural misunderstanding has led to dire political and mortal consequences. Yet people often fail to acknowledge or take responsibility for their own prejudices. I believe that comedy is an effective tool for exposing the roots and everyday expressions of ignorance in a digestible, nonjudgmental way. If we can laugh at our own ignorance, then we have already identified it. And that's a start.

Before evolving into a full-length play, *Browntown* was performed in November 2003 at the Krane Theatre in New York to kick off the first ever New York Arab-American Comedy Festival, co-founded by Maysoon Zayid and Dean Obeidallah and co-produced with Nibras. It was directed by Abigail Marateck. The cast was as follows:

OMAR	Omar Koury
MALEK	Sam Younis
VIJAY	Debargo Sanyal
ANN	Rana Kazkaz
SHERRY	Alison Poluga

The full-length version of *Browntown* premiered at the Lucille Lortel Theatre during the New York International Fringe Festival in August 2004. At the close of the festival, the play was given a 2004 FringeNYC Award for Overall Excellence in Playwriting. It was directed by Abigail Marateck. Set design was by Jisun Kim. Lighting design was by Nick Hung. The stage manager was Mary Stone. The cast was as follows:

OMAR	Omar Koury
MALEK	Sam Younis
VIJAY	Debargo Sanyal
ANN	Whitney Arcaro
SHERRY	Alison Poluga

The character of Hamilton was written into the play after the close of the New York International Fringe Festival production. An abridged version of *Browntown* was presented in Los Angeles in 2006 when the Arab-American Comedy Festival made its first visit to the West Coast. It was directed by Abigail Marateck. The cast was as follows:

OMAR	Waleed Zuaiter
MALEK	Ryan Shrime
VIJAY	Sam Younis
CASTING DIRECTOR	Neil Potter
SHERRY	Bethel Caram

Characters

OMAR FAKHOURY, a jaded and disheveled actor, Arab-American, mid-thirties

MALEK BIZRI, an earnest and well-groomed actor, Arab-American, mid-twenties

VIJAY GOVINDU, a confident Juilliard-trained actor, Indian-American, mid-twenties

ANN DAVIS, a well-established casting director, mid-thirties

SHERRY HOLLOWAY, an attractive and inexperienced actress, works as Ann's audition reader, early twenties

HAMILTON JEFFRIES, Senior Vice President of Casting for a major studio, Ann's boss and liaison to the studio executives, fifties; this character may be visible or may be played by an offstage voice

Setting

The New York City office of Wide-Net Talent Casting, November 2003. Most political and cultural references are deliberately specific to the surreal months directly following the 2003 U.S.-led invasion of Iraq. Each scene transpires in either the waiting room or the audition room of the office.

Note

A glossary of select terms appears at the end of the play.

For my incredible wife, Abby, and son, Gabriel Theodore
Younis, born September 9, 2008. For all members of the
Younis, Chidiac, Marateck and Finch families living in
the United States and abroad. Thanks for all the love and
support you have offered over the years!

Acknowledgments

I owe a great debt of gratitude to Dean Obeidallah and Maysoon Zayid—the visionary co-founders of the Arab-American Comedy Festival—and to all members of Nibras. Without their belief and passion, *Browntown* would have never been written. I am deeply grateful to my wife, Abigail Marateck, for her expertise in directing the play and for her undying support. I would also like to thank my loving parents and brother and sister for their encouragement throughout my artistic career. Finally, I thank Dr. Holly Hill and Dr. Dina Amin for conceiving this vital anthology, and for including *Browntown*.

Scene 1

THE WAITING ROOM

The Wide-Net Talent Casting office in Midtown Manhattan, Tuesday, eleven o'clock A.M. *Omar Fakhoury sits perusing* Maxim *magazine as he awaits his chance to audition for* The Color of Terror, *a made-for-TV movie. Malek Bizri enters the waiting room, signs his name on a clipboard, sits, pulls out his audition material, and begins quietly mouthing his lines to himself. Though physically animated, he is inaudible. Eventually, he notices Omar and greets him.*

MALEK: Omar! What's up, dawg! Figured I might see you here.

OMAR: You, too, man! I saw you come in, but I didn't wanna bug you. You were in "the zone" with your sides over there.

MALEK: It's cool, man. Just some last-second prep work.

OMAR: Nice. So, you staying busy these days?

MALEK: Well you know, just doing the audition-slash-catering thing. Kinda slow right now don't you think?

OMAR: Catering or auditioning?

MALEK: Both, really.

OMAR: Yeah, but it'll pick up soon. The summer's always dead.

MALEK: Hey, I didn't see you on the clipboard. Did you sign in?

OMAR: Oh shit, I forgot.

(Omar stands, scurries to the clipboard, signs in, and takes an extra moment to scan the names of the many actors who have signed in before him.)

Karim Fustok, Fawaz Qaddumi, Raj Patel, Julio Ramirez—Jesus, they're seeing all of Browntown for this one!

MALEK: I know, it's crazy, man!

(Beat.)

So where have you been? Still doing car shows out of state?

OMAR: Yep. Just got back two weeks ago.

MALEK: What exactly do you *do* at those shows?

(Omar suddenly launches into a rapid-fire version of his intolerable auto show speech. He has delivered this exact speech a thousand times. Malek may interrupt in the middle of the speech.)

OMAR: "Welcome to the Subaru display at the Louisville auto show. Subaru offers a complete line of award-winning vehicles, in terms of both safety and value. Subaru is the only company to offer Symmetrical All-Wheel Drive as standard equipment on every vehicle we sell . . ."

MALEK *(Miserable, interjecting)*: Dude—enough. I get the picture.

OMAR: Such horseshit. I'm glad to be out of Kentucky, tell you that much. Talk about a red state.

MALEK: You gotta find a new gig, man. That job's sucking your soul.

OMAR: I know, that's why I came back.

(Beat.)

So, do you know anything about this TV movie thing?

MALEK: It seems kinda interesting. I finally finished reading the script on the way here and I thought it was *way* better than—what was that last one we both auditioned for a couple of months ago?

OMAR AND MALEK *(Simultaneously)*: Geronimo Jihad!

MALEK: That was it. Ya know, I think Sameer actually booked that one.

OMAR: Really? Good for him. That's great.

MALEK: Yeah, he's in Morocco shooting it right now.

OMAR: Hey, at least they cast Sameer, and not one of those poser Indian guys.

MALEK: Whatever, who cares, man.

OMAR: Is Sameer cool with all the "lu-lu-lu-lu-lu"? *(Mimicking the "crazy Arab" sounds)*

MALEK: Yeah, he's game. They made him grow out a long beard and behead a Dutch journalist.

OMAR: That's ridiculous.

MALEK: I know, but he hadn't worked in a while so . . .

OMAR: Glad he's working then. That's an awesome break for him.

MALEK: So what did *you* think of the script?

OMAR: I quit reading it halfway through.

MALEK: Why?

OMAR: I dunno. I wasn't crazy about it. *The Color of Terror!* Just seems like another scary brown-guy movie.

MALEK: Hey, at least the Arab in this one is a *valiant* terrorist.

OMAR: What do you mean?

MALEK: I mean he has heroic reasons for blowing up the supermarket.

OMAR: Heroic reasons?

MALEK: He cared about his family. Al Qaeda was gonna kill his baby if he didn't comply, so Mohammed had no choice.

OMAR: But that's the thing, man. Why is his name *Mohammed*? Why do *all* terrorists gotta be named Mohammed in these movies?

MALEK: Well, Mohammed *is* the most popular name in the world.

OMAR: I know, but it's like these writers have never even heard of another Muslim name. It's always Mohammed! I mean, I'd love to play an Islamic militant named Tarek or Fadi for a change. Hell, I'd even settle for Moustafa.

MALEK: But at least this writer is trying to justify Mohammed's *reasons* for doing what he does.

OMAR: Why should she justify it? Why should anyone? Terrorism is fucked up. Is her *justification* supposed to make me feel better about it?

MALEK: I take that back. She's not exactly justifying his actions, but at least making him more human. And did you notice—they even called him a "freedom fighter" in the breakdowns!? "Freedom fighter." That's some progress right there! You can't be a snob about this shit, man.

OMAR: I'm not, I'm just saying, you gotta draw the line somewhere. For Chrissake, this Mohammed's got four wives, he hates all Jews, he drives a Mercedes that he bought with his family's oil money, and he's conspiring with a guerilla group called "Allies for Allah." They may as well put him on a camel and strap a bomb on to him in the opening scene. This is basically the same shit as *True Lies* or *Not without My Daughter*! There are consequences for perpetuating these stereotypes.

MALEK: Weren't you in *True Lies*?

(A beat. Omar's busted.)

OMAR: Look, all I'm saying is—why can't I—just once—play a normal guy? A paramedic, a musician, a stockbroker, a journalist. Why can't I be the brown John Cusack? You know? Some dude who's just chillin' at Al Bustan, eating some falafel, smoking some shisha and watching all the hot Lebanese chicks stroll by. I would kill to play a *normal* bad guy. Like an ethnically nondescript . . .

MALEK: Bank robber!

OMAR: Or con artist—

MALEK: Or serial rapist! That would be awesome . . . *(Has an epiphany)* You know what? Why don't we just stop bitchin' already and write our own screenplay?

OMAR: About what?

MALEK: I don't know, *good* Arabs.

(Another young brown actor, Vijay, enters wearing headphones and trendy shades. He drags a noisy, compact rolling suitcase behind him.)

OMAR: Actually, that's not a bad idea— *(Noticing Vijay)* Oh shit, man.

MALEK: What?

OMAR: Look who just walked in.

MALEK: Who, Vijay? Yeah, so what?

OMAR: That fucker keeps taking our parts.

MALEK: *Our* parts?

OMAR: He just got cast in *Hijacked at Home* and *Baby Bombers*. Don't get me wrong, he's a nice guy. I just don't understand why they keep hiring an Indian guy for specifically *Arab* roles.

MALEK: Cuz he's good! That guy played every mainstage lead at Juilliard.

(Vijay, unzipping his hooded sweatshirt, conspicuously reveals his Juilliard T-shirt.)

OMAR: But why don't they just let us represent *ourselves* for a change? We don't need some Indian guy speaking for the Arab community.

MALEK: Oh gimme a fucking break, dude. You're just jealous.

OMAR: I'm really not! I don't want that role! I told you, I'd prefer not to play these terrorist roles, unless they are really high paying. All I'm saying is, if you're not gonna give it to me, at least give it to another *Arab*. Give it to you. Or to Sameer. Don't give it to some Indian who's ignorant of our culture—

VIJAY *(Takes off his headphones)*: Hey, Omar! And, Malek, right?

OMAR AND MALEK *(Awkwardly, feeling busted)*: Yeah! Hey, man!

VIJAY: Oh, I'm not interrupting something, am I? Some serious conference?

MALEK: No, not at all!

OMAR: No. It's good to see you, man. You're a busy man these days, right?!

VIJAY: *These* days, yes. We'll see how long the luck can last.

OMAR: Must be nice juggling two films.

VIJAY: I'm just happy to be working at all! Enough about me. Omar, didn't you just get back from Louisville?

OMAR: Yeah.

VIJAY: So . . . how was *Indian Ink*?!

(An awkward pause.)

You played the lead guy—Nirad Das, right?

OMAR: Yeah, Nirad. It was a lot of fun, man. I was psyched to be in a Stoppard play. His shit is brilliant.

MALEK: *Indian Ink?* I thought you said you were in Louisville to show Subarus.

OMAR: I was, at first. Then Actor's Theatre had an open call and I booked it. So I quit the car show. I can't believe they cast me—the whole Indian thing.

VIJAY: Hey, I'm sure you were great as Nirad.

MALEK: Shit. I wanted to audition for that, but my agent said they were only seeing "straight-up Indians."

OMAR: Well, my guess is they really don't know the difference.

VIJAY: Tell me about it. Ever since I filmed *Hijacked at Home*, it's been one Ahmed after another for me.

OMAR: Go figure.

MALEK: Hey, at least you're working.

VIJAY: Very true. No complaints here.

(Ann, the casting director for The Color of Terror, *enters.)*

ANN: Malek Bizri? Right this way.

MALEK: Omar, let's do some brainstorming after this—movie ideas.

OMAR: Sure, if you don't mind waiting for me.

MALEK: Not at all.

VIJAY: Break a leg, man.

Scene 2

THE AUDITION ROOM: MALEK'S AUDITION

Sherry, the reader, enters with Ann.

ANN: Okay, Malek. Which set of sides do you have prepared for us today? Do you wanna try the courtroom scene or the terrorist training camp scene?

MALEK: I'd like to start with the courtroom scene, but I have the other one ready too in case you'd like to—

ANN: Okay. Courtroom it is! This is Sherry, she'll be reading the part of Prosecutor Jenkins. Any questions before we get started?

MALEK: Nope, I think I understand what's going on.

ANN: All righty then. Sherry will begin whenever you're ready.

(Malek, playing Mohammed, and Sherry, playing Jenkins, read the courtroom scene. They both hold their scripts. Malek uses a Lebanese accent. He works with various props throughout the audition—Arab prayer beads, a handkerchief, etc. Sherry has great enthusiasm, though her acting is far from subtle.)

SHERRY *(As Jenkins)*: Isn't it interesting that all four of your wives have testified that you were not at home around eight-thirty A.M., when the explosion occurred? They said you left early to go to the supermarket.

MALEK *(As Mohammed)*: Foolish American. I feed and take care of my wives, but I never tell them where I am going. You can force them to lie to you, but you cannot accuse me without presenting evidence. I understand American justice system. I am smarter than weak woman.

SHERRY *(As Jenkins)*: Since you are so much smarter than your wives, is it safe to assume that you know their every move?

MALEK *(As Mohammed)*: Of course, they do nothing without first asking my permission.

SHERRY *(As Jenkins)*: Then you must know that your third wife, Jumana Al-Sharif-Aziz-Khalife, provided the police with documents that described in Arabic the kinds of explosives you used to carry out this attack.

MALEK *(As Mohammed)*: Jumana would not dare deceive me, for she knows that such betrayal would cost her her head.

SHERRY *(As Jenkins)*: I see. Mohammed, did it sadden you to learn that forty-eight children, most of them Jewish, were killed in that ruthless attack?

MALEK *(As Mohammed)*: It is a shame for any child to die, unless it is an infidel Jew. When I read the paper, I mourned only because there were not more Jews in the market.

SHERRY *(As Jenkins)*: So then you would not object to the murder of innocent Americans who happen to be Jewish?

MALEK *(As Mohammed)*: They do not object to the slaughter of my people. And neither do you. Every dead Arab is a victory for America. And every dead Jew counts as a victory for Allah.

(Ann brings the actors back to reality.)

ANN: Okay, hold for a moment please, Malek. Really good work. Great intensity. I just wanna give you one small adjustment. Keep in mind that this is a guy who has probably spent most of his life in some Arab country—like Afghanistan or Pakistan. In other words, he's crazy! We are dealing with a backwards moral code. When you talk about women, there can't be any sense of reverence or love. We need to see that you're gonna go back home and show them who's boss. You know?

MALEK: Yeah, okay. It's just that . . .

ANN: Those wives are not even supposed to talk to anyone other than you. Much less cooperate with the police! You know?

MALEK: Okay, I was just thinking that . . .

ANN: It's great! It's great! What you are doing is great. But you don't need to be so respectful. When you say, "I take care of my wives," you mean, "If they cross me, they die," you know? Just keep in mind that this guy is a super devout Muslim. You know what I'm saying?

MALEK: Absoultely, for sure. Yeah. Can I try again?

ANN: Of course. Start from the part where you find out that your third wife, Jumanji, cooperated with the police. And this time, don't be a sweetheart. When you're talking about her, show the courtroom that you mean business! *(She makes a beheading gesture by drawing her finger across her neck)*

MALEK: Okay. Just one second.

(Malek takes a moment, then speaks again as Mohammed.)

(As Mohammed) Jumana would not dare deceive me, for she knows that such betrayal would cost her her head. *(He makes the beheading gesture, in the exact same manner as Ann had demonstrated before)*

ANN: Malek, stop please. I didn't mean for you to literally make that gesture.

MALEK: You didn't?

ANN: Not necessarily. It's not about the gesture. Look, Jumanji has just ratted you out. That's a sin against Allah! Where she's from, they'd probably cut off a limb. Mohammed is not a happy camper here. You just have to find a way to make him more . . . threatening. Ideally, the whole courtroom is terrified of you in this moment. This guy is dangerous. I mean, who knows? Maybe you have a bomb on you right now!

MALEK: Well, realistically I don't know if I'd be able to sneak one into the courtroom but—

ANN: Okay, that's not what I'm getting at. This is an Arab terrorist we're talking about, Malek. You're not afraid to detonate yourself at any moment, because your religion is telling you that you'll go to Heaven for it. You're angry, and you want those virgins. That's what's driving you. You're a walking time bomb.

MALEK: I think I know what you mean now. It needs more arrrrgh. *(A noise which indicates vigor)*

ANN: Exactly!

MALEK: I can definitely try that. Should I start again from the same place?

ANN: Actually we are running a bit behind. That's all we need to see for now.

MALEK: Oh . . . okay.

ANN: Thanks for coming in and reading for us today, Malek.

MALEK: It was my pleasure. Take care.

(Malek exits, with forced cheeriness.)

ANN *(To Sherry)*: He's such a sweetie, isn't he?

SHERRY: Yeah.

Scene 3

THE WAITING ROOM: SOUTH ASIA VS. THE MIDDLE EAST

Omar and Vijay sit with one chair between them. The animosity is palpable.

OMAR: How the hell did you know I was doing *Indian Ink*?

VIJAY: Sameer told me. It's his all-time favorite play, so he was hoping for a callback.

OMAR: Sameer didn't get a callback?

VIJAY: Apparently not.

OMAR: Oh well. At least he booked *Geronimo Jihad*. Sameer is the only Arab I know that even got a callback for that.

VIJAY: Actually, Sameer's not Arab, he's Indian.

OMAR: No he's not.

VIJAY: Trust me, I know all the Indo-Pak actors. Sameer's Indian.

OMAR: What the fuck are you talking about? That's bullshit!

VIJAY: Hey, take it easy, Omar. Just stating the facts.

OMAR: He's not Indian! I saw him eating a shawarma sandwich the other day.

VIJAY: So?

OMAR: Hello! Hindus don't eat cow, right? Sameer eats beef. *Beef* shawarma. Halal. Because he's Muslim. My mom saw him the other day at that huge mosque on Atlantic. Hindus don't hang out at mosques, do they?

VIJAY: Okay—*wow*—that's some ignorant shit you just said. Not all Indians are Hindus. Indians can be Muslims, too. I'm Indian and atheist, my family is Catholic, and I'll have you know I eat beef shawarma all the fucking time! Last time I saw Sameer we had a whole conversation about how much we hate Bollywood movies and how much we want to take Hindi lessons. Have you ever noticed that Sameer spells his name with two "e's" instead of an "i"? That's the Indian spelling of Sameer. I don't understand why it matters or why you feel so threatened by this newsflash, but Sameer is, most definitively, a Muslim Indian!

(Ann enters the waiting room. Malek follows her in.)

ANN: Omar Fuckree? Right this way please.

OMAR *(Under his breath)*: I can't believe I'm doing this shit. *(To Malek, whispering)* I'll see you in a bit. I'm gonna make this quick. And I mean really quick.

MALEK: Do what you gotta do. See you in a bit.

(Omar exits into the audition room as Malek sits.)

VIJAY: Well?

MALEK: What?

VIJAY: How did it go in there? Did they put you on camera? If so, what's the frame? How was the reader? What about Ann—

MALEK: Vijay. There's no camera. You'll be fine. They're pretty nice in there.

VIJAY: Why are you all mopey then? It couldn't have been that bad.

MALEK: I'm starting to think I'm not cut out for this shit.

VIJAY: That's absurd. Don't take anything these people say seriously.

MALEK: They always ask me to change what I'm doing. She basically told me that I wasn't acting "Muslim" enough.

VIJAY: Direction's good. Trust me. It means she's interested.

MALEK: Interested in what? At this point it looks like she's interested in getting me to behead my wives. Omar's right, this is all degrading nonsense. I should be able to turn down scripts for the sake of my own dignity! I hate to agree with Omar, but I gotta draw the line!

VIJAY: Technically, it's too late to "draw the line." You already auditioned. And please—don't listen to Omar's self-righteous crap. Scripts like this can get us on TV in a heartbeat. That's a good thing.

MALEK: Maybe for you. You're the one they keep hiring for the Arab parts.

VIJAY: And the smelly Indian parts, too. And you know what? I'll take 'em all! Give 'em to me. Cab driver with a turban, angry deli owner, math geek, computer hacker, terrorist—what's the difference? They're just roles. I don't give a fuck who gets offended.

MALEK: And you're proud of this? Have you no shame?

VIJAY: What is there to be ashamed of? I have no qualms about doing *my job*. Neither should you.

MALEK: We should all have major qualms with this one. *The Color of Terror?* It's, it's, it's . . . Brownsploitation. That's what it is!

VIJAY: Stop. You're overanalyzing this. It is not "Brownsploitation." I think you just need to take a step back and—

MALEK *(Having a mini breakdown)*: Why do I do this shit? Why?! Why do I go to audition after audition and pray that some asshole will give me the opportunity to slander my own culture on network television?

VIJAY: A better question is—why are you so fucking protective of your "culture"? Blacks have to play gangsters, Latinos play drug dealers, Chinese play tourists, and we both play Al Qaeda operatives on *24*. All actors deal with this shit. Get over it and do your job.

MALEK: With all due respect, Vijay, you and I are not in the same predicament when it comes to stereotypes. We are in far deeper shit than you are. You can't even compare.

VIJAY: Do you know how many third-world bodega owners named Sanjay I've auditioned for in the past three years?!?

MALEK: It sucks to be pigeonholed that way, but at least your people have *Monsoon Wedding*. You have *Bombay Dreams*. You have *Harold and Kumar Go to White Castle*.

VIJAY *(Sarcastically)*: A crowning cinematic achievement—

MALEK: You even get positive coverage on CNN—you have Dr. Sanjay Gupta! Everybody loves him!!

VIJAY: Oh please—

MALEK *(Continuing)*: But who do we *Arabs* have as our media correspondent? Some asshole who makes threats on a camcorder in the mountains of Pakistan!

VIJAY: And you'd prefer to believe that Arab terrorists don't exist. That they haven't killed innocent people. That they are just a media construct designed to make Arabs look bad. But you're deluding yourself, Malek. They do exist, and people find them very interesting. That's why they're on TV.

MALEK: I know they exist, you idiot. That's not what I'm saying.

VIJAY: Then what are you saying? That you deserve sympathy? Fine. I award you the "most likely to be vilified" trophy. But, while you sit here and complain, have you noticed what's happening in studio two?

MALEK: No.

VIJAY: It's an audition for Long John Silver's, and they're only seeing black and Latino actors. I saw Javier over there—his agent told him to dress "ghetto casual." It's a seafood commercial in fucking Ebonics!

MALEK: Well, I'd rather do that than this whole political thing.

VIJAY: Me, too, actually. It's more pay for less work. Forty thousand bucks just to say: "Long John Silver's—mad eats on the fresh tip, yo."

MALEK: "The fresh tip, yo"?

VIJAY: I told you—Ebonics! That's my point! They're the ones who should be bitching, not you.

MALEK: I know, I know, I know, you're right, I shouldn't bitch. It doesn't help. I just get frustrated.

(Malek takes out pen and a notepad.)

VIJAY: That's because you try too hard. You should ease up a bit. You're so fucking eager. These auditions don't have to control your future. Don't give them that power.

MALEK: Vijay, I think I've had enough of the advice column for one day, thank you very much.

(Vijay gives Malek a moment to cool off. Malek is furiously scribbling on his note pad.)

VIJAY: What are you jotting down over there? A suicide note?

MALEK: Ha ha ha. It's a script idea I've been working on. You'd probably think it was stupid. And honestly, I don't think you'd get it.

VIJAY: Oh, I see. It's an "Arab" thing.

MALEK: Okay, yes, maybe it is. Omar and I are gonna come up with a film concept, a new idea that will, that will—

VIJAY: That will do what? Reverse centuries of negative depictions of the brown man? Yeah, good luck with that.

MALEK: See, that's why I didn't wanna tell you. I knew you'd try to shit on it.

VIJAY *(Patronizingly)*: I'm not shitting on it. I think it's cute. It's a fun little idea. Go, Malek!

MALEK: Yeah, well, you keep on being a sellout, and I'll keep dreaming. Shut the fuck up, please.

VIJAY: Fine. Don't mind me. Go back to your pity party.

(Vijay puts on his headphones. Loud hip-hop/bhangara fusion music blasts. Malek glares at Vijay, who jams to his music.)

Scene 4

THE AUDITION ROOM: OMAR'S AUDITION

ANN: Which sides do you have prepared for us today, Omar?

OMAR *(With sarcasm)*: Well, they're both so riveting that I can't decide. Why don't *you* make the call!

ANN: Okay, why don't you read for the terrorist training camp scene, please.

OMAR: All right. In that case, I was wondering about—

ANN: Oh! I almost forgot to tell you, this is Sherry, she'll be reading the part of Chemical Ali.

SHERRY: Hi!

OMAR: Hi there.

ANN: And you know the basic gist of this, right? Mohammed is trying to prove his allegiance to Al Qaeda in front of his terrorist drill sergeant, Chemical Ali.

OMAR: See that's what I'm wondering about. Isn't Chemical Ali from Iraq?

ANN: Yes.

OMAR: And Chemical Ali's out of a job now that Saddam's gone, right?

ANN: I would hope so, he gassed his own people!

OMAR: True, but his government was toppled. How could Chemical Ali be running a terrorist training camp in Afghanistan? He's in prison!

ANN: Prison or not, you gotta know he's got something else up his sleeve. He was the King of Spades!

OMAR: "The King of Spades"?

ANN: You know, on that deck of cards. The Department of Defense's Most Wanted Iraqis.

OMAR: Oh that's right. That clears everything up. Thanks.

ANN: Omar, the thing I would say about this scene is this: Mohammed has a major decision in front of him. He has two choices. He can either abandon the Jihad and do good deeds, or choose evil to feed his own hatred. We have to see that Mohammed chooses hate. And that Ali lures him into that hatred by promising him riches and virgins and all that BS. Know what I'm saying?

OMAR: Ummm . . . no. I mean, yes—I understand the situation, but having these two people in the same country in a terrorist training camp makes no fucking sense, wouldn't you agree?

ANN: Omar, I can't speak for the writer, but it's clear that she's trying to go out on a limb here. She's trying to show us what is really going on in those countries, like it or not. I don't like to face it either, but . . .

OMAR: No, I think I'm ready to face it now. Let's just get this over with now . . .

ANN: You don't have any more questions—

OMAR *(Yelling)*: I said NOW!

(Ann, startled by Omar's tenacity, is now truly afraid of him.)

ANN: Okay, great. Sherry, go ahead with Chemical Ali.

(Scripts in hand, they play the "terrorist training camp scene." Sherry, playing Chemical Ali, uses no accent, but has tremendous energy.

Omar, playing Mohammed, uses an Indian accent in an effort to throw the audition.)

SHERRY *(As Chemical Ali)*: So, you think you are a true soldier of Allah. You think you know the meaning of intifada. You think that you are ready to dine with the virgins. But I ask you—are you ready to become a martyr?

OMAR *(As Mohammed)*: I have always told you that it is my mission in life to destroy the Zionist enemy! ALLAH AKBAR!

SHERRY *(As Chemical Ali)*: But why do you hesitate? I see the fear in your eyes! You fear to die!

OMAR *(As Mohammed)*: I do not hesitate. I do not wish to live. I wish only to do the will of Allah! Allies for ALLAH!!!

SHERRY *(As Chemical Ali)*: Do not lie to me, you coward! I know where your family lives. If you lie to me, I will poison them with my chemicals.

OMAR *(As Mohammed)*: I will do the will of Allah! I will do the will of Allah!

SHERRY *(As Chemical Ali)*: I have sooo many chemicals! Your mother's eyeballs will pop out of her skull. Your sister's skin will peel off like the skin of a fig!

OMAR *(As Mohammed)*: Death to Israel, death to America! ALLAH AKBAR! ALLAH AKBAR!

ANN: Stop right there, please. Omar—excellent reading. Have you been taking classes?

OMAR *(Leaving, incensed)*: No. And you know what else? This really isn't my thing. The whole Al Qaeda plot. It's fucking bullshit!

ANN: Wait, wait, wait. I was gonna say, whatever you're doing is GREAT. Dead ON!

OMAR *(In disbelief)*: Are you serious?

ANN: Yes! Here's a new set of sides that I'd like for you to prepare for later this afternoon. Do you mind sticking around for a few?

OMAR *(After a significant pause)*: No. Not at all.

ANN: These will also be the ones that you'll use if we decide to send you out to L.A. for a screen test with the producers.

OMAR: The producers?

ANN: Yes.

OMAR: Okay. Yes. Fine. Sure.

ANN: Great, Omar. I'll need you to harness some of the . . . *fury* . . . that you the actor brought into the audition room today and really focus it into Mohammed.

OMAR: Okay, sure. Harness it. Whatever.

ANN: Great! See you in a few.

(Transformed, Omar jets back into the waiting room. Ann pulls out her cell phone, begins dialing.)

SHERRY: Hello, attitude!

ANN: Sherry, Mohammed should not be that nice of a guy! The studio wants someone edgy and dangerous, not a sweetheart.

SHERRY: But I would be freaking-out if a casting director told me she liked my work. I'd be like, "Oh my God, thank you, thank you, thank you." You know? Omar was just so—

ANN *(Silencing Sherry, into the phone)*: Hi, this is Ann from Wide-Net Casting, may I speak with Hamilton? Okay, how long are we talking about? Because I do have more actors to see, so the sooner . . . Okay, fine.

(Ann holds on speakerphone. "On hold" music plays "Foolish Heart" by Journey.)

Oh God. Why the music? As if holding wasn't bad enough, now there's Steve Perry . . .

SHERRY: I love him! He's the only one who's ever used my name in a song.

(Ann does not know the song reference, but coincidentally exclaims:)

ANN: Oh, Sherry . . .

SHERRY: Exactly!

ANN: Well, Sherry, I hope you're learning from all of this. Being a reader is valuable training.

SHERRY: For sure. A major thing I've learned is that—

(Hamilton, Senior Vice President of Casting for the studio, answers via speakerphone. Perhaps we actually see him onstage, or perhaps we only hear him.)

HAMILTON: This is Hamilton.

ANN: Hi, Hamilton, Ann from Wide-Net Casting.

HAMILTON: Hi. How are things going over there?

ANN: I've seen a lot of ethnic talent today, and so far one actor has been a clear standout.

HAMILTON: Really. Look, I need real terror from this guy. Is he fierce?

ANN: Yes, he's very fierce, I was genuinely fearful. He even used the "f" word while he argued with me, it sent chills down my spine.

HAMILTON: Hmm. Does he speak Arabic?

ANN: Well, based on the accent he used during his read, I would imagine he does.

HAMILTON: Are you sure? Where is he from?

ANN: I didn't ask. I'm sure you know there are all these unspoken rules about that—

HAMILTON: Listen, I need to know what country to be sure. What's your best guess?

ANN: If I had to guess what country he's from—I'd say . . . *(She has no idea and gestures for help from Sherry)*

SHERRY *(Whispers)*: Yemen.

ANN: Yemen. Or maybe Pakistan. He's got that ethnic look, so don't even worry about that. The thing is, he was so angry! It was really authentic. Like he was about to explode. It just seemed right. I think you and Barry would agree.

HAMILTON: That's good. Authenticity is really important. It's Barry's number-one priority. So from now on you really need to ask these guys where they're from. Barry was very explicit about that, okay?

ANN: Okay, tell Barry that I will from now on. Ta.

(Ann and Sherry exit.)

Scene 5

THE WAITING ROOM: BROWNTOWN RECONVENES

OMAR: Good news for you, Vijay!

VIJAY: What?

OMAR: I was trying to throw the audition by being a total prick and by doing an Indian accent, but it didn't work. They want this terrorist to sound like an Indian!

MALEK: Wow.

OMAR: Vijay, you're a prick, *and* you're Indian, so you oughta go in there and nail it, no problem.

VIJAY: That's bullshit, you did *not* use an Indian accent in there. *(An afterthought)* Actually, I can't even do a good Indian accent.

MALEK: But you're Indian! Just imitate your parents!

VIJAY: My parents are from Queens!

OMAR: Just think of Apu from the Simpsons, but as a terrorist. That's what I did.

VIJAY: I've tried channeling Apu! But I somehow end up sounding like the friendly Arab guy from *Raiders of the Lost Ark*.

OMAR: The one with the monkey?

VIJAY: Yeah, I love that guy.

MALEK: So wait a minute—does this mean you get to read for *Barry*?

OMAR: Yep. She gave me new sides, and she even mentioned the possibility of a screen test in L.A. for the produ—wait a minute—Barry?

VIJAY: Umm, you may have heard of him before: Barry Juckheimer?

OMAR: Is *that* who's producing this thing? I didn't even know he did TV movies.

MALEK: Yeah, it's his new thing. It's written right there in the breakdowns—

VIJAY *(Interjecting)*: Yup, Barry's a really cool guy. Really down to earth.

MALEK: You know him?

VIJAY: Yeah. I met him during *Baby Bombers*. We really clicked.

MALEK: Well *I've* still never read for the producers on anything.

(Deafening silence. Vijay makes a faux sympathy gesture and puts on his headphones. Omar is fixated on his new audition material.)

So, Omar—I've been thinking about movie ideas . . . Here's what I came up with: Jordanian astronauts. Crown Prince Abdullah teams up with Bush, and they send astronauts from Jordan and America on a peace mission to the moon.

OMAR: A peace mission?

MALEK: Yeah. And maybe Sharon sends an Israeli, too! It would be so cool to explore the Arab-Israeli conflict in an environment of weightlessness.

OMAR: Listen, Malek, I should probably focus on this new material.

MALEK: Yeah, that's cool. I thought you wanted to come up with concepts for—

OMAR: Not now, man. This could be a really big break. I need to figure out how to do this new scene.

MALEK *(Hurt, gathers belongings)*: Okay, man. Cool. Great. I guess *The Color of Terror* has grown on you a little.

OMAR: Well, not really. It's just that, if I ace this, I might have a chance to read for Barry Juck—

MALEK: No need to explain. You work on that stuff. I'll just . . . yeah. I'll be around. I gotta go.

OMAR: Okay. I'll call you after—
MALEK *(Almost completely gone)*: Break a leg. Both of you.

(Malek abruptly leaves.)

OMAR: Vijay.
VIJAY: What?
OMAR: Can I ask you something?
VIJAY: You just did.
OMAR: How do you end up getting all these terrorist parts? Is there some secret?
VIJAY: There's no secret. I just play the scene.
OMAR: But—I mean, if you're not Arab, and you have so much diffi-culty with accents— Wait a minute—what kind of accent *do* you use?
VIJAY: I don't know *what* you'd call it. It's pretty . . . special.
OMAR: But I guess it works.

(Ann quietly enters and checks the clipboard.)

VIJAY: Well, I shouldn't jinx it, but yes. So far so good.
ANN: Vijay Govindu?

(Vijay exits to the audition room with Ann.)

Scene 6

THE AUDITION ROOM: VIJAY'S AUDITION

ANN: So, Vijay—I see you just finished *Baby Bombers*! I've heard noth-ing but good things about that project!
VIJAY: It's been a great experience. I've been very fortunate to work opposite Chuck Norris.
SHERRY: I love him!
ANN: Lemme guess: Chuck saves the day at the end.
VIJAY: Yes, at the very end he manages to intercept a bunch of Palestinian children from Al Qaeda before they are forced to become human bombs. After killing off the bad guys, he offers the Arab kids a better life as cattle herders on his ranch in Billings, Montana.
ANN: Sounds terrific.

(Beat.)

So this is Sherry, she'll be reading the role of Prosecutor Jenkins.

VIJAY: Hi, Sherry, I'm Vijay.

SHERRY: Hi, Vijay!

ANN: Before we get started, Vijay, I was just wondering: Where are you from?

VIJAY: I'm from Queens.

ANN: No, I mean, originally.

VIJAY: Well my mom is from New Dehli and my grandparents on my dad's side came from Bombay back in—

ANN: Okay, good. I was just making sure, because the director really wants to go with Arab talent—

VIJAY: Well, technically, I'm not Arab, I'm—

ANN: I know, I know: You're an American, first and foremost. But you have roots in India, so—for our purposes—I think we're safe, don't worry.

VIJAY: Ummm, okay.

ANN: Great, Vijay. Sherry will begin whenever you are ready. And why don't you skip down to the middle of page two, where it starts to get juicy. Sherry will give you your cue line and we'll just go straight through till the end.

(They read the scene, Vijay, playing Mohammed, uses a deliberate, controlled, yet menacing, faux British accent, the kind that the "intelligent" chief hijackers always use in movies with terrorists. He contrasts his quiet, measured threats with moments of abrupt furious yelling.)

SHERRY *(As Jenkins)*: So then you would not object to the murder of innocent Americans who happen to be Jewish?

VIJAY *(As Mohammed)*: They do not object to the slaughter of my people. And neither do you. Every dead Arab is a victory for America. And every dead Jew counts as a victory for Allah.

SHERRY *(As Jenkins)*: So let me get this straight—your "God" rewards the murder of innocent Jews?

VIJAY *(As Mohammed)*: Yes. He is pleased to see the enemies of Islam suffer. All Muslim men will enjoy multiple virgins and countless fine fruits once the occupier has been destroyed. The blood of the American Zionists will flow like a river into the sea. Mark my words! If the United States does not become an Islamic state within the next forty-eight hours, you will all face the wrath of Allah!

SHERRY *(As Jenkins)*: No further questions, Your Honor.

(Ann brings the actors back to reality.)

ANN: Terrific, Vijay. I can see that you are very experienced with these types of roles. And come to think of it—that sort of mature, "aristocratic" accent would really work for the character of Chemical Ali.

VIJAY: Really?

ANN: Absolutely. I'd like for you to read for Chemical Ali in this new scene, and I wanna have you read opposite Omar, who will be reading for Mohammed. I'm gonna take a quick lunch break, then I'll come back and get you both in a few minutes. Be sure to tell Omar that you'll be reading together, okay?

VIJAY: Okay, sure. No problem. See you in a few.

(Vijay rushes into the waiting room with his new sides, which he begins highlighting. Ann throws on her jacket, grabs her purse, and moves to exit. Sherry's words stop her.)

SHERRY: I guess I haven't been reading very well.

ANN: Why would you say a thing like that?

SHERRY: Because. You don't want me to read anymore.

ANN: On the contrary! Sherry, I've been very impressed by your work. On occasion you've brought some real depth to Chemical Ali.

SHERRY: Really?

ANN: Absolutely. Now, obviously, you aren't right for Ali—type-wise, but I am going to talk to Hamilton about getting you seen for the part of Jumanji.

SHERRY: Oh my God, that would be amazing! Oh my God, oh my God, oh my God. Does this mean I should start, like, tanning?

ANN: Tanning?

SHERRY: Yeah. So I can look, like, you know . . . Arabian.

ANN: Sweetie, they're gonna have her covered from head to toe, so it really won't matter. You just need to be ready to cry on cue. Jumanji is very emotional in her interrogation scene.

SHERRY: That's so perfect! I'm taking a class on sense memory right now. We're learning how to access our emotions by thinking of all the bad things that have happened to us. Like the time that my ex-boyfriend and I were out in the woods, and there was this hitchhiker—

ANN *(Not listening at all, grabbing a Virginia Slim from her purse)*: That's wonderful, Sherry. I'll fax your agent the sides and the appointment time. *(She darts out, cigarette in mouth. Shouting from offstage)* Thanks for your help today, Sherry. Go on home!

SHERRY *(Calling after Ann, who is long gone)*: I don't have an agent, but I just did an industry mailing so . . . Thank you, Ann! *(Still no response from Ann)* Bye!

(Sherry exits, walking on clouds.)

Scene 7

THE WAITING ROOM: BROWN BRAWL

OMAR *(Noticing Vijay's script)*: Why are you highlighting Chemical Ali's lines? I thought you were reading for—

VIJAY: I'm reading for Chemical Ali, and you're reading for Mohammed. That's the way she wants it. Don't ask me why—I mean, Chemical Ali has no dramatic arc whatsoever—but that's what she—

OMAR: We have to read this scene together?

VIJAY: Yes.

OMAR: Oh, that's just great! I can barely tolerate this script as it is.

(Malek enters, scribbling furiously on his notepad. He is wearing a bandana on his head. It is the same bandana that he used as a handkerchief in his previous audition. He deliberately sits far away from Omar and Vijay.)

VIJAY: Why don't you leave then, Omar? No one's forcing you to stay. Why are you still here?

OMAR: For that matter, why is Malek still here?

VIJAY: He's *your* butt-buddy, not mine. Why don't you go ask him?

OMAR: Why don't you go ask *your mom*?!

VIJAY *(Incredulous of Omar's lame comeback)*: Okay, this is the part where I tune you out.

(Vijay puts on headphones, begins his vocal warm-ups—loudly. Omar crosses to talk to Malek.)

Buh. BUH! Duh. DUH! Muh. MUH! Kuh. KUH! Guh. GUH!

OMAR *(To Malek, incredulous)*: What an asshole.

(Beat.)

So have you come up with anything else?

MALEK: Huh?

OMAR: Isn't that what you're writing about? The Jordanian astronauts thing? You know, I was thinking . . . maybe instead of ice cream they could eat powdered baklava up there.

MALEK: Actually, I'm writing some lyrics.

OMAR: Lyrics?

MALEK: Yeah, for the Long John Silver's audition next door. They want us to make up a rap about hush puppies.

OMAR: Dude, are you really gonna crash that audition?

MALEK: Yeah. I actually signed in as Malek Rodriguez so I wouldn't rouse any suspicion.

OMAR: Don't worry, you totally pass for Nuyorican. So why aren't you over in studio two with everybody else?

MALEK: It was too loud in there. I couldn't concentrate while everyone was hip-hopping out loud. *(More Vijay warm-up noises are heard)* Not that this is any better!

OMAR: And how's your hush puppy rap coming along?

MALEK: It's pretty bad. My flow is a little rusty. But, I gotta say, this stereotype is the *bomb*! Listen to this tagline: "Long John Silver's—mad eats on the fresh tip, yo!"

OMAR: Let's hear what you've got.

MALEK: She could call you in at any minute. You should look at your own stuff.

OMAR: I'm just gonna wing it. It's not like I've never played a terrorist before. You're the one who needs practice.

MALEK: Yeah, but I don't know if you wanna hear this . . .

OMAR: Oh, will you shut up and *rap*!

MALEK: Okay fine, but I need a beat.

(Omar beat-boxes like an old-school hip-hopper. Malek raps, occasionally consulting his notepad to read his own lyrics.)

I was eating fries at the Long John Silvie's,
When I noticed every G was munchin' hush puppies.
Then, a dark-skinned Latin beauty caught my eye.
I had to come up next to her and trade her my fries,
For a handful of puppies, yo, this ain't no joke!
Them hush puppies make me high,
Just like the diz-zank smoke.

(Beat-box interlude, verse two:)

> Rollin' in the Benzo, eatin' hush puppies,
> Got some bitches in my ride and motherfuck I'm feelin' lucky—

VIJAY *(Exploding)*: Oh my God, shut up! How RUDE! I am trying to focus. Why don't you take your wack-ass rhymes over to studio two!
MALEK: Okay, okay . . .
VIJAY: Inconsiderate dick-wads.
OMAR *(Picking a fight)*: What did you just say?
VIJAY: You heard me. I will not allow you two *clowns* to sabotage my preparation. Don't make me say it twice.
OMAR *(Shoves Vijay)*: And what the fuck are *you* gonna do about it, curry-ass bitch?
VIJAY *(Shoves back)*: Your face is about to find out, falafel-fucker!

(Omar and Vijay continue to talk trash and are on the verge of an all-out brawl. Malek makes a vain attempt to intervene as their ethnic slurs and chest shoves escalate. Just as they are about to start taking swings at each other, Ann enters.)

ANN: Omar and Vijay, great prep work! I should've known you two were "method"! Ready?
OMAR: Sure.
VIJAY: Yes.

(Omar and Vijay try to compose themselves. They follow Ann into the audition room. Malek exits.)

Scene 8

THE AUDITION ROOM: TERROR TRAIN

ANN: Okay, I know I sort of threw this at you last minute, but let's get started. The most important thing for the audience to see is that Mohammed is torn between his family and his desire to blow people up.
OMAR: Great. That helps.
VIJAY: Thanks. Now I think I'm ready.
ANN: Great, go ahead.

(Holding scripts, they play the scene. Omar, playing Mohammed, again uses an Indian accent, but this time with great earnestness, as he now

really wants the role. Vijay, playing Chemical Ali, again uses his menacing faux British accent.)

OMAR *(As Mohammed)*: Ali, keeper of the chemicals, why have you brought me here? And why are we dressed like our enemies, in this beach clothing?

VIJAY *(As Chemical Ali)*: The most bloodthirsty wolf wears the clothes of a sheep. Young soldier of Allah, this is the final test of your devotion to the Holy Brigade of Allies for Allah. You must prove to each of these passengers the strength of our God.

OMAR *(As Mohammed)*: But why must we fight the infidels *here* on the Long Island Rail Road?

VIJAY *(As Chemical Ali)*: The train to Montauk is always packed with rich Americans going to the Hamptons. Their tax dollars pay for the bombs that kill our people.

OMAR *(As Mohammed)*: But how shall we proceed? We have no firearms. How will we make the passengers do as we say?

VIJAY *(As Chemical Ali)*: Have you forgotten everything I taught you?

OMAR *(As Mohammed)*: I am sorry.

VIJAY *(As Chemical Ali)*: You must do precisely as I command.

OMAR *(As Mohammed)*: Of course.

VIJAY *(As Chemical Ali)*: First, you must distract the conductor.

OMAR *(As Mohammed)*: The one punching holes in all the tickets?

VIJAY *(As Chemical Ali)*: Yes, you fool! I will attack him from behind and gain control of his hole-puncher. It will be our most effective weapon.

OMAR *(As Mohammed)*: The hole-puncher?

VIJAY *(As Chemical Ali)*: Of course! After I have gained control of the train, I will announce a prayer to Allah over the loud speaker. Then I will release my chemicals into the air.

OMAR *(As Mohammed)*: But, Ali, how shall we escape the effects of your deadly chemicals?

VIJAY *(As Chemical Ali)*: I will pull the emergency brake, and run out of the train.

OMAR *(As Mohammed)*: And I will follow you?

VIJAY *(As Chemical Ali)*: You will not escape. As I said before, this is your *final* test. You will stay, and become a martyr.

OMAR *(As Mohammed)*: I wish very much to leave the train with you.

VIJAY *(As Chemical Ali)*: If you leave, your death shall be much worse. Your family will be sodomized, tortured and executed with you if you survive the train crash.

OMAR *(As Mohammed)*: And yet, my wives will die of grief if I am killed.

VIJAY *(As Chemical Ali)*: Why worry about the loss of four wives on earth when you will have seventy-two ripe virgins in the after-life?

OMAR *(As Mohammed)*: You speak the truth, Ali. I am ready to perform the will of Allah. Allah Akbar! Allah Akbar!

(Ann stops the scene.)

ANN: Okay, that seems like a natural stopping point. Omar, you really delved into the Arab mindset. I was just blown away.

VIJAY: No pun intended.

ANN: Vijay, you're free to go. So, Omar, here's the thing—

VIJAY: Did you wanna see us switch roles?

ANN: No.

VIJAY: Because—I was really prepared to read for Mohammed, and that's the character I most connected with—

ANN: No, you're free to go, Vijay.

(Vijay absorbs this and heads into the waiting room.)

Omar, I want to send you home with some additional material. I need to make a phone call, and then I'd like to meet with you one more time before I let you go.

OMAR *(Strutting into the waiting room)*: Sure, no problem.

Scene 9

THE WAITING ROOM: OMAR'S TRIUMPH

OMAR: That went all right, all things considered.

VIJAY: Speak for yourself! What the fuck was that ridiculous accent?

OMAR: I was about to ask you the same thing. Not that it matters. I totally nailed that.

VIJAY: Congratulations, Omar. I'm really happy for you. Just think: If this works out, you'll soon be on cable-TV as a Hindu-sounding Arab terrorist with a deadly hole-puncher!

(Vijay exits.)

Scene 10

THE AUDITION ROOM: HAMILTON STRIKES BACK

Ann, pacing rapidly with a Bluetooth device in her ear, dials Hamilton, who answers his office phone.

ANN: Hi, Hamilton, Ann from Wide-Net. I'm telling you, this Omar kid has really got something. I'd love for you and Barry to see him test in L.A. Would you mind faxing me any updates to the script so I can send this actor home with—

HAMILTON: Actually, I have some great news. The studio has been looking for some name power, and we found someone who is ready to take a risk and stretch his acting career. At first, Barry thought it was a long shot, but—

ANN: Wait—what? Who expressed interest?

HAMILTON: Have you seen Colin Farrell play villain roles? Cuz I have. And let me tell you, you won't find anyone more convincing.

ANN: Well, I don't know about *convincing*, he's certainly handsome. But you have to understand: Nobody told me that you guys were pursuing star talent over there.

HAMILTON: Things have been moving fast, it's hard to keep everyone in the loop.

ANN: But Colin's not Arab.

HAMILTON: It's all about wardrobe and makeup, Ann. You know that!

ANN: He could maybe *pass* for Arab, I guess, but that's really not the point.

HAMILTON: Haven't you ever noticed those dark, deepset eyes?

ANN: I know he has dark eyes, but why not go with someone who is actually—

HAMILTON: Do you want people to see this movie or not? Need I remind you that this is a Juckheimer production? We need a *name* actor! Tony Shalhoub wants nothing to do with us. His agent won't even return our calls. But *Colin* on the other hand—*Colin* is all fired up about this project. He's black Irish, which is as close as you're gonna get to Arab if you're talking about *stars*.

ANN: Black Irish or not, he simply doesn't look the part.

HAMILTON: Ann, I think it's time for you to think about the best interest of the movie—

ANN: Believe me, I am. And I would certainly never question your judgment, or Barry's, but it will come back to haunt us if we—

HAMILTON: Ann, do you really wanna fight us on this? Don't force our hand. *The Color of Terror* would not be the same without you.

(Beat.)

ANN: Is that supposed to be some kind of threat?

HAMILTON: Why can't you see how great this is? Colin Farrell! That's a name you'll turn on your TV for. "Omar Al-whoever" is not gonna cut it. Period.

ANN: Hamilton, please hear me out on this. It's great to have name talent, but you have to consider the impact on the quality of the piece. You mentioned the importance of authenticity. So can I at least put Omar on tape so you can compare him with Colin?

HAMILTON: Are you crazy? Colin is "offer only" on this one. Listen, Ann. There's no way Barry will go for an "unknown." You're totally over-thinking this—

ANN: No, you listen to me, Hamilton! Why did you hire me if you won't even let me do my job? I have been busting my ass over here to find you the perfect actor of color and you're telling me that this has been a huge waste of everybody's time because Colin fucking Farrell wants to "stretch" his acting career? I have an excellent actor waiting in the other room, is *that* what you want me to tell him?

HAMILTON: You're on thin ice here, Ann. I wouldn't advise standing in the way of what the studio wants. They've already started Colin's paperwork.

ANN: Fine, fine. By all means, don't let me interfere. Pick whomever you want. Call up Danny Devito and offer him Chemical Ali for all I care. Or maybe even Andy Griffith! It's your movie, you pick the fucking stars! *(Hangs up, furious)*

Scene 11

THE WAITING ROOM: GOING WEST?

A revitalized and confident Malek strolls in.

MALEK: You'll never believe this.

OMAR: What?

MALEK: Call back for Long John Silver's. Tomorrow. 2:35 P. Izz-em.

OMAR: That's bad-ass! Way to represent!

MALEK: I do what I can. How'd it go in there for you?

OMAR: I've never felt so good about a role before. I think Ann really likes me for the part. It's like I can do no wrong with this woman.

MALEK: That's awesome! Do you think they'll send you to L.A. for a screen test?

OMAR: I hope so. The way I look at it, if I book this—no more Subaru shows for at least two years. *And* I'll have enough money to focus on gigs that I actually care about.

MALEK: Maybe you could even produce one of my script ideas.

OMAR: I don't know, Malek. Jordanians being allowed onto a spaceship is a pretty tough sell.

MALEK: Forget that idea, I thought of a better one: a Fosse-style musical about the lives of Arab detainees called *Guantanamania!*

OMAR: We'll see. I don't want Ashcroft on my ass. Anyway, I shouldn't count my chickens right now. Anything can happen. But I do have a solid feeling about this one. I'm tellin' ya—

(Ann enters, visibly shaken and furious after her argument with Hamilton. She struggles to appear composed and pleasant.)

ANN: Omar. Thanks for being patient.

OMAR: Not a problem.

ANN: I had you stay just in case the L.A. people wanted us to put you on tape, but it turns out that it won't be necessary. You're free to go.

OMAR: Okay. But, didn't you say there was more material for me to—

ANN: I think I've overworked you as it is. I'll be in touch with your agent about the status of your audition.

OMAR: Thanks! I look forward to hearing from him.

ANN: Take care, both of you.

MALEK: Okay.

OMAR: Bye for now.

ANN *(Pained, deeply sincere)*: Omar. I hope you realize that I have almost no influence on how things will unfold from this point on. I just want you to know that you did *excellent* work today— no matter how the cards fall.

OMAR: Thanks. I appreciate that.

(Ann exits.)

She was kind of gloomy, huh? What do you make of that "cards" comment?

MALEK: What do you mean?

OMAR: "No matter how the cards fall"? It just sounds . . . I don't know, man. Like she's doubtful.

(Malek knows Omar is right, but offers assurance.)

MALEK: Well she can't just come right out and tell you she's sending you to L.A. She's gotta call your agent and iron out the details. That's probably the "cards" she's talking about.

OMAR: Yeah, you're right. For all I know, she could be talking about the Department of Defense's "Most Wanted Iraqi" cards. She mentioned them earlier.

(Malek and Omar's next lines overlap:)

MALEK: That's gotta be it. She's really into your work—

OMAR: She even went out of her way to say it—

MALEK: She's just being coy—

OMAR: Yeah. I rocked that audition—

MALEK: You're the man—

OMAR: Yes, sirrie! I'm going to L.A.—

MALEK: Totally. You *own* this Mohammed.

OMAR: Yep. The role's mine. I can just feel it!

(A significant pause as their excitement deflates, replaced by doubt. Malek breaks the awkward silence.)

MALEK: Whaddya say we get out of here and head to Mamlouk. I'm jonesing for some kafta.

OMAR: Yeah, I think I've had enough of Browntown for one day. *Yallah.*

MALEK: True dat. *Yallah. Imshe.*

(Blackout.)

END OF PLAY

Glossary

Yallah	"Let's go."
Yallah. Imshe	"Yeah, come on, let's go."

Actor-writer **SAM YOUNIS** is a Lebanese-American Texas native. He received an undergraduate degree in Spanish and sociology from Vanderbilt University, where he also studied theatre. He then earned an MFA in acting from Columbia University. *Browntown* marks Sam's playwriting debut. Sam has performed on Broadway, in numerous New York and regional productions, in television and in film. Favorite theatre credits include *The Tale of the Allergist's Wife* (Broadway, Ethel Barrymore Theatre), *1001* (The Theater @ Boston Court, Pasadena) and *Baby Taj* (TheatreWorks, Palo Alto). Recent television credits include *Worst Week*, *The Starter Wife*, *The Unit* and *24*. Sam now lives in Los Angeles with his wife, Abigail Marateck, and son, Gabriel Younis.

The Black Eyed

Betty Shamieh

Author's Statement

The point of publishing a preface to a play, particularly when written by its author, is to seduce readers into making the commitment to turn the page and experience the work itself. By putting into print lofty proclamations about your intentions and the motivating factors that compelled you to write a particular work, you are teasing your readers, hoping to excite within them a desire to see if you succeeded in doing what you set out to do. Again, it's about getting them to begin at the real beginning.

I myself love author introductions. They feel as if they are addressed to young writers or at least that is how I usually experience them. Tennessee Williams's introduction to *A Streetcar Named Desire*, first published as an essay entitled "The Catastrophe of Success," is a piece of writing that I often find myself rereading and recommending to my students. Picking up his introduction on a Sunday morning in the summer of 2000 would change the course of my playwriting career. It would help me begin the journey I needed to take before I could produce a play like *The Black Eyed*, a work in which I tried to capture the complexity of being a Palestinian-American woman living in New York in the wake of September 11.

Tennessee's introduction, a meditation on how external validation can give an artist no pleasure that compares with the satisfaction of creation, has little to do with the play itself. It can stand alone as an essay, but it shouldn't. By that, I mean, Tennessee's declarations on how money/fame/adulation can never provide lasting joy are much more fascinating because it is he—the man capable of writing *The Glass Menagerie* and *A Streetcar Named Desire*—who is making them.

In 2000, I graduated from the Yale School of Drama and was in the process of making my big move back to New York in the hopes of becoming a professional theatre artist. I had begun writing plays in high school and had written several by the time I got to Yale. One of my first works was a one-act written in blank verse in which Shakespeare's tragic characters come to life in order to harass him into changing the endings of their stories. I mention this to highlight that, from my earliest days as a writer, I wrote plays that dealt with my ethnic identity and plays that did not. I continued to do so in graduate school, but I chose not to have my plays that dealt with Arab-American themes produced. I didn't want to be pigeonholed. I had seen what usually happened to writers of color and I didn't like it one bit. Initially, a colorful playwright gets perhaps a bit more attention and has access to a few more grants, but, over the course of a career, it seemed that it was the writers who were seen as "truly" American who were being sustained. Their work was viewed as universal.

I wanted to be smart about my career choices. Though I never denied my ethnic heritage when questioned about it, I decided to allow the "reality" of how the current American playwriting market seemed to work to become an influence on which plays I would let the world see first and which plays I would keep to myself. Until I had made a name for myself in the theatre. Until I felt safe, which is hard to feel when you're in your early twenties anyway, particularly if you are a minority trying to break into a field where few or no members of your race are working.

Of course I also knew that if I produced my plays that dealt with my ethnic identity first, I would have to talk about my personal and family history, which have been very much shaped by the Palestinian-Israeli conflict. Why tackle a subject as polarizing and controversial as the modern Middle East? Especially if you enjoy being well liked as much as I do? The answer, of course, is that you absolutely should not. Unless you have to.

September 11 would change how I as an Arab-American was seen, but it was picking up *A Streetcar Named Desire* and rereading its introduction, only about a year before that tragedy occurred, that would change how I saw the seminal works of American theatre. It would also change how I thought about what might be my place in American theatre if I were brave enough to try.

I have never been good at unpacking boxes of books, because it is hard for me to put books on a shelf without feeling the need to reread one of them immediately. On that day, I picked up *A Streetcar Named Desire* and promised myself that I'd only read the last line of Tennessee's brilliant introduction before I went back to unpacking. That line, in which Tennessee writes that "the monosyllable of the clock is Loss, Loss, Loss, unless you devote your heart to its opposition," had become a sort of mantra for me. Of course, my mantra convinced me that it would be a Loss, Loss, Loss, to spend my morning unpacking when I felt consumed with the desire to reread my favorite American play instead. So, I delved into the world of Blanche DuBois. She was a character that reminded me of many of the powerful, sharp Arab women that I had known (too) well all my life. Women who loved sex and tried to pretend otherwise in order to get the affection of men. Women who were unpleasant houseguests, who had a particular combination of being mindnumbingly entitled and heartbreakingly vulnerable, which made them so easy to destroy.

Up to that point, I had viewed Tennessee Williams as a white writer, but I realized then that his best work always seemed tied to his very specific cultural identity. Southern-American writers who wrote about their culture were illuminating a subset of our society that felt as distinct and specific as African-American or Arab-American culture. I, like too many American theatregoers and academics, just chose not to see it that way. I had fallen into the trap of viewing the world of American writers as either white or not white, universal or limited, "us" or "them." I then picked up a few of the plays I had written in graduate school (yes, it took me months to unpack). It quickly became clear that the plays that dealt directly with my ethnic heritage were my best works thus far and that I had to start trying to get them produced. I realized I could write not only *despite* my fear of being pigeonholed, but also *about* my fear of being pigeonholed and of having my opportunities limited because of who I was.

Chocolate in Heat and *Roar* were my first works that were produced in New York, and *Roar* became the first play by a Palestinian-American playwright to premiere Off-Broadway. Both were plays that I had written, but never shown to anyone in their entirety, while I was a graduate student. Though they were about the Arab-American immigrant experience and had exclusively Arab-American characters in them, they did not deal directly with the Middle East conflict. *The Black Eyed* is my first play that does.

I began working on *The Black Eyed* right after September 11. Because it is an extremely political and nonlinear play written in free verse with a chorus, I half believed I would never find a major producer willing to take it on, and that freed me to write in a way I had not attempted to write before. It's a cliché to say that your best work as an artist happens when you aren't trying to please anyone but yourself, but I don't think it is an accident that *The Black Eyed* was my first play to have multiple productions and be translated into different languages.

Having this play produced in Greece was one of the nicest things that has ever happened to me, perhaps because it required the least amount of development of any of my previous productions. All I did was hand a script to a Greek actress whom I had met by chance, telling her, "I think Greek audiences might dig this play. It has a chorus." Less than a year later I was being flown to Athens for its opening. I expected the Greek producer and artists involved to be highly politicized and informed about Middle Eastern politics. But, the questions that the director and actors had for me were all about the play's structure and the characters' specific personality traits. After a bit of ouzo on opening night, I took the producer aside and asked her why she felt it was important to do a play about four Palestinian women in Greece. She looked slightly surprised at my question. Then she said that she never really thought about the play as being about four Palestinians. She said she thought the story was about four strong people.

Enough teasing. I hope you will enjoy *The Black Eyed*.

Production History

The Black Eyed premiered at Magic Theatre (Chris Smith, Artistic Director; David Gluck, Managing Director) on May 14, 2005. It was directed by Jessica Heidt. Set design was by Kris Stone. Lighting design was by Chris Studley. Costume design was by Callie Floor. The production stage manager was Leslie Grisdale. The cast was as follows:

AIESHA	Nora El Samahy
TAMAM	Bridgette Loriaux
THE ARCHITECT	Atosa Babaoff
DELILAH	Sofia Ahmad

The play opened in Athens, Greece at Fournos Theater on April 25, 2007. It was directed by Takis Tzamargias. The translation was by Athina Paraponiari. Sound design was by Platonas Andritsakis. The cast was as follows:

AIESHA	Anna Koutsaftiki
TAMAM	Evdokia Statiri
THE ARCHITECT	Kalliroe Myriagou
DELILAH	Stevi Fortoma

The play opened Off-Broadway at New York Theatre Workshop (James C. Nicola, Artistic Director; Lynn Moffat, Managing Director) on July 31, 2007. It was directed by Sam Gold. Set design was by Paul Steinberg. Lighting design was by Jane Cox. Sound design was by Darron L. West. Costume design was by Gabriel Berry. The production stage manager was Rachel Zack. The cast was as follows:

AIESHA	Aysan Celik
TAMAM	Lameece Issaq
THE ARCHITECT	Jeanine Serralles
DELILAH	Emily Swallow

Characters

AIESHA, a woman

TAMAM, a woman

THE ARCHITECT, a woman

DELILAH, a woman

Setting

The stage is very sparse.

Note

It is indicated in the text where the characters speak as part of a chorus.

To my much-loved and loving parents,
Charles and Ghada Shamieh,
who always made the improbable seem possible.

Acknowledgments

The journey I took when I began *The Black Eyed* was made cheerful by May Adrales, Vanessa Aspillaga, Dalia Basiouny, Lee Breuer, Geraldine Brooks, Chris Burney, Henry Chalfant, Kathleen Chalfant, S. Allen Counter, Sally Eberhardt, Jennie El-Far, John Clinton Eisner, Drew Faust, Tracy Cameron Francis, Frank Hentschker, Philip Himberg, Roxanne Hope, Tony Horwitz, Tera Hunter, David Henry Hwang, Todd London, Florencia Lozano, Marc Masterson, Salem Mekuria, Maude Mitchell, Hala Nassar, Eve Troutt Powell, Najla Said, Joan Shigekawa, Seret Scott, Susan Terrio, Marisa Tomei, Liesl Tommy, Naomi Wallace, Craig Watson, Mac Wellman, Torange Yeghiazarian, José Zayas and countless others. This play would not have had the life it had without the extraordinary creative insight of the directors Sam Gold, Jessica Heidt and Takis Tzamargias. *The Black Eyed* was developed with support from the Radcliffe Institute for Advanced Study at Harvard University, the Rockefeller Foundation, the Sundance Institute Theatre Program, the Lark Play Development Center and Yaddo.

I must acknowledge the late Dr. Edward Said, who attended the first public reading of *The Black Eyed* at the New York City Tenement Museum in January 2002. His support emboldened me. I have no doubt I could not do the work I do if he hadn't paved my way. Tony Kushner's brilliant theatrical imagination has always thrilled me. His incomparable moral courage, kindness and generosity of spirit as a mentor and fellow traveler are also astounding. Tony continually inspires me to be a better artist and a better person. Thank you to Kia Corthron, who was incredibly good to me as I made the haphazard transition from student to playwright. Lynn Nottage was assigned as my mentor when I was a New Dramatists Van Lier Fellow in 2001, and I have relied enormously on her wisdom and wit as I attempt to navigate the sordid world of American theatre since that time. I have to acknowledge Scott Elliott, Ian Morgan and Geoff Rich for being the first to take a chance on me, and for making me a part of the New Group family at an early stage in my career. I will forever be indebted to Chris Smith for producing the world premieres of two of my most "unconventional" plays at the Magic Theatre. I was blessed to work with my Greek translator Athina Paraponiari ("It's all Greek to me," never stops being funny) and the formidable Stevi Fortoma. Special thanks to Jim Nicola, Linda Chapman and the amazingly dedicated team at New York Theatre Workshop for all their support and for making their leading institution a true home for several Palestinian and Arab-American artists Off-Broadway. I believe their deeply honest and unparalleled commitment to locating, developing and producing playwrights from arguably the most marginalized segment of our society has already and will continue to make American theatre a more inclusive and, therefore, more culturally relevant, art form. Joseph and Natalie Shamieh's presence at the Off-Broadway opening of *The Black Eyed* meant the world to me. I salute the entire Shamieh and Ghannam family for giving me enough material for a lifetime, and for not minding when that material ends up onstage (yet) as long as the characters inspired by them are played by very good-looking actors.

Aiesha is alone onstage, facing the audience.

AIESHA:

Unanswered questions,
unquestioned answers.
I do someone good dead.
I do someone dead good.
What is the point of the revolution that begins with the little hand?
Any little hand?
(Lifts her right hand and looks at it)
This little hand?
Unanswered questions,
unquestioned answers—

(Delilah, Tamam and The Architect enter. They do not notice Aiesha at first.)

TAMAM:

(Points toward the audience)
There's the door!

(The three women see Aiesha.)

DELILAH:
   (To Aiesha:)
   We heard a rumor.
   We heard that all the martyrs
   were sitting in the one room
   in the afterlife.

THE ARCHITECT:
   (Points toward the audience)
   The one right there!

TAMAM:
   The room no one knows anything about,
   the room no one but martyrs have dared to go in.

DELILAH:
   And no one who goes in

THE ARCHITECT:
   comes out.

CHORUS *(Delilah, Tamam and The Architect)*:
   Should we believe it?

(Pause. Aiesha looks at each woman carefully before she finally speaks.)

AIESHA:
   Tell me who you are.

CHORUS *(Delilah, Tamam and The Architect)*:
   And you'll know who we're looking for?

TAMAM:
   My name is Tamam.
   It means "enough."
   I need to see the thing that started out smaller than me
   and got bigger.
   I need to see my brother.

DELILAH:
   Women were his only weakness.
   I was his only woman.

They called me Delilah.
I'm here for Samson.

(Pause.)

TAMAM:

(To The Architect:)
Answer her questions, girl. She may help us.
(To Aiesha:)
I don't know her name.

THE ARCHITECT:

I'm the architect
of the unseen, underlying structures,
the buildings that have never been built.

TAMAM:

I don't know who she's looking for.

THE ARCHITECT:

I'm here for answers from the only one who can give them to me.

CHORUS *(Delilah, Tamam and The Architect)*:
Let us in.

AIESHA:

Go right ahead.
(Motions toward the audience)
The door is unlocked.

(Pause.)

Afraid? Tell me why and I'll tell you if you have good reason to be.

(Delilah, Tamam and The Architect all begin speaking at once.)

DELILAH:

(Overlapping:)
Women were his only weakness, and I was his only woman.

TAMAM:

(Overlapping:)
Started out smaller than me and got bigger. I want to see my
    brother.

THE ARCHITECT:
> *(Overlapping:)*
> He passed me and knew I was an Arab.

AIESHA:
> Hold on!
> Women and weakness?
> You'll speak first.

DELILAH:
> Women were his only weakness
> and I was his only woman.

CHORUS *(Tamam and The Architect)*:
> Yeah, right.

DELILAH:
> Okay, the only one that mattered.
> And I asked—

CHORUS *(Tamam and The Architect)*:
> Will you have me?
> Do you want me?
> Do you love me?

DELILAH:
> I asked him:
> "What makes your strength weak?
> Show me the crack in your armor, so I may lick and seal it together.
> Let me keep you safe from
> those who hate you and wish you dead."

AIESHA:
> So you refused to put out till he told you, right?
> Crudeness is necessary for clarity.

DELILAH:
> Basically.

CHORUS *(Tamam and The Architect)*:
> It comes down to the basics.
> You knew the only power
> you had over men was sexual.

AIESHA:

Those were your means.

DELILAH:

I used them.

AIESHA:

You acted justly, Delilah.
You saved your people.

DELILAH:

My people!
My people called me a whore.
I overheard a young man from my own clan say:

CHORUS *(Tamam and The Architect)*:

"The whore did her job and she did it well."

DELILAH:

He didn't call me
the daughter of an honorable man,
or a good woman who loved her people—

CHORUS *(Aiesha, Tamam and The Architect)*:

but a whore.

DELILAH:

But not at first.
No, not . . . of course.
The elders came to me after my brother died.
They knew I was alone,
they knew I intended to stay that way.

AIESHA:

So they made you seduce Samson?
They forced you into it?

DELILAH:

Worse.
They made me think it was my idea.
They asked me to take my father's place at their meetings,
even though I was a girl,
because my only brother was dead.

We talked of many things.
They listened as if my opinions mattered,
as if I mattered.
They were polite.

CHORUS *(Tamam and The Architect)*:
Too polite.

DELILAH:
I told them my ideas about how to prevent the cattle from dying
and why our well always ran dry.
Out of the blue, my father's best friend brought up Samson.
We rarely talked about Samson in our villages.

CHORUS *(Tamam and The Architect)*:
The problems that are the most pressing

DELILAH:
are the ones you tend to ignore.
He stated the obvious.
He said if Samson isn't stopped

CHORUS *(Tamam and The Architect)* AND DELILAH:
it won't matter whether we have enough to eat next season.

DELILAH:
My father's friend said our men can't win against him.
We don't want to lose more men like your unparalleled brother,
your brother with a face like the moon.

TAMAM:
I want to see my brother.

AIESHA:
Let the girl tell her story.

DELILAH:
He said the only weakness that man has is for women.
And then, in perfect time, they all turned and looked at me.
It was then that I offered to try.

AIESHA:
You offered?!

DELILAH:

    I should have known by the way they were talking
    that they wanted something from me.
    And they sure knew how to get it.
    My father's closest friend took me aside after the meeting,
    as if he had a secret to share about my father.
    But all he told me was what my father himself told me often
        enough,

CHORUS *(Tamam and The Architect)*:

    If I had known I could make daughters like you, Delilah,
    I would have wished for a dozen.

DELILAH:

    Their words were honey.
    Sweet,

CHORUS *(Tamam and The Architect)*:

    without substance in heat.

DELILAH:

    Everyone thought I did it,
    because my brother had been killed by Samson in the last battle.
    My brother was the first of a hundred men to charge at Samson.
    Being in the front was dangerous,
    almost suicide.

CHORUS *(Aiesha, Tamam and The Architect)*:

    Suicide!

DELILAH:

    Only fools fought in the front,
    but someone had to be a fool
    if there was to be a fight at all.
    Samson snatched up my brother first,
    but killed him last.
    He made a game of dangling him,
    choking him in the crook of his arm,
    while he,
    with his other iron fist,
    continued to knock the heads off the necks
    of all my cousins, neighbors and friends.

THE ARCHITECT:
>   Hands change!

DELILAH:
>   *(Ignoring The Architect's outburst)*
>   Not only everyone you loved,
>   but everyone you knew,

CHORUS *(Aiesha and Tamam)* AND DELILAH:
>   lost someone.

DELILAH:
>   A wife of a man killed charged at Samson,
>   roaring, livid, full of a uniquely female fury
>   that when you witness
>   makes you sure
>   this woman can punch through a wall,
>   kill a lion if it chanced on her path,
>   till a man flattens her with a half-of-his-strength hit.

AIESHA:
>   He hit her?

DELILAH:
>   That would be tacky.
>   Samson was a lot of things, but he wasn't tacky.
>   He grabbed her and kissed her passionately,
>   and she scratched and bit and pushed at him.
>   He told her:

CHORUS *(Tamam and The Architect)* AND DELILAH:
>   "I like 'em kinky."

DELILAH:
>   It was then that I saw my brother was not moving.

AIESHA:
>   Now your story makes sense.
>   You're here to see your brother.

DELILAH:
>   I am not here to see my brother.

TAMAM:

My brother!
Have you seen him?
He looks like me:
black hair, black eyes—

AIESHA:

Hold your horses, Tamar!

TAMAM:

It's Tamam.

AIESHA:

Whatever.
(To Delilah:)
So who are you here to see?

DELILAH:

I told you before. Samson.

AIESHA:

To spit in his face, right?

DELILAH:

He might kind of dig that, but no.

CHORUS *(Tamam and The Architect)*:
Gross.

DELILAH:

That's my Samson. He's quite special.

AIESHA:

How did you wrench from him the secret of where his power lied?

DELILAH:

You mean, what's so bewitching about little ole me?
I'm a pretty woman.
It's not a boast,

CHORUS *(Tamam and The Architect)*:
it's a fact.

AIESHA:
 But pretty enough to die to have?

DELILAH:
 But you want to know precisely
 what he loved about me,
 so you'll understand why he told me his dark secret.
 Do you want to know why he put the power of his fate
 in the nest of my interlaced hands?

AIESHA:
 Obviously I want to know. I already asked you, bitch.

DELILAH:
 What does it matter?
 What good does it do for you to know?
 We're all dead.
 There's no hope of using the knowledge to seduce.

CHORUS *(Aiesha, Tamam and The Architect)*:
 But it can't hurt.

DELILAH:
 Women, what do you do when you want a man?
 This is what I did and this is what I suggest:
 go to where he frequents,
 dress well, dress in a way that makes it obvious you are a *(Pause)*
  woman.

CHORUS *(Tamam and The Architect)*:
 Men can never tell the difference
 between a beautiful woman

DELILAH:
 and a person dressed like one.
 He'll take you,
 because you're there and available.
 Then, he'll probably leave you alone,
 like Samson did to me,
 immediately and for days, weeks, months, years.

CHORUS *(Tamam and The Architect)*:
 Or did it just feel that way?

DELILAH:

Either way, the waiting killed me.
What's the difference between a thing that feels like it kills you
    and the one that actually does?

AIESHA:

Plenty,
but go on.

DELILAH:

I almost went back to my people,
gave up.
But then one morning,
I opened my door and there he was, about to knock.
He didn't say hello. He just announced:

CHORUS *(Tamam and The Architect)*:

"You can live with me for a while."

DELILAH:

. . . And I said, "Yes, I can."
I didn't know that there would be his other lovers living there, too,
all Philistine women,
like myself.
I had never met any of them before. They were poor girls.
At home, we did not run in the same circles. Do you understand?

CHORUS *(Tamam and The Architect)*:

We understand.

DELILAH:

I was surprised, my pride was wounded.
But I thought to myself:

CHORUS *(Tamam and The Architect)* AND DELILAH:

"I am in the process of erasing you,"

DELILAH:

"I will watch you cower and then crumble
into dust before me."

CHORUS *(Tamam and The Architect)* AND DELILAH:

"You will pay for every pleasure you exact from my pain."

DELILAH:

    Believe that and it's surprisingly easy not to be jealous.
    My indifference made me different
    so he began to prefer me.

CHORUS *(Tamam and The Architect)*:

    "Preference" is the first domino of human feeling.

DELILAH:

    Hit it hard, and it knocks over "like," "need" and, finally,

CHORUS *(Tamam and The Architect)*:

    "love."

DELILAH:

    I need to go inside.

TAMAM:

    Go, I'll follow.

DELILAH:

    I should.
    (Points toward the audience)
    He's in there. I know it. It's like I can feel him watching me.
    (Addresses the audience as if she sees Samson:)
    Samson!
    I begged my people not to hurt you.
    They promised, I almost believed.
    When they blinded you, I could not see,
    how to show you though I loved my people more,

CHORUS *(Tamam and The Architect)* AND DELILAH:

    I still loved you.

DELILAH:

    Surrounded by darkness, I knew you,
    who loved me without lights on,
    would recognize

CHORUS *(Tamam and The Architect)* AND DELILAH:

    my touch.

DELILAH:

> I touched, muttering a skeleton of apologies.
> You sliced through the bone saying:

CHORUS *(Tamam and The Architect)*:

> "Leave! Your presence torments me."

DELILAH:

> I stayed, you cursed me.
> I fled your cries and the cruelty you learned from me.
> Outside, looking in,
> I saw you framed in the doorway
> of that great hall that stood so tall

CHORUS *(Tamam and The Architect)* AND DELILAH:

> that seemed only God's hand could make fall.

DELILAH:

> You, with your head cocked as you watched me with your ears.
> Your arms stretched out.
> The pillars exploded.

CHORUS *(Tamam and The Architect)*:

> The world went flat.

DELILAH:

> You spared me.
> Your people dug and found you
> under the layers of mine.
> I prayed that you would rest softly in their soil.
> I wished your God could have kept you safe

CHORUS *(Tamam and The Architect)* AND DELILAH:

> from she who loved you,

DELILAH:

> but still wished you dead.

AIESHA:

> Nice story. But I don't suggest you stick to it.

DELILAH:

> Why not?

AIESHA:

Trust me, you won't be welcome in there if you tell that story.

DELILAH:

How do you know?

AIESHA:

Maybe because I've been in there.

TAMAM:

What? Really? Did you see my brother?

AIESHA:

I wouldn't know him if I did.

TAMAM:

How did you get in? Why did you leave?

AIESHA:

It's a long story.

DELILAH:

I don't believe you. No one who goes into that room comes out.

AIESHA:

Don't believe me. Go in. Tell your story. See what happens.

DELILAH:

If it's true you went in,
why didn't you stay?

AIESHA:

Like I said, it's a long story.

THE ARCHITECT:

Why is everybody always talking about length? There are other
factors to consider.

(Pause.)

AIESHA:

What?

TAMAM:

> Excuse her. She's not very articulate.

DELILAH:

> You'll get used to her.

TAMAM:

> She means to ask why do people mention the length of a *story*
> as a reason not to tell it?

DELILAH:

> When there are far more important factors to consider—
> like how badly we need to know it.

AIESHA:

> Okay.
> It's not a long story, it's a very short one and it ends with a real
> bang.

THE ARCHITECT:

> Hands change!

AIESHA:

> I ask the questions.
> How long have you been together?

CHORUS *(Delilah, Tamam and The Architect)*:

> A long time.

TAMAM:

> Not long enough to hate one another,

DELILAH:

> but long enough to know

CHORUS *(Delilah, Tamam and The Architect)*:

> we eventually will.

TAMAM:

> Please try to remember if you've seen my brother.
> He was about this tall *(Frantically indicates a height that would
> suggest a tall man)* and had—

AIESHA:
> What was his name?

TAMAM:
> Muhammad.

AIESHA:
> Muhammad? Do you know how many Muhammads are probably
> in there?

TAMAM:
> No more than there are Johns.

AIESHA:
> True.

CHORUS *(Delilah, Tamam and The Architect)*:
> *(Speaking together as if chanting a prayer:)*
> Help us take our first step towards that room.

TAMAM:
> Water goes from solid to liquid,

THE ARCHITECT:
> people don't just cease.

DELILAH:
> Our loved ones are allowed an afterlife,

TAMAM:
> just like every other misguided soul who murdered and raped.

DELILAH:
> Some of our martyrs were mistaken,

THE ARCHITECT:
> cruel,

TAMAM:
> even insane.

CHORUS *(Delilah, Tamam and The Architect)*:
> But the fact remains,
> they are not worse than the worst of them that are here.

DELILAH:
> We believe in
> our loved ones
> who are sitting in that room in front of us.

THE ARCHITECT:
> *(Points to the audience)*
> That room! And we only need to go in.

TAMAM:
> To see our brothers.

DELILAH:
> Our lovers.

THE ARCHITECT:
> Our strangers.

CHORUS *(Delilah, Tamam and The Architect)*:
> We are in Heaven.
> And when we woke up here,

THE ARCHITECT:
> there was a mint on the pillow
> beside the one we slept on
> and a note that had fallen off the bed.

TAMAM:
> The note said:

CHORUS *(Delilah, Tamam and The Architect)*:
> Welcome to Heaven,
> where everything you believe to be true is true.

> *(The prayer ends.)*

THE ARCHITECT:
> But we can't control what we believe.

TAMAM:
> That's what makes our Heaven such hell.

DELILAH:

> I don't care. I want to see Samson. I'm sure they'll welcome me
> in the martyr's room when they know how much I love him.

AIESHA:

> If you believe that, I've got a peace process I can sell you.

THE ARCHITECT:

> *(To Aiesha:)*
> What's your name?

AIESHA:

> Aiesha.

THE ARCHITECT:

> You look so familiar. Do I look familiar to you?

AIESHA:

> No.

THE ARCHITECT:

> Were you famous?

AIESHA:

> Yes, but you wouldn't know me.

THE ARCHITECT:

> Maybe I do. When were you alive?

AIESHA:

> Listen, half-wit. I said you didn't.
> You speak out of turn again and I'll make you go stand with one
> of the other groups of women that are around here.
> But they probably won't have you either, so you'll be all alone.
> You want to be alone?

THE ARCHITECT:

> *(Looking at Tamam and Delilah)*
> But . . .

AIESHA:

> Don't look at your friends. Keep looking at me.
> They're not going to help you.

TAMAM:

> We have to do what she says.

DELILAH:

> She may get us in the room.

TAMAM:

> Don't be difficult!

AIESHA:

> They know I'm right.
> Look at me and answer my questions.
> Do you want to be alone?

(The Architect shakes her head.)

> Listen, you worthless waste of a human soul. I'm going to ask
>> you again— Do I look familiar?

THE ARCHITECT:

> Yes, but—

(Aiesha approaches her, menacing.)

> No.

AIESHA:

> That's what I thought.

DELILAH:

> What you think, we think.

TAMAM:

> You're certainly not a religious figure.

AIESHA:

> What makes you say that?

TAMAM:

> Maybe you are, but I didn't read about you when I scoured the
>> holy books of every religion that ever existed. Looking for a
>> trace of what all the world religions say happens to martyrs,
>> so I can figure out where my brother might be.

Do you think you can go in and ask about him now?
If you wouldn't mind . . .

DELILAH:

Forget her brother. You'll notice Samson. He's the big guy. He'll
probably hit on you. Tell him to come out and get me.

TAMAM:

I knew I should never have let you follow me here.

DELILAH:

I didn't follow you! I've looked at all those books, too. I did just
as much work as you did to get here.

TAMAM:

You were wandering.
You saw that this girl *(Points to The Architect)* was following me.
At least she stays quiet, except when she screams something
about hands and change.

THE ARCHITECT:

Hands change!

TAMAM:

Like that.
I went to talk to all the gods and prophets
of all the religions that ever were.
They tried their best to tell us where to locate the martyrs in the
afterlife.
None had a clue, except this God that humans prayed to before
they made it to the *sapiens* part of the *Homo sapien*s.

THE ARCHITECT:

It was at the *Homo erectus* point in the chain of human development.

DELILAH:

Homo erectus?

TAMAM:

You'd know that if you did the research.

DELILAH:

Okay, I didn't do all the research you did.
I just stood around and said,

(Flirty:)
"I need a little information.
Does anyone want to help me out?"
Then this monkey-like god appeared,
ready to, you know, help out.

TAMAM:

What was this monkey god's name?

DELILAH:

"Oo-oo-oo" is what he called himself.

TAMAM:

I can't believe Oo-oo-oo told you where he thought the martyrs
might be.

DELILAH:

What's the big deal?

TAMAM:

Oo-oo-oo told me I was the only person he was going to tell.

DELILAH:

Well, if it makes you feel better, it wasn't easy to get it out of
him. It took a lot of persuasion.

TAMAM:

You persuaded him, too?

AIESHA:

You're obviously pretty good at persuasion, Delilah.

DELILAH:

It has been said that I am.
I got him drunk on banana wine, and I had my share, too.
Then he began to talk.
He said,
(Delilah mimics Oo-oo-oo for the next section in quotes:)
"Look, I'm going to get into trouble for telling you this.
I don't like to mess with the martyrs.
No one does. But there was this room at the corner of Heaven,
where the colobus monkeys who sacrifice themselves,"

297

AIESHA:
"who run towards the predators"

DELILAH:
"so their loved ones have time to get away,"

AIESHA:
"who run towards their predators
so the weaker ones aren't certain prey."

DELILAH:
"They used to hang out in this room, long before humans were
invented.
We gods have talked and we figured out this is the place where
the human martyrs must be, too."
That's the story he tells if you persuade him enough.

TAMAM:
Yes.
But banana wine is cheap, and persuading a monkey is easier
than you might think.
The Monkey God obviously likes all kinds of women.

AIESHA:
That's right. Women of all different cultures and all centuries
have come here to look for their martyrs.

CHORUS (Delilah, Tamam and The Architect):
They get stuck here, too stubborn to give up searching,

AIESHA:
too afraid to go in.

(In the following exchange, each woman points to different areas of the
stage to indicate the different groups of women.)

DELILAH:
There must be the Japanese women, whose men kamikazied
their way here and haven't been seen since.

TAMAM:
Over there, are Iranian mothers, who helped convince their
children it was their duty to run through land riddled with
land mines.

DELILAH:

    Here are the Tamil women, sisters of the Black Tigers who sit for
        centuries,

THE ARCHITECT:

    waiting.

DELILAH:

    There! Those are the Buddhists,
    mostly mothers of monks who made love to fire
    and died in its embrace.

THE ARCHITECT:

    The Irish girls are over there,
    whose fathers starved themselves in the hope of tasting freedom.

AIESHA:

    They tend to sing to pass the time.

TAMAM:

    There are the Jewish ladies,
    the relatives of the unsung
    heroes of the Holocaust,
    unnamed, because anyone who might have seen or been told
        about their brave acts died almost immediately after them,

THE ARCHITECT:

    unknown,

DELILAH:

    except to their loved ones who will not rest
    till they find them again.

CHORUS *(Delilah, Tamam and The Architect)*:
    There is no hatred here.
    Each of us wishes each of them well.

DELILAH:

    Here we wait in Heaven, at the gate of the martyrs' door.
    Though none of us seem to have discussed it or decided upon it,

TAMAM:

    somehow we have managed to separate ourselves
    into the groups,

THE ARCHITECT:
the races,

CHORUS *(Delilah, Tamam and The Architect)*:
we identified with while we were alive.

AIESHA:
So, you three are all Palestinians?

CHORUS *(Delilah, Tamam and The Architect)*:
Yes.

TAMAM:
Even in Heaven, you can breathe more easily with your own
people.

DELILAH:
Here we are

TAMAM:
and here we have
segregated ourselves

THE ARCHITECT:
almost by accident.

AIESHA:
All except for her.

DELILAH:
Philistine is how you pronounce Palestine in Arabic in my day
and in yours, Aiesha. You know that.

AIESHA:
All I know is that you like kosher dick, bitch.

THE ARCHITECT:
Ugly! No hands! Change!

TAMAM:
Aiesha, I want your help.
But that kind of talk is not necessary.

AIESHA:

It's not necessary to speak my mind but I'm going to do so anyway.

DELILAH:

Don't worry, Tamam. I can handle her. I like men and all the different flavors they come in. And trust me, when they do come, it is in different flavors.

AIESHA:

Forbidden fruit rots quickly.
You know why he liked you so much?

THE ARCHITECT:

Oh, no!

DELILAH:

You don't know anything about what he felt for me.

AIESHA:

Because, while having you,
he was able to relive murdering all your men.

THE ARCHITECT:

Hands!

AIESHA:

(To The Architect:)
You shut up!
(To Delilah:)
So why don't you go join the Jewish women, Delilah?

TAMAM:

Aiesha, that's enough.

DELILAH:

Just because I love someone else doesn't mean I become something else.

AIESHA:

Whatever.

THE ARCHITECT:
> You seem so familiar.

AIESHA:
> Don't you start with that again!

DELILAH:
> You were never in that room.

AIESHA:
> Yes, I was! I went in and came back out.

TAMAM:
> Not possible.

AIESHA:
> I am a martyr.
> There are female martyrs, too, you know.
> I built something more intricate than the human heart,
> hugged it to my chest,
> and walked into the biggest crowd I could find . . .

DELILAH:
> How could you do that?
> It's so angry.

CHORUS *(Delilah, Tamam and The Architect)*:
> It's so male.

AIESHA:
> Let's put it this way.
> Oppression is like a coin maker.

TAMAM:
> That's what my brother said!

AIESHA:
> Can you keep it to yourself, Reham?
> I'm trying to tell my story.
> I suggest you listen to it. It may be of some interest to you and
>   yours.

TAMAM:

> Sorry. It's Tamam, by the way.

AIESHA:

> You should be.
> Unlike some people, I didn't stand on the sidelines,
> seducing my way into saving my people's skin

DELILAH:

> It worked.

AIESHA:

> Not for long.

DELILAH:

> Samson only killed the Philistines in the banquet hall.
> Had he lived and had I not wrung his secret from him,
> he would have slaughtered us all.
> Check your sources, remember who wrote them.
> If you do, angry woman, you might find out
> you're closer to me than you think.
> I might be your ancestor.

AIESHA:

> We've heard enough out of you.
> Go hang out with the Jewish women.

DELILAH:

> Religion doesn't mean anything here.
> I was born before your religion even existed.
> *(To The Architect and Tamam:)*
> Let's go speak with those Iranian mothers,

CHORUS *(Tamam and The Architect)*:

> No.

DELILAH:

> Let's ask if they want to walk in with us.

AIESHA:

> That's a bad idea, whore.

DELILAH:

Words like that don't mean anything here,
because up here we know
there isn't a woman alive who doesn't sell herself . . .

(Pause.)

CHORUS *(Delilah, Tamam and The Architect)*:
. . . short.

AIESHA:

Maybe that's true of weak women like you,
but women like me take matters into our own hands
and we get our rewards.
The minute I got to the afterlife,
I had a hundred men of every hue.
That's what I believed I'd get.

CHORUS *(Delilah, Tamam and The Architect)*:
So that meant that's what you got.
We do know that all religions are wacky

DELILAH:

And if you don't buy that,

TAMAM:

you haven't read your own book with honest eyes.

DELILAH:

Everyone picks and chooses what's convenient
about their own religion,

CHORUS *(Delilah, Tamam and The Architect)*:
and should keep that in mind

AIESHA:

before they start judging someone else's.
I believed my book
when it said
Heaven is indescribable in human terms,

CHORUS *(Delilah, Tamam and The Architect)*:
    i.e., you just won't get it.

AIESHA:

    So, to describe indescribable delight,
    it said that men who live virtuously
    don't actually get to have a bunch of sexy, dark-eyed women,
    but they have pleasures
    that will feel like
    what can only, in inferior human terms,
    be understood as

CHORUS *(Delilah, Tamam and The Architect)*:
    hanging out with a bunch of houris,
    who were hot

AIESHA:

    virgins whose virginity is continually renewed,
    also known as

CHORUS *(Delilah, Tamam and The Architect)* AND AIESHA:
    the Black Eyed.

AIESHA:

    I interpreted that to mean that if I blew myself up and took
        others with me,
    because no one would give a shit about my people's plight
        unless I did,
    I would have a hundred men of every hue.
    who were lined up like fruits at the market,

CHORUS *(Delilah, Tamam and The Architect)*:
    ready for the picking and the plucking.

AIESHA:

    Men, forever chaste with their chastity renewing throughout
        eternity, untouched, eager.
    I had them all.

TAMAM:

    In what religious text did you find that if you blew yourself up
        you'd have a hundred men of every hue?

AIESHA:

Okay, my interpretation is a rather loose one.
But, hey, it's Heaven.
That's what I believed, that's what I got.

THE ARCHITECT:

How could you leave a hundred men of every hue?

DELILAH:

Did you happen to miss that she said that these men had no
sexual experience?
How many times can a woman scream:
"That's not it."

CHORUS *(Delilah and Tamam)*:

"That's not near it."

DELILAH:

"That's so far away,"

CHORUS *(Delilah and Tamam)*:

"you might as well be rubbing the soles of my shoes
without them even being on my feet."

(The Architect laughs hysterically.)

AIESHA:

It isn't that funny. Why are you laughing?
(To Tamam:)
Make her stop.

TAMAM:

Actually, it is funny.
You're a pretty girl, Aiesha.
It's not a compliment. It's a fact.
And you blew yourself up
and ended up with a hundred male virgins in Heaven.

DELILAH:

When any girl could have twice that number on earth if she
wanted to.

(All three women laugh at Aiesha.)

AIESHA:

Shut up. Shut up.

DELILAH:

And now you're hanging out with us,
because for some reason, the martyrs don't want you in there
    with them.

AIESHA:

I could go back there anytime.

TAMAM:

Then, go!
Ask our loved ones if they want us to visit.

AIESHA:

The door is unlocked.
Just walk in.
Your loved ones are in there.
Don't you think they want to see you
as much as you want to see them?

DELILAH:

You go first.
Help us and we'll be in your everlasting debt.

AIESHA:

Everlasting debt is overrated and hardly ever paid in full.

TAMAM:

I can't take it anymore. Go in there right now and ask about my
    brother!

AIESHA:

Shut up!

TAMAM:

You go in there right now.

THE ARCHITECT:

Stop fighting.

AIESHA:

> We're not fighting, Retard. I'm ignoring her.

TAMAM:

> Tell my brother I have something to say to him.
> Go!

CHORUS *(Delilah and The Architect)*:

> Hold on a minute.

DELILAH:

> We agreed.
> We're in this together.
> If we're asking her to go in, she should ask about all our loved ones.

TAMAM:

> No, you're going to ask about my brother first,
> before you look for anyone else.

AIESHA:

> Heyam, I don't care about you or your stupid—

TAMAM:

> My name is Tamam.
> It means "enough."
> I was called that because my family wanted

CHORUS *(Delilah and The Architect)*:

> no more daughters.

TAMAM:

> I am the last of seven sisters, good luck for the family.
> Because, after me, a brother was born.
> The only one.

CHORUS *(Delilah and The Architect)*:

> Why do our people rejoice when a boy child is born?

TAMAM:

> Because times like these call for soldiers,
> to fight
> the Europeans and their Holy War,
> crusading against we people who lived here before,

CHORUS *(Delilah and The Architect)* AND TAMAM:
    and will live here afterwards.

TAMAM:
    I want to talk about something smaller than me

CHORUS *(Delilah, Tamam and The Architect)*:
    that became bigger.

TAMAM:
    I want to talk about my brother.
    He was caught with a weapon in his hand
    and a curse on his lips.
    I went to the jail to pay a ransom for his release.
    Most of my people looked at the crusaders
    with every ounce of hatred a human heart can hold,
    their faces twisted not like they tasted something bitter,

CHORUS *(Delilah, Tamam and The Architect)*:
    like something bitter was being forced down their throats.

TAMAM:
    I was smarter than that.
    I knew I must navigate through the maze of might,
    and did my best to be kindly,

CHORUS *(Delilah, Tamam and The Architect)*:
    polite.

TAMAM:
    Hoping perhaps that I would
    remind them of a woman
    that they knew.

CHORUS *(Delilah and The Architect)*:
    Or would have liked to know.

TAMAM:
    So when they beat my brother,
    that thing that started out smaller than me and became bigger,
    they would, perhaps, maybe for my sake,

CHORUS *(Delilah, Tamam and The Architect)*:
>   lighten their touch.

TAMAM:
>   I am a pretty woman.
>   It's not a boast.

CHORUS *(Delilah and The Architect)*:
>   It's a fact.

TAMAM:
>   Looks are a commodity, an asset, a possession I happen to possess.
>   It's why my grandmother said:

CHORUS *(Delilah and The Architect)*:
>   "No,"

TAMAM:
>   when my sister's brother-in-law asked for my hand.
>   The family that was good enough
>   for my plain sister wasn't good enough for me.
>   I'm a pretty woman.
>   It's not a boast.

CHORUS *(Delilah and The Architect)*:
>   It's a fact.

TAMAM:
>   And I smiled my best smile
>   When the soldiers opened the gate for me,

CHORUS *(Delilah and The Architect)*:
>   weighed down with baskets of food.

TAMAM:
>   I brought extra,
>   hoping to create the illusion
>   that that dirty jail was one place
>   where there was enough and extra for all
>   the guards to eat twice.
>   Otherwise, my brother would get none.
>   unless there was enough and extra.

CHORUS *(Delilah and The Architect)*:
>   They thanked me

TAMAM:
>   for the food.
>   And they raped me in front of him,
>   forcing my brother's eyes open so he had to watch.
>   They wanted to know something

AIESHA:
>   that he apparently preferred not to tell them.

TAMAM:
>   They skewered the support for their argument into my flesh.
>   The crusaders believed rape would enrage our men.

CHORUS *(Delilah and The Architect)* AND TAMAM:
>   Enraging a man is the first step on the stairway

TAMAM:
>   that gets him to a place
>   where he becomes impotent,
>   helpless.
>   Say what you want about Arab men and women
>   and how we love one another,
>   there is one thing that's for certain:
>   there are real repercussions for hurting a woman in my society.

CHORUS *(Delilah, Aiesha and The Architect)* AND TAMAM:
>   There are repercussions.

TAMAM:
>   When the first hand was laid upon me, we both screamed.
>   The evolutionary function of a scream is a cry for help.
>   They tied down the only one who could,
>   so I silenced myself.
>   That was the only way to tell my brother
>   I didn't want him to tell.
>
>   I flinched when I had to,
>   but I kept my breathing regular.
>   My brother tried to look every other way,

but realized I needed him,
to look me in the eyes
(Pause)
and understand.
They thought making us face one another
in our misery would break us.
But we were used to misery.
It's like anything else.

AIESHA:
You can build up a tolerance for it.

TAMAM:
Someone else told them what they wanted to know,
so they released my brother two weeks later.

CHORUS *(Delilah and The Architect)*:
That's when he joined a rebel group organized in a prison.

TAMAM:
The group sent each man alone at the same time
to a different part of the crowded crusader marketplace,

CHORUS *(Delilah and The Architect)* AND TAMAM:
Each with a knife and a double-ball battle mace,
killing as many as they could till—

DELILAH:
Is that an arm?

THE ARCHITECT:
A hand. Who does it belong to?

TAMAM:
Full of men, women, children.

DELILAH:
No, it's a spine. Look at the ridges.

THE ARCHITECT:
Who does it belong to?

TAMAM:

> Pilgrims—not warriors.
> People—not parts of flesh strewn everywhere,
> until my brother and the others got there.
> My brother's parts mixed in
> with the people he believed could not stand him.
> Because he believed they could not stand him.

CHORUS *(Delilah and The Architect)*:

> Who does it belong to?

TAMAM:

> I was not allowed to bury what I gathered,
> what I believed to be

CHORUS *(Delilah and The Architect)* AND TAMAM:

> parts of him.

TAMAM:

> The crusader mourners pulled
> the one hand

CHORUS *(Delilah and The Architect)* AND TAMAM:

> that I was sure was his

TAMAM:

> out of mine.
> They smeared it and his head with pig fat,
> as they did to desecrate the bodies of our soldiers.
> They hung my brother's head and hand with them
> on pikes above the city walls.
> The head I barely recognized,
> but I wanted to bury his hand

CHORUS *(Delilah and The Architect)*:

> to show who it belonged to.

TAMAM:

> The day he did it,
> he told me over breakfast:
> "Oppression"

AIESHA:
>   "is like a coin maker."

TAMAM:
>   "You put in human beings,
>   press the right buttons and
>   watch them
>   get squeezed, shrunk, flattened
>   till they take the slim shape of a two-faced coin."

TAMAM:
>   "One side is a martyr,"

AIESHA:
>   "the other a traitor."

TAMAM:
>   "All the possibilities of a life get reduced to those paltry two.
>   The coin is tossed in the air
>   it spins once for circumstance,
>   twice for luck,
>   and a third time for predilection
>   before it lands flat.
>   The face that points down"

CHORUS *(Delilah and The Architect)*:
>   "towards Hell"

TAMAM:
>   "determines not only who you are,"

CHORUS *(Delilah and The Architect)*:
>   "but how you will become that way."

TAMAM:
>   What he was really saying was:

AIESHA AND TAMAM:
>   "Good-bye."

TAMAM:
>   Had I known, I would have said something more than:
>   "Brother, it's interesting you think oppression
>   makes us turn into a form of money, a currency."

CHORUS *(Delilah and The Architect)*:
"How odd."

TAMAM:

Listen, I don't agree with killing innocent people
under any circumstances,

CHORUS *(Delilah and The Architect)* AND TAMAM:
ever.

TAMAM:

I am the kind of human being
who refuses to get addicted to

CHORUS *(Delilah and The Architect)* AND TAMAM:
the intoxication of hate.

TAMAM:

In my opinion,

CHORUS *(Delilah and The Architect)* AND TAMAM:
that's the only kind of human being there is.

TAMAM:

In other words, no one is going to reduce me to a coin.
There are absolutes,
it's wrong to kill, period.

THE ARCHITECT:
Hands! Movement!

AIESHA:

(Overlapping with The Architect's line, above:)
Not always.

Tamam

I should have known what my brother was bound to do,
I could have stopped him.
I said every time he went out to fight:
"Don't go.
We'll achieve peace by peaceful means."

CHORUS *(Delilah and The Architect)*:
"Don't be a pawn."

TAMAM:
"Let others risk their lives.
With all their weapons,
these foreigners can never truly win."

CHORUS *(Delilah and The Architect)*:
"They can't kill us all."

TAMAM:
I'd always say:

CHORUS *(Delilah and The Architect)* AND TAMAM:
"Don't go."

TAMAM:
But I didn't say:
"You are the most precious thing in the world to me.
The fact that you exist makes the earth spin on its axis,
it's rolling for joy because you are here.
The sun shows up to see you,
and the moon chases the sun off to be in your sky
and none of them love you like I do, Brother."

CHORUS *(Delilah and The Architect)*:
"Not even close."

TAMAM:
"If you think this is a gift for me,
the box will be empty, Brother."

CHORUS *(Delilah and The Architect)*:
"How can it not be?"

TAMAM:
"Everything will be empty, if you're not here.
I will not forgive you if you leave me.
I will not be comforted.
I will not be."
Instead I said:

CHORUS *(Delilah, Aiesha and The Architect)*:
"Don't go,"

TAMAM:

and I didn't say it loud.
Brother, they burned down our entire village
because you killed those people.
What you did wasn't about my honor.
It was about yours.
It is braver,

CHORUS *(Delilah and The Architect)* AND TAMAM:
harder,

TAMAM:

to live in a place
where no one wants us to live
than to die and leave me like that.
I didn't want revenge.
I wanted my brother alive.
My name is Tamam.
It means "enough."
Go tell my brother I'm here.

(Pause.)

AIESHA:

Boo hoo. Boo hoo. Boo fucking hoo.
What a horrible life you had on earth.
Get over it.

TAMAM:

I'm over it. Now go on and ask about my brother.

AIESHA:

And you actually think he's going to want to see you, Miss Enough?

TAMAM:

Yes.

AIESHA:

So you can insult him? Was your brother the type that took well
to having his choices questioned?

TAMAM:

> Why does it matter?

AIESHA:

> If you don't think it matters, go right in.
> I'm sure you'll be fine.
> It's only a room full of, um, I don't know, let me see . . . martyrs!
> So I suggest that you don't go in telling some story that
> dares to question the value of self-sacrifice.

TAMAM:

> So what do I say instead?

AIESHA:

> You could start by acknowledging your story is not unique. You
> were raped and lost a brother to war. That happened to millions
> of women throughout history. In fact, the crusades were
> nothing compared to the Palestinian and Israeli wars I lived
> through.

TAMAM:

> The solution to that one was so easy, Aiesha.

DELILAH:

> Yes, Aiesha.
> The Palestinian-Israeli problem was solved ages ago.

CHORUS *(Delilah, Tamam and The Architect)*:
> One state called
> the United States of Israel and Palestine.

DELILAH:

> Pal-rael for short.

TAMAM:

> The posters for travel agents everywhere boast first-class packages
> to Pal-rael that say:

CHORUS *(Delilah, Tamam and The Architect)*:
> "Come to Pal-rael.
> It's safe
> because the Palestinians and Israelis are now real pals."

TAMAM:

"Come see the Pal-rael museum of the centuries of war."

THE ARCHITECT:

"It was built so both peoples of Pal-rael could be reminded of
their dark past."

DELILAH:

You go to remember that all the killing and struggling on both
sides was in vain.

AIESHA:

My struggle,

TAMAM:

in vain.

AIESHA:

The death of our loved ones,

THE ARCHITECT:

ourselves,

TAMAM:

in vain.

AIESHA:

It's true. I can't believe it.

DELILAH:

And it happened in your lifetime. Or rather would have if you
had stuck around a bit longer. Now, there are other hot spots
in the world.

TAMAM:

Flash points of pain.

THE ARCHITECT:

The Swedes have now gone buck wild,

TAMAM:

are angry that the Maltese continue to make fun of the fact that
they have no eyelashes.

DELILAH:
> The Swedes insist we have eyelashes, but they are blond and
>> therefore invisible to the naked eye.

CHORUS *(Delilah, Tamam and The Architect)*:
> War ensued.

TAMAM:
> It may sound kind of amusing.
> And you can laugh and laugh,

CHORUS *(Tamam and The Architect)*:
> unless . . .

DELILAH:
> you're a Maltese mother who watched a soldier slit her son's throat

CHORUS *(Tamam and The Architect)* AND DELILAH:
> from ear to ear,

DELILAH:
> or a Swedish sister whose brother walked out one day

CHORUS *(Tamam and The Architect)* AND DELILAH:
> and never came back.

TAMAM:
> Unless you lost someone who was everything to you.
> I've been in Heaven for over hundreds of years.
> I have seen every person, even the guards who raped me,
> who apologized profusely.
> And, what they believed,
> what they feared even as they raped me,
> would eventually happen, did happen.
> I was the first person to greet them in the afterlife
> and I was allowed to cut off their genitals.
> But I chose not to and said I'll be back to do it later,
> because I didn't want to hurt them once and be done with it.
> I wanted them to fear me forever.

CHORUS *(Delilah and The Architect)*:
> Wouldn't you rather let it go?
> It would be a sign that you have grown, healed.

TAMAM:

Hell no.

Those soldiers killed more than my brother did, I'm sure.

And yet they are still here, roaming free.

I have seen everyone,

except the dearest person in the world to me.

So, if the war I suffered under is truly over,

why is my brother in that room?

Why is he not with me?

THE ARCHITECT:

Tell her.

(Pause.)

Tell her.

AIESHA:

Maybe I will, maybe I won't.

THE ARCHITECT:

Tell her and tell me why did I have to die like that?

AIESHA:

I don't know how or why you died.

I'm getting tired of you, you little idiot.

THE ARCHITECT:

I may be inarticulate.

Have always been.

It's not that I'm not thinking clear thoughts,

I'm thinking too many of them.

Hands, movement, change!

(To Aiesha:)

Murderer!

TAMAM:

(To Architect:)

That's enough, honey.

THE ARCHITECT:

(To Aiesha:)

I know your face.

AIESHA:
    Do you have something to say?

THE ARCHITECT:
    Yes!
    But can I say it?
    Why must I speak in words when I think in images?
    Hands! Movement! Change!

    I'm an architect of unseen structures
    and buildings that will never be built.
    I am the mother of children who will never be born,

CHORUS *(Delilah and Tamam)*:
    the lover of men who will remain unloved.

THE ARCHITECT:
    No, men who are loved beyond compare,
    but will never know it.

CHORUS *(Delilah and Tamam)*:
    Or how their lives would be changed if they did.

THE ARCHITECT:
    Right.
    It was all the Half-Breed's fault.
    Meeting that son of a bitch led to my murder.
    This, like so many things, all started with a

CHORUS *(Delilah and Tamam)*:
    job interview.

THE ARCHITECT:
    He had an Arab last name.

CHORUS *(Delilah and Tamam)*:
    Half-Breed.

THE ARCHITECT:
    I was always falling for the half-breeds.
    I can even see him in front of me now.

(Addresses Delilah as if she is the Half-Breed:)
I walked into your office, Half-Breed,
applying for an assistantship.
I read all about you in *Architectural Digest*.
Your daddy's a Christian Palestinian,
like my parents are.
But your mama's

CHORUS *(Delilah and Tamam)*:
    white.

THE ARCHITECT:
    You're a son of bitch with that sideway smile,
    that you flash when I walk in.
    You were discussing Gehry's new museum with your minions.
    Nice as hell you were,
    asking me what I thought of the new museum,
    as if my opinion mattered,
    as if I mattered . . .
    You were polite,

CHORUS *(Delilah and Tamam)*:
    too polite,

THE ARCHITECT:
    to someone applying to be an assistant.
    And everyone in the room knew it.
    Sidelong glances and smirks from your minions.
    "He's at it again," their eyes say.

CHORUS *(Delilah)*:
    "I'm at it again,"

THE ARCHITECT:
    your eyes say.
    I'm glad you asked me.
    Architecture is the only thing I can be articulate about.
    "I think Gehry's work is over . . . "
    Your eyes never leave mine as
    your head cocks to one side.
    "-indulgent."
    I meant to say "-rated!"

CHORUS *(Delilah)*:
> "Why do you say that?"

THE ARCHITECT:
> The answer is: you make me nervous.
> You make me say "overindulgent" when I meant "overrated."
> If you didn't, I'd still be articulate
> about the one thing I can be articulate about.
> If that flash in your eyes wasn't signaling,

CHORUS *(Delilah)*:
> "We don't have to be here.
> You and I.
> We could, in fact, be somewhere else."

THE ARCHITECT:
> While your lips are asking me,

CHORUS *(Delilah)* AND THE ARCHITECT:
> "How would you"

CHORUS *(Delilah)*:
> "do it?"

THE ARCHITECT:
> If I was articulate, I'd say, "Hire me and find out."
> But I'm not,
> so I pull out the drawing I happen to have,
> the draft I made on the train coming over.
> You see I do little projects.
> I take

CHORUS *(Delilah and Tamam)*:
> the requirements and dimensions

THE ARCHITECT:
> that clients give to far too many overrated white men like Gehry
>> to make a museum
> and make my own drawings
> of how I would do it
> if some gave me

CHORUS *(Delilah and Tamam)*:
>a chance.

THE ARCHITECT:
>And on the ride over to meet you, Half-Breed,
>I happened to be working on
>my version of the museum
>you and your minions—in your jealousy—were denigrating.

CHORUS *(Delilah and Tamam)*:
>An exercise,

THE ARCHITECT:
>you might say, if you didn't know
>how desperate I get on trains.
>I have what I call

CHORUS *(Delilah and Tamam)* AND THE ARCHITECT:
>"day-mares."

THE ARCHITECT:
>Every time I step on a train, I think,
>"What if"

CHORUS *(Delilah and Tamam)*:
>"what if"

THE ARCHITECT:
>"what if
>I'll always be stuck in this place
>where no one is allowed to talk to one another
>while trying to get to a place where people hopefully do?"
>So I take out a piece of paper and sketch
>and scrap and sketch again.
>I never show the work I do on trains to anyone.
>Why I gave it to you,

CHORUS *(Delilah and Tamam)*:
>God only knows.

THE ARCHITECT:
>You appraise it, the way you appraise everything in your path,
>including me in my well-tailored suit.

If you were to touch me, Half-Breed,
I would pull out handfuls of your hair,

CHORUS *(Delilah and Tamam)*:
   not against,

THE ARCHITECT:
   but towards me!
   I can already feel how your hands
   will work,

CHORUS *(Delilah and Tamam)*:
   sculpt,

THE ARCHITECT:
   grasp
   fingers full of my flesh
   like clay in your arms.
   I'll want to tell you:
   "It's like you're shaping me!"

CHORUS *(Delilah and Tamam)*:
   "You're shaping me!"

THE ARCHITECT:
   But I'm not articulate, so I'll probably just—

CHORUS *(Delilah and Tamam)* AND THE ARCHITECT:
   pant.

THE ARCHITECT:
   I'm thinking all this while you are
   still staring at my draft, my exercise.

CHORUS *(Delilah and Tamam)*:
   Buying time.

THE ARCHITECT:
   Though there might be none for sale.
   I would marry you in a heartbeat.
   Our children will have an Arab last name
   and I will raise them in the culture you do not know
   and you will not understand why I'm still a virgin at thirty.

CHORUS *(Delilah)*:
> My father's tongue is not my mother tongue.

THE ARCHITECT:
> I don't speak hardly a lick of the Arabic language either,
> but I can make out the morsels that count.
> You will not know
> that the only thing you've got going for you is
> you have a chance of understanding
> the two languages I was born to learn and love.

CHORUS *(Delilah and Tamam)*:
> Arabic and architecture.

THE ARCHITECT:
> I live with my parents,
> always have,

CHORUS *(Delilah and Tamam)*:
> always will,

THE ARCHITECT:
> till a man takes me from my father's house.
> Half-Breed, can I explain why
> if you want me
> it's important your people come to my home on the day we marry,
> so that you know I do not come from nothing?
> The bejeweled old peacock-women of my clan
> who you pray I won't look like in forty years,

CHORUS *(Delilah and Tamam)*:
> though I'd be proud to have half the strength of the least of them,

THE ARCHITECT:
> will come to my house to make their presence known.
> To trill and clap, but really to show you
> that if you hurt me . . .
> these bejeweled old women
> can fly up like birds and peck out your eyes.
> What they're saying by showing up to my house early,
> witnessing your people escort me from it,
> is:
> "We are watching . . ."

CHORUS *(Delilah and Tamam)*:
> "If you fuck with her, you fuck with us."

THE ARCHITECT:
> But you won't know our customs.
> Half-Breed!
> Your mother wasn't Arab.

CHORUS *(Delilah and Tamam)*:
> Mothers teach their children early
> the customs and morals and superstitions that stick.

THE ARCHITECT:
> My mother always told me

CHORUS *(Tamam)*:
> Marry an Arab man.
> They have a little sense of decency.

THE ARCHITECT:
> She means they don't often abandon their families.
> My mother thinks if a man doesn't leave you,
> that means he loves you,

CHORUS *(Delilah and Tamam)*:
> in the way men know how to love.

THE ARCHITECT:
> I would marry you in a heartbeat, Half-Breed.
> Give you my hand
> and hope you learned how to be a man from your father.

CHORUS *(Delilah and Tamam)* AND THE ARCHITECT:
> I have designs on your heart.

THE ARCHITECT:
> But I don't know how to execute them.
> Why can't love be as easy as architecture?
> Half-Breed, you like me and I like you.
> I wish I could just show you
> a draft of the nest I would build for us,
> with a room for each child I want to have.

A house with no master bedroom.
A house with no masters.
The only thing I'll have to say is:

CHORUS *(Delilah and Tamam)*:
"Do you like this house? Just say yes or no."

THE ARCHITECT:
And you will understand my question to mean,

CHORUS *(Delilah and Tamam)*:
"Do you want to live here with me forever? Yes or no."

THE ARCHITECT:
"Put the plans in motion or no.
Lay down the first twig of our nest in the nook of a tree
that won't be felled or"

CHORUS *(Delilah and Tamam)*:
"no!"

THE ARCHITECT:
All this I think of as I look at you looking at my draft.
I stare at you, Half-Breed.
And from the time it takes you to lift your eyes
from the page to mine,
this is what I think on:
"Will our children have your doe eyes or my black ones?"
I think of how I will stop making drafts on subways,
because I want our youngest son to recite for me his ABCs
    and 123s.

"Our daughter is so arrogant already.
Just like me."

Arrogance is confidence that is snuffed out,
resuscitated,
and is never quite the same again.

CHORUS *(Delilah and Tamam)*:
Weaker and meaner.

THE ARCHITECT:
>Unrecognizable.

>Arrogance is what happens to a confident girl
>when the whole world, or even just her mother,
>tells her that she's nothing and she finds out
>she's really something.

CHORUS *(Delilah and Tamam)*:
>Really something.

THE ARCHITECT:
>I'll tell myself,
>"It's no big tragedy that I rarely sketch anymore.
>It's my choice, really."
>You tell me:

CHORUS *(Delilah)*:
>"Get a nanny, if you want to . . ."

THE ARCHITECT:
>As if what I want ever has anything to do with what I get.
>Occasionally a female architect like Zaha Hadid succeeds,
>but it's mostly men like Gehry and you, Half-Breed Husband,
>who get to design museums.
>I wipe asses because they are the most beautiful perfect little
>>asses imaginable,
>and no one would wipe them the way I do!

>I content myself with helping you with your work,
>showing you where you falter, and you falter often enough.

CHORUS *(Delilah and Tamam)*:
>It's not sound. It's not sound,
>and it's being built on a fault line.

THE ARCHITECT:
>Was your head up your ass when you designed this?!

CHORUS *(Delilah and Tamam)*:
>Or was it up someone else's?

THE ARCHITECT:

But I can't say that.

I'll have to be vague and suggest

a reinforcement or two.

I have to be careful not to bruise your ego.

CHORUS *(Delilah and Tamam)*:

Because we all know what happens when that happens.

THE ARCHITECT:

You have your women.

But you never leave me.

That's cold comfort and I'm in the winter of my life.

CHORUS *(Delilah and Tamam)*:

But it's comfort just the same.

THE ARCHITECT:

I'm like cement

You pour me, I fit the mold of a wife, and stay there

AIESHA:

until you crack.

THE ARCHITECT:

I'll smile softly when I overhear them saying about me—

CHORUS *(Delilah and Tamam)*:

"She's an architect in her own right, too."

THE ARCHITECT:

"In my own right," they will say,

which always makes me think

my relationship with you makes

what is my right somehow in question.

CHORUS *(Delilah and Tamam)*:

Why must one speak in words when she thinks in images?

THE ARCHITECT:

You lift your head from my page,

Your eyes finally meet mine.

You smile.

CHORUS *(Delilah)* AND THE ARCHITECT:
    I can make you fall in love with me

THE ARCHITECT:
    but never feel secure in that love.
    I know that, if I encourage you, twenty years

CHORUS *(Delilah, Tamam)*:
    from now,

THE ARCHITECT:
    I will be sitting on the toilet
    in a hotel ballroom
    on a night you get some award
    for a project I did at least half the work on.
    Two girls will enter,
    about the age I am now,
    and one will be bragging in a sing-song voice to the other:

CHORUS *(Tamam)*:
    "I did it with him again on Sunday. In his office."

THE ARCHITECT:
    She won't have to say his name for me to know,
    which him she's singing about.
    My half-breed husband!
    My mind will flip back to Sunday afternoon
    when you said:

CHORUS *(Delilah)*:
    "I'm going to the office to finish up the project I'm working on."

THE ARCHITECT:
    Sunday is my day.
    You take the children and I do my work
    But I don't insist, you usually give me my Sundays.
    I don't complain because the one time I tried,
    you told me:

CHORUS *(Delilah)*:
    "Give me a fucking break.
    Whose work pays the bills?"

CHORUS *(Delilah and Tamam)*:
"Who pays the bills?"

THE ARCHITECT:
I don't cost much to feed nowadays.
You're a big fat motherfucker now.
I weigh much less than the day you married me
because I have to stay
thin,
gaunt,
hollow.

CHORUS *(Delilah and Tamam)*:
Take up less space!
Take up less space!

THE ARCHITECT:
I stay thin so no one can say that I'm not trying

CHORUS *(Delilah and Tamam)*:
to be in control!

AIESHA:
Stay in control.

CHORUS *(Delilah)*:
"Who pays the bills?"

THE ARCHITECT:
If I was articulate, I would say,
"I do!
I organize every aspect of your life
so you can do your life's work."
But I know that's not what you mean.
Most people ask for one day of rest, I beg for one day of work
and you

CHORUS *(Delilah and Tamam)* AND THE ARCHITECT:
can't give it to me!

THE ARCHITECT:
But I don't complain on that Sunday
and you go to work on

CHORUS *(Delilah and Tamam)*:
    your project.

THE ARCHITECT:
    And that was the day I slapped my daughter hard
    across the face.

(Tamam and Delilah clap once at the same time.)

    She gave me a look that said:

CHORUS *(Tamam)*:
    "I did not deserve that."

THE ARCHITECT:
    "I will not forget that you did that to me and I didn't deserve it."

CHORUS *(Tamam)*:
    "Not even the day you die."

THE ARCHITECT:
    That was last Sunday.
    I will leave the bathroom and join you at the table of

CHORUS *(Delilah and Tamam)*:
    honor.

THE ARCHITECT:
    You smile when our eyes meet from across the banquet hall.
    I think about what you told me on the way over here:

CHORUS *(Delilah)*:
    "My wife's still a pretty woman.
    It's not a boast, it's a fact."

THE ARCHITECT:
    I sit next to you, Half-Breed Husband.
    You can tell I'm upset.
    Everyone can tell.

CHORUS *(Delilah and Tamam)*:
    You cock

THE ARCHITECT:
>your head to the side,
>questioning at first:

CHORUS *(Delilah)*:
>"What's wrong, honey?"

THE ARCHITECT:
>Then you see the look in my eyes, you don't ask again.
>You let it go.
>
>I'll tell myself to just lighten up and get over it.
>There are people dying in Palestine.

AIESHA:
>There are people dying in Palestine.

THE ARCHITECT:
>And I very easily could have been one of them.
>In marriage, there are worse crimes than infidelity.

CHORUS *(Delilah and Tamam)*:
>He still falls asleep
>stroking your cheek.

THE ARCHITECT:
>I now even think it's endearing that he is jealous of my work,
>that he needs all my time and attention when he's home.

CHORUS *(Delilah and Tamam)*:
>Like a child.

THE ARCHITECT:
>Soon enough, I'll be staring at you in your coffin.
>Our three-quarter-breed children will be crying,

CHORUS *(Delilah and Tamam)*:
>"Baba!"

THE ARCHITECT:
>Because I made our three-quarter-breed children use the Arabic
>>words for family members.

Always.
They'll be crying:

CHORUS *(Delilah)*:
"Excuse me, would you like to go somewhere and" *(Pause)* "have
coffee?"

THE ARCHITECT:
Your question interrupts my thoughts, Half-Breed.
It startles me.
I didn't notice you were done looking at my exercise and holding
it out for me to take back.
I think to myself,
"Why are you talking to me?
Can't you see I'm in the middle of envisioning our future together?"
I realize that I've done it again.
In my mind, I planned a whole life—

CHORUS *(Delilah and Tamam)*:
birth,
death,
remembrance—

THE ARCHITECT:
with a guy
before he even asks me out.
Why does my mind flip a lifetime ahead?
We might go out and not hit it off.
I mean, for God's sake, you could be gay.
I could be reading all the signs wrong.
It has happened to me before.
You've just asked me for coffee.
Why am I imagining your funeral
with our children standing before you screaming:

CHORUS *(Delilah and Tamam)*:
"Baba!"

THE ARCHITECT:
Why am I sure
as I stare into your eyes, trying to decide if I want to have coffee
with you,

that, if I say yes, one day
I'll be staring at your corpse in your coffin,
thinking a thousand thoughts,
not the least of which will be,
"There lies your body. Your flesh,
that you valued more than my heart, my love, our family and
    my life.
Let. It. Rot!"

CHORUS *(Delilah)*:
    I said: "Would you like to have coffee with me?"

THE ARCHITECT:
    "No! No! No!"

CHORUS *(Delilah)*:
    "Tea?"

THE ARCHITECT:
    And I decline that, too, saying: "I have to go right back home."
    We worked together for a summer and he's always

CHORUS *(Delilah and Tamam)*:
    polite

THE ARCHITECT:
    but he never offers to quench thirsts with me again.
    (Pause)
    Then, I was murdered.
    And, as a result, I died.
    Do you understand now?
    Do you see now that she's lying?

CHORUS *(Delilah and Tamam)*:
    No.

AIESHA:
    Ha! I knew you were a half-wit.

THE ARCHITECT:
    (To Delilah and Tamam:)
    She's going to try to distract you
    She's going to keep you here.

AIESHA:

All right you two. If you want my help—

THE ARCHITECT:

Stop pretending you're going to
eventually lead them through that door.

AIESHA:

Stop pretending you know something about me.

THE ARCHITECT:

(To Aiesha:)
I'm getting to how I know who you are.

TAMAM:

What does this encounter with a half-breed
have to do with this woman?

DELILAH:

Why shouldn't we trust her?
Can you tell us in a way we will understand?

THE ARCHITECT:

Yes.
My contract with the Half-Breed's company was not renewed.
I was told I was not a team player.

CHORUS *(Delilah and Tamam)*:

Five years passed.

THE ARCHITECT:

I stayed friends with his assistant so I could keep tabs on the
    Half-Breed.
On my thirty-fifth birthday, I called him.
You see I had promised myself
if I'm not married by thirty-five,
I would stop being precious and just have sex
with a man I wanted to love me,
whether or not he did.

CHORUS *(Delilah and Tamam)*:

Why thirty-five?

THE ARCHITECT:
>   Because it's no longer cute
>   that you're a virgin at thirty-five.

CHORUS *(Delilah and Tamam)*:
>   I called him.

THE ARCHITECT:
>   I told him my name. He said:

CHORUS *(Delilah)*:
>   "You're the girl who worked as an assistant that summer,
>   who walked into the interview
>   with a plan for a museum,
>   right?"

THE ARCHITECT:
>   "I want to come see you. I want to come stay with you."

CHORUS *(Delilah)*:
>   "Get on the next flight."

THE ARCHITECT:
>   And I do so!
>   I've got two fantasies—day-mares—about flying.

CHORUS *(Delilah and Tamam)*:
>   First fantasy I have as I'm going through
>   the security check

THE ARCHITECT:
>   on my way to see the Half-Breed.
>   It's totally stupid, okay?
>   But you've got to understand,
>   I grew up watching American movies
>   and so I've got this fantasy
>   that I'll be on a flight, okay, and it'll be hijacked by my people—
>   Arabs.

CHORUS *(Aiesha)*:
>   Sounds stupid.

THE ARCHITECT:

    I already admitted it was.

    But in my fantasy

    I'll hear the shouts first in my mother's tongue

    that my mother never bothered to teach me to speak.

    And I understand what they're saying.

    I realize the power of language—

    that being able to listen and understand is a different kind of
        articulacy

    and one I possess.

    Like how I can't speak Arabic, but I can comprehend

CHORUS *(Delilah and Tamam)*:

    and know what's going on before everyone else does.

THE ARCHITECT:

    In my fantasy

    all the men are fit and handsome.

    They don't intend to kill anybody.

CHORUS *(Delilah and Tamam)*:

    They've lived lives that would break the hardest of men.

THE ARCHITECT:

    They only want to be heard.

    Dramatic music will play.

    I will stand up,

    perfectly manicured and dressed to meet the press,

    I will say in perfect Arabic to the men—

CHORUS *(Aiesha)*:

    But you can't speak Arabic.

THE ARCHITECT:

    This is my fantasy, goddamn it!

    And in it, I speak perfect Arabic.

    I will stand up

    and talk those men out of their plans.

    I will tell them:

CHORUS *(Delilah and Tamam)* AND THE ARCHITECT:

    "So what if terror helped bring down apartheid in South Africa?"

CHORUS *(Tamam)*:
> "So what if the Black Panther movement got civil rights workers
>> moving
> just a little bit quicker?"

CHORUS *(Delilah)*:
> "So what if the American government supports corrupt leaders
> in our countries and then kills
> hundreds of thousands of Arabs
> when those leaders don't do"

CHORUS *(Delilah and Tamam)* AND THE ARCHITECT:
> "what they say
> when they say it?"

THE ARCHITECT:
> "All that still doesn't make it right to kill."
> I would say to them:
> "You're hijacking this plane full of people who are ignorant,
> who are looking at you and saying:"

CHORUS *(Delilah and Tamam)*:
> "What kind of people could do such violent, cruel things?"

THE ARCHITECT:
> "They don't know that it's the kind of people
> the American government has been doing
> just as violent, cruel things to
> in its people's name for generations.
> Maybe they don't care.
> But they're not worth killing yourself over.
> They call us terrorists."

CHORUS *(Delilah and Tamam)*:
> "They are wrong!"

THE ARCHITECT:
> "We're too good a people to do such harm."
> I would tell them,
> "I am a Palestinian.
> I lived like an Arab in America.
> I even only dated my own kind,

because I wanted someone who understood
the first words my family taught me to mean love—

CHORUS *(Delilah and Tamam)*:
Ha-beeb-tea.

THE ARCHITECT:
"Even after I realized,
just because a man knows the right words
doesn't mean that he will say them
and, even if he says them,
it doesn't mean that he means them."
I will tell those men:

CHORUS *(Delilah and Tamam)* AND THE ARCHITECT:
"I was never ashamed of who I was."

THE ARCHITECT:
"I knew I had to synthesize all the signals about who I was
in a way
that made me not want to be anything else.
I knew if I was not proud to be a Palestinian,
I could not live a life with dignity.
I knew if I did not love my people, no one would."
I would tell them all this

CHORUS *(Delilah and Tamam)*:
and more!

THE ARCHITECT:
And, when I tell them about my life, it will seem like it has
a relevance,
a grace,
an arc,

CHORUS *(Delilah and Tamam)*:
a worth

THE ARCHITECT:
that I didn't realize it had before.
They will realize it, too.
I would no longer resent being a bridge between two cultures,
or ask myself,

CHORUS *(Delilah and Tamam)* AND THE ARCHITECT:
> "What does a bridge ever do except get stepped on?"

THE ARCHITECT:
> Because I was so articulate in my perfect Arabic,
> the plane would touch down safely.
> All the Americans in the plane would listen to the grievances of the
> men who were willing to kill and die to be heard.

CHORUS *(Delilah and Tamam)*:
> They would be moved by stories of those they feared.

THE ARCHITECT:
> In fact, they'll refuse to get off of the plane,
> until Palestinians are allowed the right to self-determination.
> Iraqis are not killed so their oil can be stolen.
> The people on the plane don't buy the crap the American
>   government
> tries to sell us about trying to secure human rights,

CHORUS *(Delilah and Tamam)*:
> having the gall to use human rights

THE ARCHITECT:
> as an excuse to bomb those human beings
> while being allies,

CHORUS *(Aiesha)*:
> bedfellows,

THE ARCHITECT:
> with the oppressive Saudi royal-pain-in-the-ass regime because

CHORUS *(Aiesha)*:
> they give up their juice.

THE ARCHITECT:
> When all those conditions are met, everyone on the plane
>   leaves safely.
> There will be a movie made about me.
> I would end up on *Oprah*, telling my story.
> I will be articulate.
> One of the audience members will tell me:

CHORUS *(Delilah)*:
   "Julia Roberts does a great job playing you in the movie.
   I'm glad she acknowledged you at the Academy Awards.
   But I've got to say . . ."

CHORUS *(Delilah and Tamam)*:
   "We the PTA board members of Lansing, Michigan,
   think you're even prettier than Julia is."

THE ARCHITECT:
   Then Oprah will say:

CHORUS *(Tamam)*:
   "More importantly, she's also a brilliant architect."

THE ARCHITECT:
   But she won't have to say "in her own right."
   Before the first commercial break,
   it'll be clear that Oprah and I are now best friends.
   I'll let her announce that I've been commissioned to design
   the new United Nations building
   since the old one obviously wasn't engineered to work right.
   And, in my fantasy, the love of my life,
   who may or may not be the Half-Breed,
   because maybe when my people are no longer under siege,

CHORUS *(Delilah and Tamam)*:
   no longer a dying breed,

THE ARCHITECT:
   I won't feel I owe it to my people to mate with my own kind.
   I'll be free

CHORUS *(Delilah and Tamam)*:
   in the most important way it is to be free.

THE ARCHITECT:
   I'll be free to love who I love.
   And whoever that man who I love is,
   he will be sitting in the audience.
   Our eyes will connect for the slightest second.
   We'll remember:

CHORUS *(Tamam)*:

"We don't have to stay here much longer.
You and I, we will soon go somewhere else."

THE ARCHITECT:

I'll feel a shot of warmth in me,
like a dying fire that with one breath he can keep aglow.
I will be a hero like Dr. King or Gandhi,
but no one shoots me.
Did everyone hear that? No one shoots me.
That's not part of the fantasy I have as I go through the security
 check on my way to lose my virginity to the Half-Breed.
I don't want to die that way.

AIESHA:

Does anybody want to die that way?

THE ARCHITECT:

No. And no one wants to die the way I did, either.
Hands, change!

(Aiesha bursts into laughter.)

Small! Change hands! Movement.

AIESHA:

She speaks gibberish.

TAMAM:

(To The Architect:)
We're still listening.

DELILAH:

You're going through the security check—

THE ARCHITECT:

Right, and I think to myself,
"What a stupid fantasy that is.
I've clearly been watching too many American movies.
I will refuse to watch the one on the flight."
I think that to myself, as I give the girl at the counter my ticket.
I'm afraid to fly. So much of my life is lived in the space between

CHORUS *(Delilah and Tamam)*:
    fear and desire.

THE ARCHITECT:
    I know if my plane were to go down,
    there is one thing I would truly regret.
    And that leads me to the next fantasy I have while settling in
        my seat
    on the plane,
    which will take me to the place
    where I will lose my virginity to the Half-Breed.
    I look for the straps of my seatbelt.
    Knowing I'm a beast,

CHORUS *(Delilah and Tamam)*:
    animal,

THE ARCHITECT:
    beast, but to have been a beast with only one back all my life.
    To die a virgin!

CHORUS *(Aiesha)*:
    What a tragedy that would be.

THE ARCHITECT:
    Tell me about it.
    So my fantasy as I strap my seatbelt on—

CHORUS *(Delilah and Tamam)*:
    click—

THE ARCHITECT:
    is that if I somehow figure out that
    this plane is going to crash.
    And I realize I'm going to die a virgin.
    I'd stomp up to the

CHORUS *(Delilah and Tamam)*:
    cock

THE ARCHITECT:
    pit.
    (And who says language isn't everything?)
    And once I get to the

CHORUS *(Delilah and Tamam)*:
> cock

THE ARCHITECT:
> pit, I'd get on that loudspeaker and say:
> "Unfasten your seatbelts,"

CHORUS *(Delilah and Tamam)* AND THE ARCHITECT:
> "Motherfuckers!"

THE ARCHITECT:
> "If this plane is going down,
> someone is going down on me!"

CHORUS *(Delilah and Tamam)*:
> But one rarely has the guts to act out fantasies.

THE ARCHITECT:
> So even if the plane went down
> by accident—

CHORUS *(Delilah and Tamam)*:
> technical failure instead of the emotional kind—

THE ARCHITECT:
> I probably would not go up to the

CHORUS *(Delilah and Tamam)*:
> cock

THE ARCHITECT:
> pit and say that.
> I would have sat in my seat like I

CHORUS *(Delilah and Tamam)*:
> sat in the seat of disbelief.

THE ARCHITECT:
> When I actually did hear those men shouting in my mother's
>   tongue
> and it wasn't a fantasy.
> It was real.

It was my life.
It was awful.
I knew what they were saying and I knew what they were doing

CHORUS *(Delilah and Tamam)*:
before anyone else did.

THE ARCHITECT:
One of them passed by my row and I thought to myself—
as if I was an American with ancestors on the Mayflower
and had no understanding of America's history
in the Middle East—
I thought to myself,

CHORUS *(Delilah and Tamam)*:
"What kind of person could do such a thing?"

THE ARCHITECT:
The one who ran past me was chubby

CHORUS *(Delilah and Tamam)*:
like my brothers.

THE ARCHITECT:
Stupid me, always thinking

CHORUS *(Delilah and Tamam)*:
inappropriate thoughts.

THE ARCHITECT:
Thoughts that make me thank Heaven I am so inarticulate.
As the man tied up a stewardess,
I was thinking I like chubby men.
I don't trust men if they're too thin.
I don't trust men
if they aren't susceptible
to the least pernicious of appetites.

CHORUS *(Delilah and Tamam)*:
I think you just don't trust men.

THE ARCHITECT:
>He passed my row and our eyes met.
>Perhaps because I was the only one looking up,
>not crying.
>He froze.
>The way Arabs outside the Arab world do
>when they recognize that someone here

CHORUS *(Delilah and Tamam)*:
>is one of my kind.

THE ARCHITECT:
>He waited for me to speak
>and when I couldn't,
>he went on his way without a backward glance.
>From the look in his eyes,
>I lost all hope that any of us would live.
>I took out my sketchbook
>and sketched for the first time

CHORUS *(Delilah and Tamam)*:
>without fear.

THE ARCHITECT:
>I took out my sketchbook,
>did my work

CHORUS *(Delilah and Tamam)*:
>and saw that it was good.

THE ARCHITECT:
>I'm here to find that man who passed me and knew I was an Arab.
>He's in that room in front of us.
>I know it.
>Just like I know that I could have stopped him
>before he did what he did
>if I had the right words.

CHORUS *(Delilah and Tamam)*:
>Don't blame yourself.

THE ARCHITECT:
>It's not about blame. What's the point of being articulate when no one
>can hear anything they aren't ready to hear?

CHORUS *(Delilah and Tamam)*:
>It's not about blame.

THE ARCHITECT:
>It's about knowing that there are always words—

CHORUS *(Delilah and Tamam)*:
>words that work like spells,

THE ARCHITECT:
>something you can say
>that will stop someone from doing something

CHORUS *(Delilah and Tamam)*:
>awful.

THE ARCHITECT:
>The man who killed me is the only one who can tell me

CHORUS *(Delilah and Tamam)*:
>what those words are.

THE ARCHITECT:
>I'm here to ask him.
>If anyone gives me trouble while I'm trying to get in, I will tell them
>I died a virgin, but that was just bad luck.
>While I was alive, I did the hardest thing imaginable,
>more wonderful than a million buildings that will one day crumble.
>I am a woman who was born with a good heart
>and I designed and executed my life in a way that made sure
>that's how I would stay.
>
>The image I had in my mind
>during the last moment I was alive
>was of your face.
>I died thinking I hope people won't see me where I saw you.

AIESHA:
> You've never seen me.

THE ARCHITECT:
> The night before I boarded that plane and died on it,
> I had insomnia.
> It was my last night as a virgin.
> Or so I believed.
> I couldn't sleep.
> I was on my computer
> using search engines to seek
> out the sites of hate that cry:

CHORUS *(Delilah and Tamam)*:
> "Death to Arabs!"

AIESHA:
> Why do you look at those sites?

THE ARCHITECT:
> To remind myself that every breath I take is a victory,
> that the reason I work so hard at architecture

CHORUS *(Delilah and Tamam)*:
> and drive myself to the point of collapse

THE ARCHITECT:
> is so I will one day create a work that defies gravity itself.
> I think, maybe, if I work hard enough.
> and create something worthwhile, something of value.

CHORUS *(Delilah and Tamam)*:
> Something!

THE ARCHITECT:
> It will make people think we are just as smart, just as human,

CHORUS *(Delilah and Tamam)*:
> we exist,

THE ARCHITECT:
> we matter.
> Then, I remember I can't control what people will think.

But I can point to the buildings I'll make and ask:
"Do you want to be remembered
as the murderers of people
who make things like that?
Ask yourself."

CHORUS *(Delilah and Tamam)*:
Answer me!

THE ARCHITECT:
I go to those websites and check for updates to see what I am up
against and sometimes I see stories like yours that read:
"Palestinian female suicide bomber's only victim is one of her
own kind."
They show your picture and they show hers,
because they think it's funny.
She was a little Palestinian girl.

AIESHA:
I didn't mean to kill her.
I wanted to kill an enemy.
You can't look at the specifics
of my particular life
in order to understand why I did it.
Others around me had lived more terrible lives
and still wanted to live.
All I knew was that I couldn't breathe.

CHORUS *(Delilah and Tamam)*:
No one hears our cries.

AIESHA:
I can't breathe.

CHORUS *(Delilah and Tamam)*:
No control over our own destiny.

AIESHA:
I can't breathe, and, if I can't breathe,
then no one should be allowed to breathe easy.
But, when the time came, I was scared.
I was so scared.

I intended to get a crowd
but—

CHORUS *(Delilah and Tamam)*:
    Timing is everything.

AIESHA:
    The group I was leaning towards suddenly moved away
    at the same second
    I detonated myself.
    They knew to get away, all except for this little girl with big
        black eyes
    and a heavy key around her neck.

CHORUS *(Delilah and Tamam)*:
    She couldn't have been more than nine.

THE ARCHITECT:
    The website said seven.

AIESHA:
    Her mother took her with her across hours and hours of Israeli
        checkpoints,
    so she could work as a maid.

CHORUS *(Delilah and Tamam)*:
    Her mother was proud.

AIESHA:
    The women in the refugee camp thought she was arrogant.
    She never let them forget she was once

CHORUS *(Delilah and Tamam)* AND AIESHA:
    the richest girl in her town.

AIESHA:
    The town of Ras Abu Ammar.

CHORUS *(Delilah and Tamam)*:
    The town that no longer exists.

AIESHA:
    Have you heard of it?

THE ARCHITECT:
Of course.

AIESHA:

It was the place this woman once lived in
before her family fled to Gaza.
She's only allowed to get near her town with a worker's permit.

CHORUS *(Delilah and Tamam)*:
She's only allowed to go back to be the maid.

AIESHA:

She was proud.
She named her only daughter Amal.

CHORUS *(Delilah and Tamam)*:
It means hope.

THE ARCHITECT:
And she felt hope

AIESHA:

as she hung the heavy key of the door to the house
she once lived in
around her only daughter's neck.
It didn't matter that the house no longer stood there.
It was her house.
Her daughter would know that—

CHORUS *(Delilah and Tamam)* AND AIESHA:
she had a house.

AIESHA:

The mother hated to make her daughter
watch her clean toilets.
She hated it even more that day,
because her daughter offered to help,
and, even though she said no, Amal took a dripping brush in
    her hand.
Amal's mother slapped her.

(Tamam and Delilah clap their hands once.)

The mother thinks to herself as she watches her daughter trying
to swallow her tears,

CHORUS *(Delilah and Tamam)*:
"When my daughter grows up and can understand, I will apologize
for that."

AIESHA:
She imagines how she will one day tell her daughter
everything one cannot say with a mop in your hand
and work to be done

CHORUS *(Delilah and Tamam)* AND AIESHA:
before the curfew is called.

AIESHA:
But, years later, the mother
will still *be* sorry,
not just say or feel or act it,

CHORUS *(Delilah and Tamam)*:
but become sorrow itself.

AIESHA:
She imagines when Amal is sixteen or so,
they will be laughing.
Her mother will look at her and ask:

CHORUS *(Delilah and Tamam)*:
"Do you remember that time I slapped you for no good reason?"

AIESHA:
Amal will shake her head as if to say:

CHORUS *(Delilah)*:	CHORUS *(Tamam)*:	CHORUS *(Delilah,*
"No, that didn't	"No, I don't	*Aiesha and*
happen."	remember."	*Tamam)*: "No."

AIESHA:
And Amal's mother will tell her:
"You did not deserve that.
Is it possible for you to see that as something I did once,
not someone who I was?"

CHORUS *(Delilah and Tamam)*:
> Amal will nod.

AIESHA:
> And the mother of hope
> will know that she taught her daughter the most important lesson,
> the lesson you have to learn
> to survive this life with your humanity intact.
> She taught her daughter

CHORUS *(Aiesha and The Architect)*:
> how to forgive.

AIESHA:
> It's not something Amal's mother normally allowed.
> But on that day, she sent her outside with the Israeli teenager of
>   the house,
> who doted on her . . .

CHORUS *(Delilah, Aiesha and Tamam)*:
> Look at those big black eyes.

THE ARCHITECT:
> The teenager and her friends bought Amal a falafel sandwich,

AIESHA:
> because what else do you feed little Arab children?
> Amal saw the janitor at the shop was Palestinian.
> She smiled at him,
> so he would recognize that she was one, too.
> The man didn't smile back.
> Amal thinks to herself as she takes the first bite of her falafel
>   sandwich,
> "When I grow up . . ."

CHORUS *(Delilah and Tamam)*:
> "I will remember what it's like to be a child."

AIESHA:
> "When I grow up . . ."

CHORUS *(Delilah and Tamam)*:
> "I will greet children as if they are people."

AIESHA:

"When I grow up and have children . . ."

CHORUS *(Delilah and Tamam)*:

"if people don't greet them, I won't speak to them either."

AIESHA:

Amal thinks the sandwich the teenagers gave her was lousy,
not enough parsley.
But she didn't want to hurt their feelings,
so she thanked them
and forced herself to eat it.

THE ARCHITECT:

The teenagers bought her an ice-cream cone.

AIESHA:

And they ran and left her for dead when they saw me coming.
I don't think they meant to, but that's what they did.
It was too late to stop everything,
the one step I took back was my last.
The little girl didn't understand she was going to die.
She smiled at me.

THE ARCHITECT:

The last image I had in my mind
before I died was of her picture next to yours.
And underneath it were the words:
"Finally, they are killing one another."
I thought to myself, "Will they put my picture next to the man
     who ran past my row?"
Under our pictures, will they write the words:

CHORUS *(Delilah and Tamam)* AND THE ARCHITECT:

"Finally, they are killing one another"?

TAMAM:

So, the reason the martyrs don't want you in there

DELILAH:

is because you're no good at being no good.

THE ARCHITECT:
> No. That is no room for martyrs.
> Or maybe it is?
> We won't know till we go in that door.
> But we can't believe what we've been told.
> This can't be Heaven.
> Heaven is not a place where people segregate themselves
> according to religion or race.

TAMAM:
> We're in Hell.
> Hell is a place where we have to look for the ones we lost.

DELILAH:
> No. Earth.
> Earth is a place where—there is a door—
> where no one who goes in comes out.

AIESHA:
> No, this is Heaven.

CHORUS *(Delilah)*:
> Heaven is not a place you
> have to be convinced that
> you're in.

CHORUS *(Tamam)*:
> Heaven is not a place where
> people don't know the
> answers.

AIESHA:
> You know a lot about what Heaven is not,
> but you don't know what Heaven is.
> The only thing real is that door.

THE ARCHITECT:
> You don't know what's beyond it.
> I don't believe you've ever been inside.
> If you don't spend your life asking hard questions,
> you spend your eternity with no answers.
> I believe you've been standing here and distracting us from
> > moving forward.

CHORUS *(Delilah and Tamam)* AND THE ARCHITECT:
> You keep people here!

THE ARCHITECT:

> I believe each of the groups of women here has
> someone like you,

DELILAH:

> someone from their own race,

TAMAM:

> someone they feel they can trust,

AIESHA:

> someone who keeps them in line
> for their own sakes.
> You want real answers,
> first ask harder questions.
> Or you can stay here
> and stay safe with me

THE ARCHITECT:

> spending an eternity, separate from other people, asking easy
>> questions like:
> "Aren't they just a little different?"

TAMAM:

> "Am I supposed to feel sorry for what my great-grandparents did
>> before I was born?"

DELILAH:

> "Isn't the only way we can assure we're never oppressed is to
>> oppress other people?"

THE ARCHITECT:

> "Wouldn't they do the same to us the minute they had the chance?"

CHORUS (Delilah, Tamam and The Architect):
> "Why is violence only wrong when we use it?"

CHORUS (Delilah, Aiesha, Tamam and The Architect):
> "Isn't violence the only thing these people understand?"

AIESHA:

> For your own safety, I keep you asking the wrong questions.

CHORUS *(Delilah, Tamam and The Architect)*:
> So, we'll stay with you.

THE ARCHITECT:
> Instead of going on the quest
> to find the answer to the only question.

AIESHA:
> "How do you survive in a violent world and not be violent?"

CHORUS *(Delilah, Tamam and The Architect)*:
> Key word:

AIESHA:
> "survive."

THE ARCHITECT:
> This place feels too much like limbo.
> I've been in limbo all my life.
> I'll go first, you two can follow.

AIESHA:
> You'll be harmed.

THE ARCHITECT:
> You don't know that.

AIESHA:
> Neither do you.

THE ARCHITECT:
> Are you two coming or not?

> *(Pause.)*

DELILAH AND TAMAM:
> No.

THE ARCHITECT:
> *(To Aiesha:)*
> Then, you come with me.

AIESHA:

I'm not allowed in there.

THE ARCHITECT:

Who says?

AIESHA:

I say.

What I did was right.

I'm not going to any place where I might have to question that.

THE ARCHITECT:

Do you know why I keep searching?

What I need to tell the man who murdered me is:

"They rate our lives at nothing,

when we kill ourselves in the hope of hurting them,

we show that we agree,

that we feel our lives are dispensable."

AIESHA:

Our lives?!

He's going to laugh at you.

What have you suffered?

Did someone make fun of your parents' accents?

Didn't get an award or two because of racism?

CHORUS *(Delilah and Tamam)* AND AIESHA:

Poor you!

AIESHA:

Live my life on earth

in my dirty, crowded refugee camp

in the place that your parents abandoned.

Spend one day.

Live like that for one day

knowing that the people

CHORUS *(Delilah and Tamam)* AND AIESHA:

you love most

AIESHA:

have no choice

but to live like that

every second of their living lives.
Then, see if you think limbo
is the only honest place to be.
I am no privileged little

CHORUS *(Delilah and Tamam)* AND AIESHA:
hypocrite.

AIESHA:
You can go around searching for Heaven,
I wasn't born to have that luxury.
Maybe that door is back to earth.
Who knows?
Maybe you and me would return there together.
Maybe then we could see
which of us does any good?
Down there I didn't even have the chance to ask
who makes more of a difference
in the long run,

CHORUS *(Delilah and Tamam)*:
artists or militants?

AIESHA:
People like me or people like you?
Because I never had the chances
you had to do anything different
than what I did.
So don't you judge me.
I don't get to make pretty drawings and such . . .
and pray people
will maybe look
and maybe see
and maybe think of me as human.
No.

CHORUS *(Delilah and Tamam)* AND AIESHA:
I am human.

AIESHA:
I will be treated as such.

CHORUS *(Delilah and Tamam)* AND AIESHA:
Or else.

THE ARCHITECT:

My life and what I do with it is worth something.

AIESHA:

Because you had a life worth living.

THE ARCHITECT:

I can't stay here in limbo.
I've been in limbo all my life.
I have to tell the man who killed me—
Hands, movement, change.

(She heads toward the exit.)

CHORUS *(Delilah, Aiesha and Tamam)*:
(Chanting together and seeming to ignore The Architect:)
Here I only have unanswered questions.
Because, there, I only had unquestioned answers.
Unanswered questions,
unquestioned answers.
I do someone good dead.
I do someone dead good.
What is the point of the revolution that begins with the little hand?
Any little hand?
(Each woman lifts her right hand and looks at it)
This little hand?
Unanswered questions,
unquestioned answers.
I do

(The Architect exits. The women chant:)

TAMAM:	DELILAH AND AIESHA:
no one	someone

(Aiesha and Delilah look at Tamam. Then, all three women resume chanting together again.)

CHORUS *(Delilah, Aiesha and Tamam)*:
good dead.
I do

DELILAH:	AIESHA AND TAMAM:
no one	someone

(Aiesha and Tamam look at Delilah.)

CHORUS *(Delilah, Aiesha and Tamam)*:
    dead good.
    What is the point of the revolution that begins with the little hand?
    Any little hand?
    (Each woman lifts her right hand and looks at it)
    This little hand?

(Delilah and Tamam look at one another.)

DELILAH AND TAMAM:
    The point is

DELILAH:
    it pushes,

TAMAM:
    forces,

DELILAH AND TAMAM:
    the big hand forward!

TAMAM:
    With enough movement,

DELILAH AND TAMAM:
    the times will change.
    Little hands, enough movement,

AIESHA:
    times change.

CHORUS *(Delilah, Aiesha and Tamam)*:
    Hands, movement, change.
    Wait!

(They do not move.)

END OF PLAY

BETTY SHAMIEH is the author of fifteen plays. Her Off-Broadway debut as a playwright was the 2004 New Group premiere of *Roar*, which starred Annabella Sciorra and was selected as a *New York Times* Critic's Pick. *The Black Eyed* was produced at New York Theatre Workshop, the Magic Theatre and Theatre Fournos of Athens. Her play *Again and Against,* which was developed at the Royal Court and selected for the Public Theater's "New Work Now!" series in 2007, was presented in a Swedish translation at Playhouse Teater in 2008. *Territories* had its world premiere at the Magic Theatre in 2008. A German translation of *Territories* ran for six months at the European Union's Capital of Culture Festival in 2009. Shamieh was selected as the 2009–2010 playwright-in-residence at Het Zuidelijk Toneel, where her latest work, *Free Radicals*, will be produced in a Dutch translation in 2010. She performed in her play, *Chocolate in Heat,* at its sold-out premiere at the New York International Fringe Festival in 2001, two extended Off-Off-Broadway runs and more than twenty venues throughout the United States. Naked Angels produced her one-act play *The Machine* Off-Broadway in 2007, directed by Marisa Tomei. A cartoon of *Roar* appeared in the *New Yorker*'s "Goings on About Town" section. Shamieh received an honorable mention for her screenplay *Anonymous* from the Third Annual Writers Network Screenplay and Fiction Competition and has taught screenwriting at Marymount Manhattan College. Her essays have appeared in *American Theatre* magazine, the *Brooklyn Rail, CounterPunch* and *Mizna.*

Shamieh has been awarded a Sundance Institute Theatre Program residency, a New York Foundation for the Arts Artists' Fellowship, the New Dramatists Van Lier Playwriting Fellowship, a Ford Foundation grant, a Yaddo residency, an Arts International grant and a Rockefeller Foundation residency in Bellagio, Italy. She was selected as the 2004–2005 Clifton Visiting Artist at the Radcliffe Institute for Advanced Study at Harvard University, and is currently serving on the playwriting advisory board for the New York Foundation for the Arts. In 2007–2008, she was awarded a playwriting grant from the National Endowment for the Arts and Theatre Communications Group to spend a year as playwright-in-residence at the Magic Theatre. A graduate of Harvard College and the Yale School of Drama, Shamieh is one of the youngest artists to be named a fellow at Harvard University's Radcliffe Institute for Advanced Study. She is currently working on a new play commission from Time Warner/Second Stage and her first novel.

Call Me Mehdi

Torange Yeghiazarian

Author's Statement

 One Saturday morning I woke up in a strange mood and typed on my laptop for two hours. I laughed as I was writing, but was later embarrassed to read the draft to friends. But they laughed, too, which was a relief. That was the beginning of *Call Me Mehdi*. It embodies my two preoccupations in life: sex and politics (the sexiness of politics and the politics of sex).

Most people say *Call Me Mehdi* is about cross-cultural understanding, or lack thereof. It is. At the same time, it is about a woman claiming her own body and her own land. Don't anyone tell me who I am or who "we" are.

Often the language we use to express love is laden with politics. We claim the body of the lover the way a foreign army might a new continent. The excitement of exploring uncharted territories fills the air as the body trembles to launch its forces. Exploration often leads to possession. Boundaries disappear and "two become one." A lovely prospect unless you are the one losing everything in the process. While the Sufi ideal of love is well, lovely, I for one advocate a more pragmatic approach. Borders may be abstract and fluid but they are critical to maintaining an identity in the face of invading forces. We strive for a world without borders, yet we must first acknowledge the lover/other as an equal with boundaries of her own, boundaries that must be respected.

Most of all, *Call Me Mehdi* is a comedy about love—love is worth it. Let no one convince you otherwise. Across cultures and religions, beyond acceptable gender roles, love is worth the trouble. Don't miss out.

Production History

Call Me Mehdi was first performed at ReOrient 2005, an annual festival
of short plays exploring the Middle East, produced by Golden Thread Productions at the Magic Theatre in San Francisco, from November 11–
December 4, 2005. It was directed by Meg Patterson. The cast was as
follows:

ZIBA	Ahou Tabibzadeh
JOHN	Noah James Butler

Call Me Mehdi received a staged reading at the One World Many Voices
conference at Missouri State University on April 17, 2007. It was
directed by Sheila Gordon.

Characters

ZIBA, Iranian-American woman, attractive, thirties
JOHN, American man, pale, blond, thirties

Setting

The bedroom of Ziba and John's apartment. Four o'clock A.M.

Note

Ziba and John stay in bed the entire time. They are either naked or have minimal underwear on.

The original production used side lamps, turning them on and off as the couple spoke or did not speak. This is certainly an option but not necessary. Part of the fun of staging this play is to play around with the push/pull between Ziba and John. The stage directions are there as a guide. The actors are encouraged to find their own game.

Acknowledgments

Thanks to Motti Lerner for his thoughtful feedback that helped deepen the couple's relationship. Many thanks to Naomi Wallace for her wisdom, generosity and encouragement.

Many thanks to Q for telling me the Mehdi joke, to Jim who is a proud gringo and to Richard and Rana who first heard the play. Thanks to Norman Dog whose Bad Habits comic series was an inspiration. Thanks to Meg, Ahou and Noah for their trust and invaluable contribution to developing this piece. To Sheila, for making fabulous sense of the final moment of the play.

I would like to thank my mom, Vida Ghahremani, Iran's first screen goddess, who is an inspiration; my sister, Termeh Yeghiazarian, who is an amazing artist and a rare human being; Simin for her friendship; and Sima for making my heart sing.

The stage is in darkness. We make out the silhouette of two reclining figures whispering in bed.

JOHN: What were the two of you giggling about for two hours?
ZIBA: I don't remember.

(Pause.)

When?
JOHN: The whole time. He kept whispering something to you and you
    kept laughing.
ZIBA: Jokes. He was probably just telling me more of his silly jokes.
JOHN: Apparently you found them very entertaining.
ZIBA *(Dozing off)*: Uh-um . . .

(Silence.)

JOHN: What was it?
ZIBA: Hum? What?
JOHN: What was it? Tell me one of his jokes.
ZIBA: Whose?

JOHN: Kevin.

ZIBA: Kevin?

JOHN: Kevin. Kevin. Kevin whispering jokes in my wife's ear all night. Kevin.

ZIBA: Oh, Khashayar . . .

JOHN: K-kh-kash-ki-vor . . . *(Almost chokes on his own spit—the "kh" sound is difficult for English-speakers to make)*

ZIBA: Are you okay?

JOHN: Yeah. Why?

ZIBA: You sound weird.

JOHN: He introduces himself as Kevin.

ZIBA: He does?

JOHN: To me . . .

ZIBA: Hum . . .

(Silence.)

JOHN: Z.

ZIBA: Hum . . .

JOHN *(Reaching for her)*: Tell me one of his jokes.

ZIBA: Sweetie . . . don't.

JOHN: What?

ZIBA: I'm exhausted.

JOHN: No wonder!

(For the first time she turns to face him.)

ZIBA: What is the matter with you?

JOHN: I just want to hear one of his jokes. That's all. Not asking for much.

ZIBA: Sweetheart, you know those Persian jokes . . . they don't really translate well. They're . . . they're . . .

JOHN: Culturally specific.

ZIBA: Right.

JOHN: Yeah, you keep telling me.

ZIBA: Well, it's true.

JOHN: Try me.

ZIBA: Sweetie . . . *(John doesn't give up)* All right, fine! *(Sits up)* I don't need to sleep. Sleep is overrated anyway.

(John lifts himself up slightly, childlike in his excitement to hear the joke.)

Okay. Well, let's see. Can I remember any of them?

(Pause.)

Hum. *(Sigh)* Sweetie, really. I don't remember any of them.

JOHN: Oh, come on!

(John is watching her with a look like he will break down in sobs if she doesn't come up with a joke.)

ZIBA: Okay. Well, here's one. A *Rashti* comes home and finds his wife parading around naked. You remember who *Rashtis* are, right?

JOHN: Yeah, *Rashtis* are those guys who like boys.

ZIBA: No. Those are *Qazvinis*. Remember *Rashtis* are those from Rasht, the town in northern Iran by the Caspian Sea who have a reputation for being . . . *(John is patiently listening)* being too liberal. —Okay, forget that one . . . Let me see . . . *(Searches her brain for a while)* Here's another one. I don't think you'll find it funny—but, anyway, here it goes. So, there's this good-looking woman who decides to kill herself. She's very attractive, big boobs and all. So, she jumps out the window of a high-rise but as she's falling, she looks down and has second thoughts. She calls out, "*Ya*, Imam Zaman, save me!" Well, right then and there Imam Zaman appears and takes her in his arms. "Thank you, Imam Zaman!" she says, startled. Noticing her beauty and well endowment, he says, "Call me Mehdi."

(She laughs lightly, watching John for a reaction. He smiles. Ziba shrugs.)

I told you . . . *(Still giggling)*

JOHN: What? Like, "K-khash-ki-vor, but call me Kevin"?

ZIBA *(Lies back down, turns her back to him)*: Well, I tried.

JOHN: Well, what does it mean?

(Pause.)

Okay. So, it's too much trouble to explain. Right? Poor Johnnie here, he just doesn't get it. He can lecture on multiclient network systems in Hebrew and Turkish, but don't expect him to understand the subtleties of the Persian language. That most incomprehensible mystery of all! And you claim to work towards world peace . . . *(Turns his back to Ziba, then lies back down)*

ZIBA *(Opens her eyes and listens for a bit; ponders)*: "World peace"?

JOHN: World peace.

ZIBA *(Turns back to face him)*: World peace, what? What about world peace?

JOHN *(Faces Ziba)*: You and all your claims. You don't mean any of them. What—if you won't even take the time to—make an effort to—to—make a silly joke understood by someone outside the culture. Someone who would give his life for you. Someone— someone—you supposedly care about. Then—then what hope is there for Israel and Palestine?

ZIBA: Israel and Palestine? What—how is this related?

JOHN: You heard me. Don't pretend like you don't understand.

ZIBA: What? You want an introduction to Islam at four o'clock in the morning?

JOHN: As good a time as any. If you were trying to recruit me, you'd take the time. Any time. Right?

ZIBA: Recruit you for what?

JOHN: I don't know, jihad, a suicide bombing or two.

ZIBA: Now you're really pissing me off. What's gotten into you?

JOHN: Why is the joke funny?

ZIBA: It's not! It really isn't that funny, even in Persian. This is what I'm trying to tell you. You're not missing out on anything earth-shattering here.

JOHN: You didn't spend one minute with me tonight.

ZIBA: What?

JOHN: Not one minute.

ZIBA: Oh Christ . . .

JOHN: Stick to your own deities.

ZIBA: He is. Islam acknowledges Jesus as a prophet.

JOHN: But not as the son of God.

ZIBA: At least we don't call him a terrorist like your Senator Jesse Helms called Muhammad!

JOHN: He's not *my* Senator Jesse Helms!

ZIBA: Could have fooled me.

(Pause.)

What's gotten into you, anyway? *(Pause)* We throw a fucking party. We invite guests. And we're supposed to spend time with them.

(Pause.)

I spend time with you every goddamn day. Thousands of minutes!

JOHN: Sounds like a real drag . . . *(Turns his back to her)*

ZIBA *(Fully sitting up in bed)*: You wanna know why the joke is funny? Because everyone knows those so-called religious leaders are sexual perverts. Imam Zaman tries to pick up the woman he is supposedly saving. *(When Ziba becomes sufficiently worked up, John turns to face her)* He doesn't recite the Qur'an or inspire her with religious fervor; he makes a pass at her. That's why it's funny. Like all those jokes about priests coming on to women during confession or making out with altar boys . . . they're sick. Sick jokes. But funny. Yes, funny because we're sick people and we're sick of the hypocrisy of our religious leaders. Are you happy now, John?

JOHN: Call me Mehdi! *(Grabs Ziba)*

ZIBA: Get away! Just stop—

JOHN: I love it when you get feisty. *(Pulls her closer)*

ZIBA: Don't. Getting me all worked up . . . I hate you! *(Pushes him away, playfully)*

JOHN: Yes, that's right. Say it in Farsi. C'mon, tell me that thing about eating my liver. Come here. Stop pulling away. Don't you want a piece of my flaming kebab?

(Ziba bursts out laughing.)

Yeah, there you go. I can make you laugh, too. Can't I? Not just your Eye-ranian ex-boyfriends.

ZIBA: Stop.

JOHN: Say it. Say that thing about eating my liver . . .

ZIBA: *Jeegareto bokhoram . . .*

JOHN: Oh God—you're killing me. *(Bites her earlobe)*

ZIBA: Ow! That hurt— *(John gets busy under the sheets)* Stop . . . my . . . oh, jeez, what? Ah, that tickles. Um . . .

(Ziba is enjoying herself, moaning and groaning.)

Ah! Don't bite!

JOHN *(Appearing from down below)*: I want to eat your ear. How do you say that in Farsi?

ZIBA: Persian.

JOHN: Say it . . .

ZIBA: *Goosheto bokhoram.* *(John groans)* Sweetie, did you really mean that? You'd give your life for me?

JOHN *(Adjusts himself on top of her, looking straight into her eyes)*: You better believe it. I'm taking out my machine gun right now, baby.

Can you feel it? *(Gyrating on top of her)* My kind of jihad starts nice and slow. I like to take my time . . . earn each convert.

ZIBA: Convert those capitalist pigs who run the empire.

JOHN: Hush, you infidel. Give up your soul to Allah!

ZIBA: Oh, Father John, is it my soul you're after?

JOHN: I'm a martyr for your soul. I'm a martyr for your soul. I'm a martyr for your soul.

ZIBA: You go, cowboy . . .

JOHN: You say that to all the gringos.

ZIBA: What's a gringo doing with a timid Eye-ranian virgin?

JOHN: Huh! Now, there's a joke.

ZIBA: Fuck you!

JOHN: Say please . . .

ZIBA: So demanding . . .

(They fool around. John appears from under the covers.)

JOHN: You know, I think I seriously would give my life for you.

ZIBA: It's really not necessary, sweetie. Just keep doing what you're doing right now.

JOHN *(Sits up)*: Hum. That's a scary thought.

ZIBA: It is? Sweetie, don't stop . . . *(Pushes him under the covers)*

JOHN *(Pulls the covers off)*: Two years ago, if anyone had asked me, I would have said, "Impossible!" Not for my country, not for my God . . .

ZIBA: Hello! You're getting off track . . . can we get back to the business at hand?

JOHN: But now—for you. Anything.

(Pause.)

Hum. Interesting. *(Turns his back to her)* Good night.

ZIBA: What? John . . .

(Pause.)

Listen, buddy, you keep me awake at four in the morning with these silly revelations, and I play your game and I listen—and explain—and do all that is asked of me, and now I'm damned if I just leave it at "good night"!

JOHN: We'll pick up where we left in the morning.

ZIBA: It is the morning!

JOHN: Good morning then . . .

ZIBA: John! Get up or I swear I'll beat the shit out of you.

(Silence.)

John!

JOHN: Tomorrow . . . I promise.

ZIBA: You're the world's biggest hypocrite. "Do anything for you!" Right! That means shit. The one time we can actually have our mutual friends in one place you go around *pouting* all night and interrogating me after. Making grandiose claims when the smallest thing is too much for you. You fucking liar! *(Pulls the sheet off him and wraps it around herself)*

JOHN: Hey . . . calm down. *(Pulls the sheet to cover himself, she pulls back)* This is ridiculous. Here I open up to you in a very deep way and all you care about is sex!

ZIBA: Listen, Mr. Very Deep Way, *(They keep tugging at the sheet)* if you really cared about opening up, you'd go to Iran with me.

JOHN: Woah! Where'd that come from?

ZIBA: Want to get the jokes, check out the country. You know what I mean?

JOHN: Can I wait till they're done shouting: "Death to America"?

ZIBA: Coward!

JOHN: It's dangerous, Z. You said so yourself . . .

ZIBA: Sean Penn went!

(Pause.)

JOHN: What about the Israeli visa in my passport?

ZIBA: Get a new passport. Tell them you lost it.

JOHN: But to travel together in Iran we'd have to be married according to Islamic law, I'd have to convert to Islam.

ZIBA: It's just a stupid prayer. Say Allah Akbar three times and get a ticket to paradise. Sounds like a bargain to me!

JOHN: But I don't even believe in God.

ZIBA: Then what's the problem?

(Silence.)

JOHN: Z . . .

ZIBA: Ziba.

(John is not following her meaning.)

It's not that difficult. Say it: Zee-*ba*.

JOHN: Ziba.

ZIBA: Thank you.

JOHN: Means "beautiful."

ZIBA: That's right.

JOHN: Why is it always me who has to prove his love?

ZIBA: Because you're the one always counting. Two hours with Khashayar, two minutes with me, five jokes with Hussein, one with me, three glasses of wine—

JOHN: I can never be who you want me to be, Z. Uh—Ziba.

ZIBA: Come to Iran with me. We'll make love in the Caspian Sea.

(Silence.)

Come here, cowboy *(She pulls the sheet with him wrapped in it, close to her)* Submit your luscious lips to the Mistress of the East. *(They kiss)* Come to Iran with me. They won't take you hostage.

(They kiss. She pulls the sheet over them.)

JOHN: Promise?

ZIBA *(Pulls the cover off, ponders his question)*: Well . . .

END OF PLAY

TORANGE YEGHIAZARIAN writes, directs and acts for the theatre. She is the founder and artistic director of Golden Thread Productions, a San Francisco company dedicated to theatre that explores Middle Eastern cultures and identities. Born in Iran, and of Armenian heritage, Torange holds a master's degree in Theatre Arts from San Francisco State University. Her plays (*Call Me Mehdi*, *Waves*, *Dawn at Midnight*, *Behind Glass Windows*, *Abaga*) reflect the perspective of the culturally displaced in tackling today's world of contradictory realities and values. As part of Golden Thread's Fairytale Players, Torange has adapted a number of children's stories for the stage, including Karim Alrawi's *The Girl Who Lost Her Smile*.

As a teaching artist, Torange taught playwriting to at-risk youth, as part of the Each One Reach One program; incorporated theatre into social studies in Richmond's Washington Elementary School, as part of East Bay Center for Performing Arts' Learning Without Borders program; and led acting and play development workshops for Golden Thread Productions. A trained scientist, Torange is a licensed clinical microbiologist and is proud to have contributed to improving human health during her twenty-year career in the diagnostics field.

Among Torange's theatre writings are *Abaga* (*The Future*), a lyrical tale of two generations of forbidden love; the first, between an Armenian man and a Turkish woman in Istanbul 1915; the second, between their daughter and a Jewish immigrant in Jerusalem 1935. *Dawn at Midnight* centers on an unexpected turning point in the life of Sahar, a successful Iranian TV personality in Los Angeles; *Waves* depicts the reunion of two political activists after a seventeen-year separation; *Publicly Resting* is a farcical drama inside an airport men's restroom; *Behind Glass Windows* is adapted from a story by Sadeq Hedayat; *Operation No Penetration, Lysistrata 97!* is a contemporary adaptation of the classic Greek comedy, where Palestinian and Israeli women unite to force their men to sign a peace treaty; and the melodrama *TORCH!* created collaboratively in a workshop with the San Francisco Mime Troupe. Torange performed in Darvag's production of *The Eighth Voyage of Sindbad* by Bahram Beyzaii; Farhad Ayish's *The*

Last Supper; Franca Rame and Dario Fo's play *A Woman Alone,* as well as in the independent films *The Last Illusion* and *Surviving Paradise,* both by Kamshad Kooshan.